Innocent Subjects

Innocent Subjects

Feminism and Whiteness

Terese Jonsson

First published 2021 by Pluto Press
345 Archway Road, London N6 5AA

www.plutobooks.com

Copyright © Terese Jonsson 2021

The right of Terese Jonsson to be identified as the author of this work has
been asserted by her in accordance with the Copyright, Designs and Patents
Act 1988.

British Library Cataloguing in Publication Data
A catalogue record for this book is available from the British Library

ISBN   978 0 7453 3751 7   Hardback
ISBN   978 0 7453 3750 0   Paperback
ISBN   978 1 7868 0342 9   PDF eBook
ISBN   978 1 7868 0344 3   Kindle eBook
ISBN   978 1 7868 0343 6   EPUB eBook

Typeset by Stanford DTP Services, Northampton, England

Simultaneously printed in the United Kingdom and United States of America

Contents

Acknowledgements

My thinking and writing is fundamentally indebted to the work of the many Black feminists and feminists of colour which I draw on in this book. I want to thank and acknowledge all those who have been doing the often unrewarding and emotionally draining work of challenging and critiquing racism and whiteness within feminist theorising, politics and communities for a long time.

Throughout the process of research and writing, I have been incredibly lucky to have shared learning, friendship, support, despair and laughs with a number of amazing feminist thinkers and doers. Andrea D'Cruz, Anna Bull, rashné limki, Dyi Huijg, Naaz Rashid and Sarah Keenan have not only informed my thinking through their incisive and generous feedback on various versions of different chapters, but have also been great friends and colleagues. Ongoing conversations and collaborative scheming with Humaira Saeed have been central to the development of my ideas and analysis. Rashida Harrison's knowledge and shared enthusiasm for exploring the archives of *Outwrite Women's Newspaper* benefited my thinking about the paper's political significance. Anna Feigenbaum and other members of the Feminist Activist Forum's 'DIY feminist history group' also informed my perspective on *Outwrite*'s legacy for contemporary feminists. Conversations with Nydia Swaby enriched my understanding of the histories of Black British feminism. My analysis has also been influenced by conversations which started at the 'Feminist Complicities' meeting in 2015 and continued from there, including in particular with Nadine El-Enany (in addition to people already mentioned above). Throughout the journey of my PhD and then writing this book, I have benefited from and appreciated intellectual and political discussions with members of the Gender and Sexuality PhD forum at London Metropolitan University, the 'Race', Ethnicity and Postcolonial Studies (REPS) postgraduate network, the 'Critical Edges' organising group and event in 2019, the Citizenship, Race and Belonging (CRaB) research network, the Critical Pedagogies reading group, and the feminist reading group, the latter three all at the

University of Portsmouth. I want to thank my students at Portsmouth for inspiration, in particular those who engaged with openness and thoughtfulness in conversations on my Equality or Liberation? Theorising Social Justice module. A number of colleagues at Portsmouth deserve mention for their kindness and care in the midst of a sector which encourages the opposite, in particular Joseph Burridge, Emily Nicholls, Naheem Jabbar, Sukh Hamilton and Rusten Menard.

This book grew out of my PhD research which I completed in 2015. My supervisor, Irene Gedalof, helped me, with great care and patience, shape and carry out the research. I would like to acknowledge and thank my thesis examiners, Sara Ahmed and Sunny Singh, for their critical engagement with my work, which gave me ideas for how it could be developed. I also want to thank my MA dissertation supervisor Nirmal Puwar, who influenced my thinking and direction of scholarly travel during my MA in Gender, Culture and Modernity at Goldsmiths College in 2004–05.

Both the PhD and the book were a long time coming and there were times when it was doubtful that either were going to come at all. Many friends, older as well as newer, have provided steadfast encouragement, laughs and reality checks when I needed them. In particular, I want to thank Denise and Jackie Hales, Sam Stewart, Dan McMahon, Johanna Novales, Soley Mustafa, Yula Burin, Sarah James, Leslie Barson, Sian Fletcher and everyone at Otherwise Living.

I am grateful for David Shulman's support for my work and incredible patience in seeing this book through to completion and I would like to thank him and everyone else at Pluto Press. I also extend my sincere thanks to the anonymous reviewers of the initial proposal and chapter, whose comments were incredibly helpful in refining and clarifying my arguments and the ways in which I communicate them.

My dad, Kurt Jonsson, passed away as I was writing this book, in March 2018. It is difficult to succinctly summarise the influence he had and continues to have on my life and my work, but I am particularly thankful to him for teaching me to think critically, to ask questions and to believe that things can be changed (even though we did not always agree on what questions need to be asked or what needs to change). I am grateful to my mum, Gunilla Jonsson, and my sister, Linda Forsberg, who have both been consistently supportive of me and my various endeavours and winding paths, and who continue to be an important part of 'home' for me. Thank you to Natasha, without whose deep care, support and patience I would not be where I am today, and this book would certainly not have been completed. I also want to thank the Parker-Campbell-Hinton family for their generosity and openness. Special thanks go to my niece, Amiyah, and my nephew, Alex, for all the joy and creativity they bring into my life.

Finally, I do not have the words nor the space to fully describe the influence Lani Parker has had on me as a person and on my work. I can only thank her for her unwavering encouragement and love, her close attention to and feedback on various drafts of chapters, and for always challenging me to think deeper and act braver.

All royalty payments I receive for this book will be redistributed to the Resourcing Racial Justice fund (http://resourcingracialjustice.org/) and anti-racist feminist projects.

*   *   *

Some material in Chapter 3 has previously been published in article form, as 'The narrative reproduction of white feminist racism', in *Feminist Review*, 113 (2016).

1

'That Old Chestnut':
Feminism and Racism

In a letter published in *Spare Rib* in December 1980, reproductive rights activist Jan McKenley writes of her frustration that most white feminists around her seem to have stopped caring about racism:

> I'm beginning to feel invisible again within the WLM [women's liberation movement], having to work myself up to making 'heavy' statements that will embarrass sisters in meetings – I can see the eyebrows going up already – 'Not racism – that old chestnut again – it's so boring.' Well, if it's boring for you, white sister .... I've got no monopoly on dealing with racism – it's your problem too.[1]

Noting that the topic had been 'trendy' a year or two prior, McKenley describes being 'left feeling that racism was "last year's thing"', urging her white 'sisters' to take out 'the 1978 file' again in order to remind themselves of the anti-racist arguments they should already know but appear to have forgotten. 'And if you don't take that file off the shelf, I hope it falls on your bloody head, so don't say you haven't been warned!' the letter ends.

Fast forward 37 years. In her 2017 book *Why I'm No Longer Talking to White People About Race*, writer Reni Eddo-Lodge discusses recent feminist debates on social media and in the liberal press, highlighting how racism continues to 'cause immovable fault lines in the movement'. 'Too often', she continues, 'a white feminist's ideological standpoint does not see racism as a problem, let alone a priority'. Drawing attention to the long history of Black feminist critiques of white feminism, Eddo-Lodge questions why, if white feminists 'can understand the patriarchy', they 'struggle to understand whiteness as a political structure in the same way'.[2]

Even though over three and a half decades separate McKinley's and Eddo-Lodge's comments, the concerns they raise are similar: a lack of commitment on the part of white feminists to understanding racism, and an unwillingness to listen to feminists of colour and to see them as equal partners in shaping the movement. Between these two moments, as before and after, many other critiques have been raised about the ways in which white feminists have too often failed to take racism seriously, and the many ways in which they have marginalised, tokenised, erased and appropriated women of colour's work and experiences. This book is an attempt to act upon such critiques, drawing on their arguments and insights to develop an in-depth examination of how race and whiteness shape white-dominated feminist theorising and politics in the contemporary British context. I will elaborate on the concept of whiteness later in the chapter, but as a brief definition, this term describes how the structural dominance of white people within both Western society and globally is presumed to be natural. Whiteness positions white people as the norm within society. Within feminism, it positions white women as the normative and central subjects of theorising and political organising.

The need to resist feminist whiteness remains critical. As I will discuss, feminist theories and politics which do not adequately address race are not only flawed and irrelevant to many women, but harmful in their racist effects. The dominance of whiteness within many feminist spheres also destroys the possibility of powerful and sustainable multiracial feminist movements – ones which are urgently needed.

Britain enters the third decade of the twenty-first century as a deeply unequal and unjust society. Following 30 years of neoliberal restructuring and a decade of austerity measures, right-wing politicians and press have fuelled the flames of anti-migrant, anti-Black and anti-Muslim racism. This rose to fever pitch in the lead-up to and continuing aftermath of the 2016 referendum on European Union (EU) membership, in which the anti-migrant rhetoric of 'Leave' campaigners largely set the terms of the debate and ultimately led to its success at the polls. I finalise this book in January 2020 in the wake of the December 2019 general election, in which the Conservative Party, under Boris Johnson's leadership, gained a large parliamentary majority on the back of the election promise to 'Get Brexit done'. After three years of political deadlock over Brexit, the election results decisively reaffirmed the original results of the referendum, with Britain's ongoing shift to the right in line with global trends of resurgent nationalisms. The Brexit saga, as Nadine El-Enany argues, is intimately tied up with the country's unresolved relationship to Empire; Brexit 'is not only nostalgia for empire – it is also the fruit of empire'.[3] The 'Leave' slogan of 'taking back control' evokes a fantasy of a victimised nation under attack by migrant 'others' and European bureaucrats. It is based on a disavowal of Britain's brutal imperial past and its role in maintaining global inequalities through trade, military interventions and migration controls in the present.

The immensity of horrors unfolding at the borders of Europe provides the backdrop to the Brexit saga and the rise in racist populism, not just in Britain, but globally. As 'Fortress Europe' has shut down safe routes of travel, hundreds of thousands of people from African and Middle Eastern countries make desperate and dangerous journeys towards and across the Mediterranean Sea. Over 14,000 people have died during their attempts to cross the Mediterranean since 2014.[4] The suffering of poor Black and Brown people is the background to European life, the underlying message clear: their deaths matter less than our (way of) life. In June 2017, the Grenfell Tower fire tragically exposed how this logic operates also within Britain's borders. Starting as a small fire in a flat on the fourth floor, the 24-storey tower block went up in flames in less than an hour, giving residents on higher floors little chance to escape. Alongside pictures of the dead and missing, details soon emerged of residents' previous unheeded warnings and complaints about the lack of fire safety, of the cheap materials used and their incompetent installation in a recent refurbishment. The majority of the 72 people who died in Grenfell Tower, which sits in London's richest borough of Kensington and Chelsea, were working-class people of colour, many with a migrant background.[5]

Gender analysis is crucial for understanding the ways in which racism, economic inequality and different forms of violence coalesce in these times. Anti-migrant and anti-Muslim discourse centres on arguments about how 'they' – migrant, Muslim others – treat 'their' women and sexual minorities, and the threat they pose to 'ours' and to 'us'. Muslim women's perceived oppressed status, their clothing practices, their supposed lack of agency, education and English language skills remain a constant source of fascination and regulation for policymakers and the media. Institutional surveillance and othering of Muslims creates an environment which further legitimates popular and everyday racism and harassment. A year prior to becoming Prime Minister, Boris Johnson dedicated one of his regular *Telegraph* columns to mocking women who wear niqabs and burqas, describing them as 'looking like letter boxes' and 'bank robber[s]'.[6] As a number of us wrote in an 'anti-racist feminist statement on Islamophobia' at the time (signed by over 270 individuals and organisations), '[w]hile couched within an ostensibly liberal argument against a "total ban" of niqabs and burqas in public places, Johnson's comments were clearly and very deliberately aimed at stoking already entrenched anti-Muslim racism and appealing to the right of the Conservative Party to build support for his likely leadership bid'.[7] It worked. In the aftermath of Johnson's column, assaults and street harassment against Muslim women increased, and Johnson's dehumanising epithets were enthusiastically added to the Islamophobic lexicon.[8] Just over a year later, Johnson led one of the most historically right-wing configurations of the Conservative Party to a resounding victory in the general election, with notorious far right personalities such as Tommy Robinson (former leader of the English Defence League) and Katie Hopkins declaring their support, and the far right group Britain First urging its members to join the party in order to 'make Boris Johnson's leadership more secure'.[9]

As we further wrote in the statement,

> In affecting a concern for Muslim women's rights while peddling Islamophobia, Johnson is treading the well-worn path of gendered racism. The demonisation of Muslims in western political discourse originated with the orientalism of European colonisers, and has always proceeded on highly gendered terms, with the figure of the 'oppressed Muslim woman' operating as a symbolic shorthand to justify all manner of imperial foreign and domestic policy interventions.

Naaz Rashid's research on government policy initiatives aimed to 'empower' Muslim women as a counter-terrorism strategy reveals how this gendered racism functions, highlighting how such initiatives are based on and reproduce stereotypical ideas of Muslim women as 'victims solely of "pathological Muslim patriarchy" rather than as victims of deprived socio-economic conditions, citizenship uncertainties, or patriarchy and racism in wider society'.[10] The effect of such policies, then, as Rashid demonstrates, is not Muslim women's liberation but rather the further demonisation and surveillance of Muslim communities (and Muslim *men* in particular) within a context of institutional denial of structural racism and racialised impoverishment.

The impact of austerity is also gendered and racialised, with women of colour and disabled women hit the hardest by cuts to welfare services and jobs in the public sector, and the reduction of funding for refuges leaving many women experiencing sexual and domestic violence with nowhere to escape.[11] As the slogan of direct action group Sisters Uncut spells out, 'they cut, we bleed'.[12]

In times of ideologically constructed scarcity it becomes even clearer that to speak of women as a uniformly oppressed group makes little sense. Akwugo Emejulu and Leah Bassel's research highlights how the effects of austerity are unevenly distributed, with women of colour 'disproportionately disadvantaged due to their already existing precarity'.[13] At the other end of the spectrum, powerful women are instrumental in enforcing inequalities of gender, class, race and disability. For instance, since 2007, four women have held the office of Home Secretary as part of the British government: Jaqui Smith (Labour), Theresa May (Conservative), Amber Rudd (Conservative) and Priti Patel (Conservative). All apart from Patel have declared themselves as feminists. These women have overseen the running of immigration detention centres such as Yarl's Wood, where around 400 women are held at any given time. Run by the global private security firm Serco, Yarl's Wood has been the subject of a number of damaging reports and media exposés which have revealed detainees being subjected to sexual abuse and racism from guards, with high levels of self-harm and mental ill health among detainees.[14] Yet, in 2014, May renewed Serco's contract for another eight years, and calls for the reduction or elimination of immigration detention have been ignored by successive Home Secretaries. Now, as always, differently positioned women have widely divergent needs, interests and experiences of life, and those with more power are more likely to ally with those similar to themselves in terms of class, race, politics and nation rather than with more marginalised women. It bears noting, for instance, that the majority of middle age and older white women voted for Brexit in the referendum. The fact that many of these women saw the solution to Britain's current problems in the need for less 'foreigners' is something which, as Ruth Cain argues, feminists need to take more seriously.[15] In another sphere of social life, Nicola Rollock's recent research into the experiences of Black female professors in UK universities (of which there are, shockingly, only 25) reports that white female academics have often contributed to Black female academics' experiences of alienation and exclusion, by, for instance, aligning themselves with the views of white men 'while ignoring the contributions of women of colour'.[16]

Anti-racist feminist analyses and politics are vital to address white supremacist and heteropatriarchal oppression and violence at both local and global levels. Yet, despite long histories of such theorising and organising by feminists of colour, there continues to be a lack of critical mass of white feminists working consistently against racism. As McKenley's comments convey, the sense of having the same conversation over and over again is habitual among those who challenge whiteness within feminism – and that was so even 40 years ago. But why has race been such a persistent problem within feminist politics, considering most white feminists balk at the suggestion that they are racist? Why haven't white feminists learned from the past, considering the critiques are so well rehearsed? These are some of the questions which led me to conduct the research which forms the basis of this book.

I started asking these questions around the time that I began learning about Black British feminism, and doing some research into the British feminist archives of the 1980s. Dominant white accounts of British feminism's recent past too readily cast the 1980s as a period of decline and fragmentation of the women's liberation movement, yet for the development of Black and anti-racist feminisms, the 1980s were a highly significant period. The ascendance of an autonomous grassroots Black women's movement in the 1970s and into the 1980s, alongside the emergence of Black British feminism as an academic project, enabled, as Julia Sudbury writes, a more 'coordinated attack on white hegemony [through which] white feminists were forced to take note of the serious challenge posed by Black feminism'.[17] This was a time of intense debate and conflict along a number of fronts – race, class, disability, sexuality. Although often painful and acrimonious, these debates and the work of marginalised feminists in pushing them forward were highly influential in developing more complex understandings of gender through its intersections with other structures of power.

Learning from feminists of colour's anti-racist analyses, parts of the white-dominated movement began to transform, resulting in increasing solidarity and coalition-building between feminists of colour and white feminists at this time. In her landmark essay 'White woman listen! Black feminism and the boundaries of sisterhood', published in 1982, Hazel Carby argues:

> ... it is very important that white women in the women's movement examine the ways in which racism excludes many black women and prevents them from unconditionally aligning themselves with white women. Instead of taking black women as the objects of their research, white feminist researchers should try to uncover the gender-specific mechanisms of racism amongst white women. This more than any other factor disrupts the recognition of common interests of sisterhood.[18]

A number of white feminist scholars, notably Vron Ware, Ruth Frankenberg, Antoinette Burton and Catherine Hall, took heed of Carby's and other Black feminists' calls, and published valuable research on white women's relationship to racism and Empire.[19]

There are many important legacies and lessons to learn from by revisiting activist archives and academic scholarship from this time, and I will explore some of these in the next chapter. But what this book is centrally concerned with is interrogating the ways in which feminist whiteness has (re)asserted itself in more contemporary times, particularly within academia and in the liberal public sphere: two significant sites where feminist thought and discourse has been institutionalised and gained increasing power. If we start with the premise that whiteness was – never wholly, but significantly – destabilised within feminist activist and academic communities in the 1980s, my analysis of contemporary feminist texts suggests that a re-centring towards whiteness has since taken place, despite claims that anti-racist critiques have been taken on board. Specifically, I suggest that a white-centred feminism is maintained through asserting its innocence of racism. Here I am drawing on a body of literature (discussed further below) which theorises claims to 'white innocence' as a manifestation of white racial power. White feminist innocence, I will argue, is sustained through the promotion of particular kinds of narratives and knowledge claims about the relationship between feminism, race and racism which repeatedly erase, marginalise or appropriate the work of feminists of colour. The book focuses on feminism as a knowledge project: the ways in which ideas, concepts and narratives are theorised, discussed and struggled over within feminist discourse and communities. In particular, my research examines the ways in which dominant forms of feminist knowledge are entangled with 'white ignorance', which has been theorised by Charles Mills as a faulty knowledge system.[20]

In the next section, I will clarify my usage of the terms 'Black' and 'white' feminisms. Following this, I will historically situate the construction of the categories of gender and race as well as the emergence of British feminism in the context of Empire. I will then elaborate on the concept of whiteness, and related theorisations of 'white innocence' and 'white ignorance'. The subsequent section addresses the questions of location, explaining the book's focus on the British context and how I see this geopolitical and historical specificity as part of a commitment to transnational feminist solidarity. Here I will also address my own positionality in relation to this work. Following this, I will briefly address the 'politics of citation', urging readers to consider critically how they use and cite this book. The chapter concludes with a discussion of the study's methodological approach, as well as an outline of the remaining chapters.

BLACK AND WHITE FEMINISMS

The term 'Black' has often been used within Black British feminism as a political term inclusive of all people targeted by racism, although this has also been a recurrent point of contention and debate. Avtar Brah describes how the deployment of Blackness as a 'political colour' is 'historically contingent' and has no essential meaning, but should be understood as having been forged through political struggle for (primarily) African Caribbean and Asian solidarity against racism in 1970s and 1980s Britain.[21] Similarly, Nydia Swaby describes 'political Blackness' as 'a politics of solidarity; nothing more, nothing less'.[22] Both Brah and Swaby stress that the term's continued relevance cannot be assumed or predetermined, and it is important to recognise that it continues to be contested and critiqued. In recent years, mobilisations of 'political Blackness', for instance within the National Union of Students, have come under increased critique for obscuring (and thereby reproducing) anti-Blackness, i.e. the colonial racial hierarchy which places people from the Black African diaspora at the bottom.[23] In an attempt to respect self-definitions, the way I use the term Black in this book varies depending on the context. However, unless otherwise specified, references to Black British feminism use Black as a 'political colour', as this is how it has most commonly been used. At the same time, I recognise that there are problems with this usage, so when it seems more accurate I use the term feminists of colour or other terms which are more specific to the context.

The term 'white feminism' originates from critiques by feminists of colour of white feminist politics which do not attend to race. Razia Aziz defines it as 'any feminism which comes from a white perspective, and universalizes it'. In Aziz's words, white feminism 'subsists through a failure to consider both the wider social and political context of power in which feminist utterances and actions take place, and the ability of feminism to influence that context'.[24] It is a theoretical and political perspective which anyone can promote or disrupt, thus there is no essential connection between white feminism and white feminists. Importantly, this distinction allows white feminism to be dismantled. The term's continued widespread use and resonance among feminists of colour speaks to the fact that this has yet to meaningfully take place.

While I use the term 'white feminism' to denote forms of feminist politics which continue to ignore race, as noted above, many white feminists today to varying extents do address, or at least acknowledge, race in their theorising and activism, and are more wary of universalising from a white perspective. To recognise this, while at the same time pointing to the persistence of whiteness as a normative framework within much contemporary theorising and politics, I often refer instead to 'white-centred' feminism. White-centred feminism retains white women as the central subjects of theorising and activism, even though women of colour and race analysis may also be visible to varying degrees within such work.

There is a danger inherent in analysing white and white-centred feminism of inevitably contributing to reinforcing its centrality. Suki Ali notes a common tendency within narratives of Western feminism to construct white, middle-class Western women as the key protagonists 'out to define the world, women and gender oppression in their own terms', while the work of women of colour is either 'erased entirely or reduced to the role of critiquing the central emergent field'.[25] In focusing its analysis on white-centred feminism, this book risks reinscribing the kind of narrative Ali warns us about, especially as it draws mainly on Black feminists' and women of colour's theory which in some way critiques this field. Therefore, I want to spell out explicitly that Black (British) feminism(s) and women of colour's thought and activism in the last 50 years emerged from a number of different historical trajectories, and have been shaped by many different routes, contexts and motivations. As Akwugo Emejulu and Francesca Sobande write, 'Black women have always been leaders of women's liberation ... Black feminism is in no way an afterthought or a derivative of white feminism but rather a radical praxis for the liberation of everyone – starting with Black women.'[26] I do not do the histories of Black women's theorising and activism justice in this book, because that is not its purpose. For readers unfamiliar with these, Julia Sudbury's 'Other Kinds of Dreams': Black Women's Organisations and the Politics of Transformation (1998), Shabnam Grewal, Jackie Kay, Liliane Landor, Gail Lewis and Pratibha Parmar's Charting the Journey: Writings by Black and Third World Women (1988), Beverley Bryan, Stella Dadzie and Suzanne Scafe's The Heart of the Race: Black Women's Lives in Britain (1985), Black British Feminism: A Reader edited by Heidi Mirza (1997), Feminist Review's two special issues on Black British feminism(s) (1984 and 2014), among other sources, provide useful starting points for learning about women of colour's thought and organising in the British context (some of which are referenced in this endnote).[27] Emejulu and Sobande's recently published collection To Exist is to Resist: Black Feminism in Europe (2019) represents a valuable addition to this literature, with contributions from Black feminists across the continent.[28]

It is important, then, while critiquing whiteness within feminism, not to over-determine its influence. As Ali suggests, over-exaggerating the whiteness of feminism 'negates the huge struggles and highly contested nature of the field from its outset'.[29] This also includes (racialised) struggles over what gets defined as 'feminism', and who uses this term to describe their work. Struggles over analytical frameworks and priorities between differently positioned women have been continuous features of feminist politics in Britain as elsewhere. This has been clearly evident in the last decade within activist politics, as feminists of colour have been able to use social media to raise the visibility of their analyses and experiences, and to build transnational networks and communities which decentre whiteness. This is a point raised by Lola Okolosie, a member of the UK Black Feminists group (which was active in the early 2010s), who writes that 'social media has enabled our attempt to position Black feminism not as existing on the fringes and in opposition to "mainstream" feminism, but as centred in our own right'.[30] The group was influential in shaping feminist debate about race and intersectionality, both in grassroots feminist communities and in the liberal public sphere (as I will discuss in Chapter 5). Alongside the work of long-standing Black feminist organisations such as Southall Black Sisters (formed in 1979), the London Black Women's Project (formerly the Newham Asian Women's Project, formed in 1987), Apna Haq (formed in 1994) and Imkaan (formed in 1998), feminists of colour have also led many activist groups in recent years, including Sisters Uncut, Sisters of Frida, Freedom Without Fear Platform and London Latinxs, as well as online media outlets such as Media Diversified, No Fly on the Wall and Gal Dem.

In other words, while this book focuses and dissects the whiteness which dominates certain sites of British feminism – specifically within feminist academia, popular publishing and the liberal press – this whiteness should not be assumed to be overly determining of feminist politics and theory as a whole. At the same time, there is no denying that whiteness remains structurally dominant, particularly within well-resourced and powerful institutions, and thus constitutes a problem which still needs addressing.

GENDER, RACE AND THE MAKING OF MODERN BRITAIN

We cannot understand the politics of gender and race without locating the meaning of these categories as they emerged in the historical context of colonialism. Kathleen Wilson's research highlights how the colonial project led European colonisers to encounter unfamiliar gender systems 'not structured by the binaries and complementarities familiar to Europeans'. As Wilson argues, gender as a 'mode of power' was central to the maintenance of British colonial control, as differences in gender arrangements were used to justify colonial conquest. Wilson highlights how a central plank of the theory of the 'natural history of man' (from 'savage' to 'civilized'), for instance, differentiated each stage of human development by how women were viewed: 'from the treatment of women as drudges and packhorses in the first, to the respect and esteem accorded to women in the last'.[31] Hypocritically, Britain constructed itself as the pinnacle of civilisation and one in which women were supposedly accorded respect and esteem, despite the fact that British women had few rights and that any woman who transgressed heteropatriarchal ideals of middle- and upper-class feminine morality was hardly 'respected'. The colonial encounter, both at 'home' and 'abroad', was thus highly significant in the development of modern ideas of gender.

With its model of patriarchy masquerading as 'respect for women', European colonisers' claim to bring civilisation to uncivilised people in fact brought a particular patriarchal gender order. In her study of the gendered effects of British colonisation of Yorùbáland, Oyèrónké Oyéwùmí argues that the British imposed a rigid gender regime where previously there was not one. Through the enforcement of a colonial state structure based on a division of the public and private sphere, Yorùbá men were given employment within the colonial state, while women, who had previously worked, were excluded. Christian missionary schools segregated pupils by gender, and taught female pupils sewing and embroidery, with the aim of 'producing mothers who would be the foundation of Christian families'. The privatisation of land also dispossessed women of previously held land rights. Thus, Oyéwùmí argues, 'colonization was a twofold process of racial inferiorization and gender subordination'.[32] While her study does not make any sweeping claim about patriarchy being uniquely Western, which it is patently not, it does highlight how the imposition of a particular Western patriarchal structure formed a central part of the colonising process.

Those who have researched the development of British feminism within the context of Empire have also highlighted the imperial worldview of most British feminists at this time. In her analysis of nineteenth-century white British women's anti-slavery and women's rights literature, Ware highlights that while these liberal women strongly condemned slavery, they were at the same time invested in the ideology of 'white superiority' and European cultural supremacy.[33] Clare Midgley highlights how both anti-slavery campaigners and feminists saw their role as saving colonised women, who were depicted as 'passive victims unable to defend themselves'. The language of the 'white woman's burden' became increasingly used during this period to describe white British women campaigners' role in relation to colonised

women. Crucially, Midgley suggests, both female anti-slavery campaigners and liberal feminists 'accepted the validity of British imperial
intervention'.[34] Midgley's, Burton's and Inderpal Grewal's research
highlight how the notion of the victimised Indian woman (believed to be
uniquely oppressed by her male counterpart) was used by white British
middle-class feminists to campaign for their own rights to partake in
the imperial project.[35] Many white British women also participated in
the machinery of Empire through work and travel. As Ware suggests,
Empire provided these women with their first opportunities for 'female
independence'. Records suggest that more than 20,000 British women
took up voluntary positions in colonised countries between 1862 and
1914, with more women emigrating and taking up work through other
connections.[36]

Then, as always, feminist politics encompassed a range of different
perspectives and analyses, and it would be incorrect to claim that all
white British feminists were pro-Empire. For instance, Grewal highlights how Sylvia Pankhurst attempted to build alliances with colonised
people. Through her Marxist approach to imperialism and patriarchy,
Pankhurst recognised that colonialism exploited women in India and
that the 'civilising' mission would thus not enable their liberation.[37]
Similarly, the Women's International League for Peace and Freedom
formally condemned imperialism at its 1926 international congress.
Yet, at the same time, Mona Siegel documents a continued ambivalence
within the British section of the League, noting that most members
were middle- and upper-middle-class reformers who were above all
concerned with promoting Western women's role and expertise in international politics.[38] A sense of national and white superiority thus tended
to infuse British feminist politics in the nineteenth and early twentieth
centuries, even those with more anti-imperial and internationalist perspectives. As Grewal notes, even Pankhurst still wrote of Indian women
using reductive colonial tropes, and idealised 'the Western woman's life
and abilities in comparison to that of Indian women'.[39]

Racialised constructions of gender relations and womanhood have
continued into the era of formal decolonisation. Examining 1940s
government reports on the British welfare state as well as Caribbean
states' transitions from colonial rule, Denise Noble highlights a tension
between the British state's desire to produce 'more White British babies'
and its need for women's labour, which was resolved through the

recruitment of Caribbean women to Britain as workers. Thus, British policy produced the Caribbean woman 'as a racialized category of female, working-class labor' in opposition to the white British housewife and mother.[40] Proper womanhood was in this way reserved for white women, with Black women's parenting practices and family structures constructed as pathological. As Carby puts it, 'black women were seen to fail as mothers precisely because of their position as workers'.[41]

Another significant fault line between white women and women of colour emerged in this era in relation to immigration and nationality law, as highlighted in Ranu Samantrai's analysis of legal reforms and debates about national identity between 1948 and 1982. Samantrai demonstrates how the dividing line between national inclusion and exclusion shifted from gender to race in this period, with white women becoming fully included in the nation at the same time as people of colour became increasingly excluded. In the 1948 Nationality Act, British citizens were defined as citizens of the UK as well as of its colonies. Through the 1960s, successive immigration legislation increasingly restricted the right of people from former colonies to enter Britain, and the 1971 Immigration Act effectively ended the right of all primary migration from former colonies by introducing the requirement that all would-be migrants could demonstrate 'patriality', i.e. that they had either a parent or grandparent born in Britain. However, nationality law still discriminated against women, as it prohibited them from being able to pass on citizenship to their children. This was rectified in 1981 with a new Nationality Act, which formally eradicated discrimination against women in the passing on of nationality. However, the 1981 Act's definition of a British citizen was sharply narrowed down so that citizenship could only be passed on through descent from a citizen. This meant that a child born to a migrant in the UK did not automatically have citizenship, whereas a child born abroad to a British citizen did. The end of discrimination against women in nationality law thus primarily benefited white women at the expense of people of colour. As Samantrai argues, 'the formation of contemporary England can be read as the process of changing the nation from the patriarchal family enshrined in the 1948 Nationality Act to the racial family of the 1981 act'.[42]

As the research discussed above suggests, in order to understand gender relations and inequality in Britain, we must account for how the very category of gender has been constructed and made meaningful through the construction of race, and the reverse is also true. The categories of gender and race as they are understood in Britain today have thus been fundamentally co-constituted through the process of colonial modernity up until the present day. The foundations of British feminism, similarly, are inextricably linked with histories of Empire, steeped in the logic of white superiority. These histories are too often and too easily dismissed as precisely that: history. But as Burton argues, feminist movements 'must be truly and continually accountable to their pasts; they must be willing to enter into a dialogue with them; and they must acknowledge the historicity of the present'.[43]

The belief that it is possible to draw a line of separation between the past and the present rests on the assumption that Britain has fundamentally changed from the colonial era to the present day. Yet, contemporary Britain continues to be structured by a deeply embedded colonial logic of white supremacy. The continuity of global structures of racial inequality is captured in the concept of coloniality, developed by Latin American and Caribbean decolonial scholars.[44] Despite the formal end to most (although not all) European colonial rule, as Aníbal Quijano argues, 'the main lines of world power today' continue to exploit, dominate and discriminate against racialised people of formerly colonised countries.[45] There is, in other words, no line in the sand to be drawn between the past and the present. This is not to suggest that nothing has changed, but it is to contest simplistic progress narratives in relation to the racialised structures of the British nation-state (as well as those of other former colonial powers). This present is the inescapable context in which contemporary British feminisms are articulated, and with which they must contend in order to resist the continuity of white supremacy.

WHITENESS: IGNORANCE AND INNOCENCE

Whiteness: that powerful place that makes invisible, or reappropriates things, people and places it does not want to see or hear, and then through misnaming, renaming or not naming at all, invents the truth – what we are told is 'normal', neutral, universal, simply becomes the way it is ...[46]

Heidi Mirza's definition of whiteness, from the introduction to the 1997 collection *Black British Feminism*, speaks both to the way in which whiteness functions to maintain white people as the 'neutral' standard within society, as well as to the way in which it functions as a form of dominant knowledge, through 'invent[ing] the truth'. This section elaborates on how whiteness functions as a form of faulty yet powerful 'truth', how this enables a discourse of white innocence, and how this operates in gendered ways.

A familiar narrative within academia is that whiteness emerged as a site of theorisation with the advent of whiteness studies in the 1990s, predominantly by white scholars. Yet, such a narrative presents a limited view of what theorising whiteness entails. As Sara Ahmed writes:

> Any critical genealogy of whiteness studies, for me, must begin with the direct political address of Black feminists such as [Audre] Lorde, rather than later work by white academics on representations of whiteness or on how white people experience their whiteness ... Whiteness studies, that is, if it is to be more than 'about' whiteness, begins with the Black critique of how whiteness works as a form of racial privilege, as well as the effects of that privilege on the bodies of those who are recognised as black.

Ahmed draws attention to the racialised politics of knowledge production: who counts as producers of academic knowledge and fields, and how white forms of knowledge (including about whiteness) come to dominate. For one, whiteness as theorised by white academics often starts with the assumption that it is invisible, but, as Ahmed points out, 'of course whiteness is only invisible for those who inhabit it. For those who don't, it is hard not to see whiteness'.[47]

Charles Mills argues that whiteness is a fundamentally faulty knowledge system, based on a systemic form of ignorance about racism. Writing about the US context, Mills argues that African-Americans have by necessity become experts in understanding and theorising whiteness. As he argues, '[w]hat people of color quickly come to see ... is that they are not seen at all'. 'White ignorance' is a knowledge system predicated on an unwillingness or inability (whether conscious or not) to recognise people of colour as fully human. Importantly, 'ignorance' in Mills' usage is not just the 'absence of true knowledge' but also 'false belief', an ignorance about racism which 'fights back'. Whiteness, Mills suggests, requires this ignorance to justify white supremacy. When confronted with evidence which contradicts the white knowledge system, white ignorance enables white people to reject this knowledge as not possible or not true. Within spheres of academic knowledge production, Mills notes how '[w]hites will cite other whites in a closed circuit of epistemic authority that reproduces white delusions'.[48]

There are distinct gendered dimensions to how white ignorance operates. For instance, when white women are held to account for racism, they frequently claim an inability to do so competently, something which María Lugones describes as an 'infantilization of judgment'. This process involves white women taking 'flight into those characteristics of childhood that excuse ignorance and confusion'. Lugones argues that this self-infantilising process is mobilised by white women in order to protect their moral innocence, and is thus in itself a form of racism, as it effectively shields the white woman in question from being held accountable.[49]

White feminists also participate in the production of ignorant knowledge about women of colour. Addressing the US context, Mariana Ortega suggests that while contemporary white feminists now claim to listen to women of colour and attend to issues of race, their scholarship and actions often perpetuate a 'loving, knowing ignorance' about women of colour. This particular form of ignorance, Ortega argues, drawing on Marilyn Frye's theory of 'loving' and 'arrogant' perception, is the consequence of white feminists looking and listening to women of colour's words, but failing to 'check and question' whether they have fully understood.[50] Because whiteness impels those anxious to remain within its field of vision to view people of colour arrogantly, the failure to check and question their perception of women of colour's scholarship can lead white feminists to appropriate it to their own needs and desires in oppressive ways. This is often done at the same time as claiming to 'know' and have 'loving perception' towards women of colour.

A related argument is made by Aileen Moreton-Robinson in her book about white feminist academics in Australia. Moreton-Robinson found that her participants, while claiming to be interested in race and advocating anti-racism in their research and teaching practice, tended to locate race as belonging solely to people of colour. This subject position refuses to recognise whiteness as itself a racialised position, and maintains white dominance through evading acknowledgement of complicity in racism. This refusal to recognise one's own racialised position on the part of white middle-class feminist academics, Moreton-Robinson argues, 'is predicated on a mind/body split that works to allow the white female body to be separated from the mind'.[51] This split enables white feminist academics to theorise from a 'disembodied' subject position, as if their theories are not produced by or shaped within the white subjectivities, histories and spaces that they occupy. As white feminists have critiqued patriarchal scholarship for producing just such a split in relation to gender, Moreton-Robinson calls attention to the hypocrisy of their reproducing it in relation to race. Both Moreton-Robinson and Ortega are concerned with white feminist practices of knowledge production, drawing attention to the relationship between knowledge production and questions of power. Whose knowledge is sanctioned and canonised versus whose knowledge is delegitimised and dismissed have, within the colonial modern project, been deeply racialised, gendered and classed questions. Yet, as white-centred feminist scholarship has fought for and found increased legitimacy within the academy, this has been achieved in complicity with the racialised system of knowledge production which validates white, colonial forms of knowledge as the only 'true' knowledge.

One way in which whiteness as a form of racial power is maintained is through the construction of white people as innocent of racism. In her book *White Innocence*, Gloria Wekker addresses the connection between whiteness and innocence – or the pernicious construction of whiteness *as* innocence – through an exploration of how the white Dutch 'sense of self' as 'innocent' and 'just' is rooted in a paradoxical process of colonial, racialised othering and a simultaneous denial of the significance of race. Her analysis foregrounds the ways in which histories of colonisation and racial violence are hidden behind the facade of innocence, noting how 'innocence speaks not only of soft, harmless, childlike qualities' but is also 'strongly connected to privilege, entitlement, and violence that are deeply disavowed'.[52] The assertion of innocence, in other words, is not innocent. The common sense logic which posits that white people are innocent and good is, as bell hooks describes it, a 'fantasy' which upholds the system of white supremacy. This fantasy stops white people from understanding Black people's lived realities of whiteness, which, as hooks puts it, has made 'its presence felt ... most often as terrorizing imposition, a power that wounds, hurts, tortures'.[53] In particular, liberal white people tend to see themselves as good white people, distinguished from bad white racists, wilfully ignorant of their own complicities in structural racism. Barbara Applebaum thus argues that 'being a good white is *part of the problem* rather than *the solution* to systemic racism' because the 'need for moral innocence can encourage a profound resistance to knowing that entrenches ignorance further'.[54]

White feminists, generally committed to progressive politics and ending (gender) oppression, have a particularly deep investment in being 'good' white people. In addressing the gendered forms of white innocence which play out in feminist academia, Wekker notes how these white feminist academics tend to respond to frank discussions about race with 'anxiety, fear, avoidance, and feelings of guilt'.[55] Her observations are consistent with those of Mary Louise Fellows and Sherene Razack, who draw attention to the difficulties which arise in feminist discussions about oppressive relationships between women. Fellows and Razack describe this as initiating a process of 'competing marginalities' which they call the 'race to innocence'. Via an historical account of the emergence of middle-class notions of respectability in nineteenth-century Europe, Fellows and Razack argue that the interlocking systems of coloniality, capitalism and patriarchy require women to disavow their complicity in other women's subordination in order to keep their own 'toehold on respectability'. The middle- and upper-class white woman in colonial Europe achieved her respectability through her association with the cleanliness of the middle-class home, which required the disavowal and othering of the domestic worker who cleaned her home and the sex worker who was constructed as intimately connected with the 'degenerate slum'. Thus, the middle-class woman was able to secure her (relative) safety from economic and sexual exploitation through complicity in other women's exploitation. The domestic worker in turn could (although more tenuously) claim her respectability through disavowing the sex worker.[56] Fellows and Razack suggest that understanding the historical contexts through which different gendered positions have emerged allows us not only to see how specific hierarchical relationships between women have developed, but also how much women's identities are invested in not feeling connected to or complicit in other women's oppression. This, I would argue, is particularly pernicious in relation to middle-class whiteness, precisely because of the colonial relationship between whiteness and innocence.

As Sarita Srivastava's research with Canadian feminist organisations demonstrates (and as anyone who has challenged white feminists on racism knows), claims to innocence are endemic whenever white feminists are confronted with their racism. Anti-racist critiques tend to be met with defensiveness, denials, anger and often tears. Srivastava draws attention to the 'moral undertones' of such responses, arguing that colonial legacies of white femininity as rooted in 'racial innocence and superiority' intertwine with 'feminist ideals of justice and egalitarian community' to produce (white) feminist communities overly preoccupied with 'morality and self'. As she puts it, 'many white feminists may feel that it is their self image – as good, implicitly nonracist people – and particularly their shared moral identity as feminists that is under siege' when they are held to account for racism.[57] Observing the way high-profile white feminists have tended to 'close ranks' to defend the white feminist project against anti-racist critiques, Eddo-Lodge notes that white feminists perceive her 'speaking up about racism in feminism' as 'a violent attack on their very idea of themselves'.[58] This sense of the white feminist self as under attack is intimately tied to the moral attachment to innocence Srivastava observes in her research. This attachment often leads white feminists to expend more energy on asserting their innocence rather than learning about and challenging racism.

The preoccupation with innocence is something Ruth Frankenberg also highlights in her study about white women and race, published in the early 1990s. Frankenberg found that the dominant 'discursive repertoire' (i.e. ways of talking about race) which her interviewees mobilised was one of 'colour- or power evasiveness', i.e. a claim to not 'see' race or consider it to be significant (this perspective is often referred to as 'colour blindness', a term Frankenberg avoids, partly because of its ableist connotation, but also because it suggests passiveness rather than an active choice). Frankenberg also identified a more 'race-cognisant' repertoire employed by some of her participants who did acknowledge the significance of racism. This repertoire was more common among those participants who identified as feminists, and who had been influenced by anti-racist critiques by feminists of colour. Frankenberg observed that the extent to which this acknowledgement resulted in anti-racist action, rather than immobilising guilt, however, was very variable. On the other hand, there was consistency across both repertoires in that the 'status of the white subject was at stake ... as much as, if not more than, that of the subject of color'. This leads Frankenberg to suggest that the 'evasion of or engagement with white guilt and complicity with respect to racism are … perhaps what is at the heart of each of these discursive repertoires'.[59]

As the analysis in forthcoming chapters will demonstrate, contemporary white-centred feminist theory tends to vacillate between power-evasive and race-cognisant framings of race, but, as with Frankenberg's participants, an attachment to white innocence too often continues to get in the way of concerted attempts to dismantle white power structures within feminist politics. Throughout the book I will elaborate on how I see such attachments functioning within contemporary white-centred feminist theorising and liberal public debate in ways which ensure the prevailing dominance of white frameworks and narratives for understanding gender oppression.

LOCATION MATTERS

There is a tendency within British feminist literature to locate its theories as part of a broader field of 'Western' feminism or, somewhat more specifically, 'Anglo-American' feminism. It is undoubtedly true that feminist theory and politics which emerge from the British context can be usefully located in such a way. There are many historical continuities between the two countries, given the US origin as a British settler colonial project, and this is reflected also in feminist histories. Ware's research, for instance, highlights some of the connections between American and British feminists and abolitionists in the eighteenth and nineteenth centuries.[60] Ann Phoenix also points towards the importance of 'transatlantic conversations' between Black feminists in the US and the UK.[61] At the same time, when 'Anglo-American' is too easily assumed as a common sense descriptor of feminist theories emerging from the British context, this can lead to a loss of historical and contextual specifics. In her comparative study of British and US feminist activism, Elizabeth Evans interrogates whether the term has much empirical value, and concludes that while there are some similarities between US and British feminisms, the term ultimately glosses over important differences between them. Evans highlights, among other aspects, how 'the role of race and class have shaped the feminist movements in the US and Britain in different ways'.[62] Although Evans' research does not itself pay adequate attention to whiteness within British feminism (as I will discuss in Chapter 4), it does usefully question the phrase's explanatory power. This book addresses a concern that the construction of an 'Anglo-American' feminist field frequently works to erase the specificities of the British context in the aftermath of Empire, which is why it focuses specifically on British feminist theory and politics.

Chandra Mohanty's influential work on the possibilities of transnational feminist solidarity emphasises the importance of a 'politics of location'. Critiquing the notion of a 'universal sisterhood' of women, Mohanty argues that feminist relationships across borders of various kinds must be formed through an engagement with differences and power inequalities rather than through attempting to transcend them. Part of this engagement requires us to ground our work within the specificities of context, location and history. While she ultimately envisions a 'feminism without borders', Mohanty argues that transnational feminist solidarity requires us to understand that the borders between us matter: that they have a history and different material effects depending on where we are located. For Mohanty, 'the unity of women is best understood not as given, on the basis of a natural/ psychological commonality; it is something that has to be worked for, struggled toward – in history'.[63] This requires, in Mohanty's anti-capitalist, decolonial feminist analysis, an understanding of how colonialism, capitalism and heteropatriarchy interlock at a global level to produce women's differentiated experiences at local levels. Rooting this book's analysis within the specific context of (post)colonial Britain, then, is done in order to historically, socially and culturally locate the feminist theories and politics which have been shaped by (and which are part of shaping) this context. This is done not in the service of parochialism, but in order to understand how feminist politics in this context are connected to Britain's history in the world.

Of course, even writing about 'feminism in Britain' or 'British feminism' flattens out and conceals differences and omissions of various kinds. Most of the material that I analyse originates from institutional locations in England, and the book does not deal with regional differences in race politics. I considered redefining my object of study as 'English feminism', but this raises political questions of (self-)definitions which are themselves connected to histories of race and empire. An immediate post-Brexit poll found, for instance, that two-thirds of those who identified more as English than British voted Leave, while two-thirds of those who identified more as British than English voted Remain.[64] Brexit was a victory for the populist and racist agenda of the United Kingdom Independence Party (UKIP) which, despite its name, in fact has largely mobilised an *English* nationalism.[65] Given its history, Englishness often resonate specifically as *whiteness*, and people of colour are much more likely to identify as 'British' than 'English'.[66] The fact that most feminists (of colour and white) in England are perhaps also more likely to identify with Britishness rather than Englishness (if either) makes writing of an 'English feminism' complicated. Furthermore, newspapers such as the *Guardian* and the *Observer*, which I analyse in Chapter 5, have a national remit. Thus, I opt for writing of feminism in Britain despite the noted dominance of English-located perspectives.

A politics of location also requires attention to the contexts which shape our personal experiences and perspectives, and the naming of the positions from which we speak and theorise. In my case, this is from a white and also class-privileged position. I am part of the context in which I write and clearly implicated in the argument that I am making. Yet, the naming of the position is not itself the work. As Ahmed points out, white self-defined anti-racist activists and scholars often name their whiteness as a way of indicating that they are aware of the privilege it brings, but unless such declarations are accompanied by ongoing work to dismantle white supremacy then it has little value. Such declarations may in fact shore up whiteness by creating space for 'good' white identities: an 'anti-racist' whiteness which still centres the actions and intentions of white people rather than the work of ending racism.[67] As should be clear from the previous section, the 'good white feminist' position reproduces colonial and heteropatriarchal notions of white feminine innocence which need to be resisted. While I try to avoid positioning myself in such a way, it is clearly a tension within the project. White people doing anti-racist work must remain attuned to the ways in which they are complicit in structures of whiteness, otherwise, as Fiona Probyn bluntly puts it, 'we've missed the whole point'.[68] Generally, I use 'they' rather than 'we' in referring to white feminists in the book not to distance myself but rather to ensure that I am not only addressing white feminist readers.

A NOTE ON KNOWLEDGE PRODUCTION
AND THE POLITICS OF CITATION

One of the risks of publishing this book is that others (particularly other white feminists) will engage with it and cite it on the topic of whiteness and racism *instead of* engaging and citing the work of feminists of colour on this topic. Of course I am writing this book in order for readers to engage with it, however, there is a clear risk that my work may end up being referenced as if critiques of white feminism originate from it, rather than for what it is: *a response to feminists of colour's critiques of white feminism and an attempt to address the content of such critiques.* Academic researchers are frequently required to justify the originality of their research, but I want to stress that many of my arguments are *not* original. Part of the problem that I am trying to address is precisely the question of why anti-racist critiques by feminists of colour have had to be made over and over again, and yet the problems persist. This is why I am especially interested in how narratives of British feminism are constructed, and pay particular attention to the ways in which Black British feminism and feminists of colour are repeatedly marginalised or erased from dominant accounts. The element of originality of the book (and, hopefully, its value) lies rather in its in-depth analysis of and extended attention to how whiteness shapes different sites of feminist knowledge production in the contemporary British context. The book aims to respond to the repeated calls which have been made by feminists of colour for white feminists to do the work of interrogating whiteness, how it operates, and, crucially, how it can be dismantled.

There may be a range of different kinds of readers of this book, with different levels of knowledge and experience in relation to the subject. For those who are well versed in critiques of white feminism, many of the points made may appear self-evident. For these readers, I hope that the in-depth examination of contemporary white-centred discourse can still provide some useful new material and evidence. For other readers – particularly white feminists – who have not significantly engaged with critiques of white feminism before, but have decided to pick up this book, I hope that it can provide an introduction to the subject and contribute towards deepened thinking and action to challenge racism and whiteness as a response. Most importantly, I hope that it will impel such readers to seek out work by feminists of colour. As I hope is clear, my analysis is fundamentally informed by and indebted to Black and postcolonial feminist and radical women of colour's theorising which addresses the connections between heteropatriarchy, white supremacy and capitalism.

As will be highlighted within the forthcoming analysis, one of the ways in which white-centred feminist theory maintains its whiteness is through the use of citations. Specifically, white-centred theorising often marginalises the scholarship of feminists of colour. Describing citations as 'academic bricks', Ahmed writes that '[w]hen citational practices become habits, bricks form walls'. When white feminists centre the work of white feminists in their theorising, the walls of whiteness are reinforced. She continues: 'I think as feminists we can hope to create a crisis around citation, even just a hesitation, a wondering, that might help us not to follow the well-trodden citational paths.'[69] Within feminist theory making, citational practices are opportunities for disrupting whiteness. I therefore urge white readers (particularly academics) to reflect on how they use and cite this book, and to ensure they do not do so instead of engaging with or in ways which decentre feminists of colour's work.

THE 'HOWS' AND 'WHYS' OF THE RESEARCH

This book grew out of a PhD project which I finished in 2015, and that PhD project grew out of my involvement with and interest in feminism since the early 2000s, both as activist politics and as academic knowledge. My formative activist experiences came from being involved in organising Ladyfest festivals and other feminist and queer networks which sprang up around and inspired these events. While there were efforts by some activists – predominantly people of colour – to discuss race and white privilege within these communities, a largely unacknowledged whiteness significantly harmed and weakened them, as was documented in the *Race Revolt* zines, edited by Humaira Saeed.[70] Intense conflicts and fallouts over racism were recurring features during these years. At various points, I found myself both in the position of being critiqued as well as critiquing others. In 2004–05, I had been lucky and privileged enough to be taught about Black British feminism by Nirmal Puwar during my MA in Gender, Culture and Modernity at Goldsmiths College. Subsequently, embroiled in conflicts about racism within these contemporary feminist and queer communities, I started to question the disconnect between Black and white feminisms and why the former was so little known or acknowledged by the latter, particularly in the British context.

The dominant whiteness of British feminism became even more conspicuous to me as I began my research degree and consequently found that most academic feminist spaces, such as conferences, were some of the whitest spaces that I regularly inhabited, both numerically and politically. At many feminist academic events race was not on the agenda at all. It is not unusual for almost all participants at such events to be white and for this to go unremarked upon, at least until the closing plenary when someone – and too often this is left to a woman of colour – draws attention to the absence of conversations about racism and the predominant absence of feminists of colour in the room. Such interventions are routinely met with awkward silences and vague commitments about 'next time'. Other events may frame their call for papers around intersectionality and difference, yet on the day, hardly anyone mentions Black feminism or racism. Then there are the events where conversations about racism in feminism do take place, but where white comfort and innocence is prioritised. In my experience, there is often intense resistance from white feminists to actually staying with the discomfort of this conversation without reframing it as a defence, or otherwise retreating into silence, particularly when it means talking about racism as something which exists in the communities and spaces we are part of and invested in.

Considering the perennial and repetitive nature of these debates and conflicts led me to think about the role of knowledge production within feminist communities in shaping how anti-racist critiques are addressed – or not. In other words, what kinds of theories and narratives about feminism and race get legitimated, written down and passed on? Who and what gets left out, erased or marginalised? This concern with formal channels of knowledge production led me towards researching the representation of issues of race and racism within white-centred feminist literature, and the arguments in this book have been developed through an analysis of contemporary feminist texts. Specifically, my research focuses on authored books as well as newspaper articles which in some way address questions about what feminism is, what it has been and what it should look like in the future: what its key concepts, ideas and challenges are.

Although simplistic distinctions between 'theory' versus 'practice', or 'texts' versus 'the world' are problematic, it is worth noting that textual analysis does in many ways not do justice to the messiness of the 'real life' politics and practices of everyday discussions and dynamics within feminist communities. The structures and practices of the publishing industry, academia and the mainstream media mean that only very select voices are legitimated through these channels. Academic accreditation and publication authorises some voices as experts while the majority of those involved with feminist politics do not have their perspectives recognised in the public domain in such a way. But this is precisely why I chose to focus on published texts in constructing my analysis: they tell us something important about what kinds of knowledge and ideas become legitimised and circulated through formal publication. Although many other perspectives and analyses circulate within feminist communities, media and publishing industries have significant power to set agendas for others to engage with (despite the increasing influence of social media, as will be discussed in Chapter 5), whether they do so by critiquing those agendas or not.

In analysing the ways in which these texts construct knowledge about race, the book centres on critique. This critical approach is likely to also garner a critical response. When presenting my work at conferences, I have been asked on numerous occasions by other white feminists whether I think it is 'fair' to critique other feminist writers in the way that my work does. The short answer to this is yes: I definitely believe it is 'fair' to critique published material. This is common practice and the building blocks of theorising and scholarship: we engage with what others have written, building on their work, which may also involve disagreeing with their analysis and responding via a critique. The fact that this is often perceived as particularly fraught when it comes to anti-racist critique brings us back to white feminist investments in racial innocence, and thus it is important to reflect on the role that this plays when anti-racist critique is understood as 'not fair' and destructive. As hooks compellingly argues, 'feminist solidarity rooted in a commitment to progressive politics must include a space for rigorous critique, for dissent, or we are doomed to reproduce in progressive communities the very forms of domination we seek to oppose'.[71] 'Internal' critique within feminist communities (too easily dismissed as 'infighting') is an essential part of their theoretical and political development.

Too often the difficult and emotionally fraught work of anti-racist critique within feminist spaces has been left to women of colour. Thus, I see this work as part of taking responsibility, as a white feminist, for challenging white-centred theory and politics – of being accountable to critiques by feminists of colour and taking calls to address the issues these have raised seriously. The purpose of the critique presented here is not to point fingers at individuals. Although the analysis focuses on particular texts which have been authored by particular people, the ideas and theories contained within them are not created in a vacuum but are formulated within the context of a wider community. Books, for instance, are the end products of various collective processes, including engagement with prior literature, conversations with and feedback from peers, review, editing, and so on. In other words, the privileging of whiteness is institutionalised within mainstream academic and popular feminism: it is the collective responsibility of white feminists, and bigger than any one individual – although each individual has a role to play.

The books analysed in Chapters 3 and 4 have all been published since 2009, while Chapter 5 takes a somewhat longer view, tracing the construction of a 'new feminism' in liberal public discourse since the turn of the century. The analysis involved close readings of the texts, looking for key words and themes which are relevant to the topics of race and whiteness, whether directly or indirectly. Similar to Ahmed, who describes following words (such as 'diversity') around as a methodological approach, I followed words such as 'race', 'racism', 'difference', 'diversity', 'ethnocentrism' and 'intersectionality' around within these texts to see what they revealed: what context they were used within, what stories they were part of, and what work they were made to do.[72] Significantly, this also involved paying attention to absences in the text – where I felt that a race analysis was missing or being evaded, or where euphemisms were employed in ways which suggested an attempt to avoid addressing racism directly.

My concern with the repetitiveness of anti-racist critique and responses to such critiques led me in particular to consider the role of narratives – how stories are told about feminism and race, and the repetition of particular stories – in how whiteness is reproduced again and again. As Clare Hemmings argues, interrogating which stories come to dominate shines a light on contemporary power structures within feminism: the power to define a particular narrative as the dominant story of feminism 'enable[s] a particular present to gain legitimacy'.[73] In her research on feminist stories, Hemmings conducted an analysis of peer-reviewed articles in academic feminist journals, homing in on any parts of an article which told a story about the historical development of feminist theory. Her close attention to the narratives which are constructed across brief segments of the articles allowed her to unpick what she calls the 'political grammar' of feminist storytelling. Hemmings' attention to the structuring and content of the stories told within and across the journal articles enabled her to track how three parallel narratives of progress, loss and return have become dominant within Western feminist theory.[74] In a similar way, I focus attention on those bits of contemporary feminist texts that tell stories about the feminist past and present. I pay particular attention to how they produce meanings about feminism in relation to race and racism. Approaching white-centred feminist literature and discourse through an examination of the dominant stories told opens up another way of interrogating and potentially disrupting the reproduction of whiteness.

More broadly, narratives are a form of representation, i.e. what Stuart Hall defines as 'the process by which members of a culture use language … to produce meaning'.[75] As not everything which I draw out from the texts could be defined as a narrative, in a broader sense the project can be understood as looking at the representation of feminist ideas and politics within the texts that I analyse. These texts are part of a larger feminist discourse, i.e. the larger sphere of talk and writing on feminist topics which together shape how such topics are known and understood.

I will end this section by acknowledging an unresolved tension within the book: while my analysis deconstructs and interrupts narratives which tell the story of feminism in particular ways, it inevitably and quite deliberately also constructs its own stories. How do we write without telling stories, given that they are central to how we make sense of the world? They anchor our understanding of a given moment or event by providing context as to how we got there and why events have taken their particular shape in the present. This is precisely why stories are political. The narratives the book constructs foreground particular events and frame their meaning according to the particular agenda of this book. It should be stressed therefore that while I do insist that they tell us important things that we need to know in order to understand the politics of race and feminism in the contemporary British context, they are at the same time partial, incomplete and subject to revision.

OUTLINE OF THE BOOK

In line with the unresolved tension on which I ended the previous section, the next chapter tells a story which provides some historical context for the book's central arguments. Tracing a partial narrative of feminist debates about race in the 1970s and 1980s, the chapter draws attention to some of the ways in which whiteness was challenged within the women's liberation movement at this time. Exploring feminist archives of the 1980s, I draw attention to some of the important legacies of conflicts, discussions and coalitions that took place in terms of the development of anti-racist feminist frameworks. After this historical account, the second part of the chapter discusses some of the key analytical frameworks and concepts emerging from Black and postcolonial feminist theorising.

Chapters 3 and 4 both analyse the construction of white-centred narratives within contemporary academic literature about feminism. Chapter 3 focuses in particular on texts which construct feminist whiteness as a problem of the past, while Chapter 4 focuses on literature which acknowledges racism within feminism as an ongoing problem. These divergent narratives pave the way for different kinds of engagements with the concepts of race and racism. In Chapter 3, I draw attention to ways in which race analysis is alluded to while it is simultaneously displaced, as well as to how white feminists are positioned as having transcended whiteness. Chapter 4 analyses the more concerted race analysis apparent in three recent books about feminist activism, finding that even though these texts acknowledge the importance of race, they also reproduce whiteness through a continued marginalisation of feminists of colour. Here, I pay particular attention to how whiteness is constructed as inevitable, and how this absolves white feminists of responsibility for addressing it.

Chapter 5 focuses on feminist politics within mainstream spheres of public debate, exploring the ways in which a 'new' feminism for the twenty-first century has been constructed within popular feminist books and the liberal press, using the *Guardian* and *Observer* newspapers as case studies. The analysis of the popular books draws attention to the ways in which the 'new' feminist subjects they construct are heavily inscribed with whiteness, through narratives which also exhibit a careless othering of racialised women and an investment in Britain's colonial history. The analysis of the *Guardian* and the *Observer* highlights the role these papers have played in promoting a small group of white, middle-class women as the intellectual leaders of twenty-first-century feminism, with depictions of these individuals reproducing colonial ideals of a noble and selfless white femininity. The chapter also explores more recent attempts in each paper to diversify its coverage of feminist activism and ideas, finding that while a more diverse range of 'voices' are now given space within the paper, the liberal framework which underpins it ultimately works to co-opt and depoliticise anti-racist feminist interventions.

Across Chapters 3 to 5 I highlight how white feminist innocence is prioritised in order to maintain and legitimate the continued centring of white women within feminist theorising and movements. In order to interrupt this systemic attachment to innocence, Chapter 6 considers what a shift from innocence to *complicity* might entail for white feminists, and what work such a shift suggests. In one sense, then, this chapter attempts to address the frequently asked question 'what should white feminists do?' while also problematising the assumptions which often underpin it.

2

British Feminisms in
the Aftermath of Empire

As Chapter 1 has established, debates about feminism, racism and whiteness are not new, but rather a perennial feature of feminist communities. In the first half of this chapter, I will revisit a few such debates in more depth, with a particular focus on Black feminist critiques of feminist whiteness and the development of anti-racist feminist analyses and political praxis in the 1980s. This provides some necessary context for the remainder of the book, as it is important to know about some of the developments which took place at this time in order to understand and situate contemporary feminist discussions about race. In focusing on this time period I am not suggesting that such debates and developments *only* took place at this time, but rather aim to highlight the significance of some of the work which *did* take place in this era. The debates that took place in the 1980s as a result of Black feminist interventions significantly challenged the pervasive white ignorance which up until that point dominated the movement. As such, they constituted important building blocks for the development of anti-racist feminist analysis, as well as for Black and postcolonial feminisms as ongoing intellectual projects. In order to elaborate this second point, the second half of this chapter draws attention to key analytical frameworks, concerns and concepts which are central to these projects, and which are highly relevant for the analysis in subsequent chapters.

The chapter should not be read as an account of the history of Black British feminism. Rather, it is a highly selective exploration of some of the discussions, conflicts, coalitional work and theorising that have been influential in shaping race-critical feminist analysis and practice in the British context. One point which is often minimised or erased in white-centred accounts of Black feminism is its significance for feminist politics as a whole, with many white feminists presuming that Black feminism has nothing to do with them, and that it is only relevant to women of colour. Yet, such perspectives expose a misunderstanding of Black feminism as an intellectual project. Heidi Mirza challenges the misinterpretation of Black feminism as being simply about claiming space for an 'authentic voice' of Black women:

> To simply 'have a place' in the academic discourse is not the project of Black British feminism. Black women do not want just to voice their experiences, to shout from the roof tops 'we have arrived! ... listen to me ... this is my story'... We are engaged in a far more subtle project, a project in which over the last 20 years we have attempted to invoke some measure of critical race/gender reflexivity into mainstream academic thinking. In telling our different story, in exposing our personal pain and pleasures, Black British feminists reveal *other ways of knowing* that challenge the normative discourse.[1]

Here, Mirza calls attention to the broader transformative aims and possibilities of Black feminist analyses, emphasising its relevance for all critical theorising and praxis.

The first section of the chapter provides a brief overview of the politics of race and racism in the latter half of twentieth-century Britain, in order to locate feminist politics within the wider cultural and political climate of the time, which involved a concerted effort to 'forget' Empire in the era of decolonisation. I will then move on to discuss the development of anti-racist feminisms from the late 1970s to the late 1980s. This will include a focus on three case studies: debates about racism, antisemitism and Zionism in the women's liberation movement magazine *Spare Rib*, the development of anti-racist theoretical analyses in the academic journal *Feminist Review*, and the multiracial coalitional work of the *Outwrite Women's Newspaper* Collective. My account of debates within these sites of feminist knowledge production is based on empirical research in the archives at the Feminist Library and the Women's Library in London, as well as through engagement with academic literature. The London-centric nature of this account must be noted and cannot be generalised as representing the level of discussion about race and racism across the country. However, each of these case studies is significant to the development of anti-racist feminist politics in Britain. The *Spare Rib* conflict led to one of the most protracted debates about racism within the women's liberation movement, its effects reverberating well beyond the members of the collective in London. *Feminist Review* underwent a significant transformation in relation to race analysis and praxis and therefore constitutes an interesting example of a collective as well as a publication which has attempted to grapple with whiteness. *Outwrite's* anti-racist and anti-imperial radical feminist perspective was ground-breaking in its time, and its legacy has been vastly under-appreciated and often obscured completely within contemporary accounts of the women's liberation movement.

Following the historical accounts, the discussion moves on to consider the development of Black and postcolonial feminisms as intellectual projects since this time, highlighting key analytical frameworks and concepts which these projects tend to foreground. This lays the ground-work for the subsequent chapters, which consider the extent to which such frameworks are acknowledged and engaged with in contemporary white-centred feminist work. This discussion also draws attention to the processes involved in the institutionalisation of feminism within academia, noting that while Black, postcolonial and race-critical feminist analyses have carved out space within academic theorising, this growth has at the same time been curtailed via the institutional margin-alisation of women of colour within the academy, with white feminist academics often complicit in this process.

FORGETTING EMPIRE

The second half of the twentieth century, up until the end of the cold war, is commonly periodised within British public culture as 'post-war'. This description tends to conceal the fact that this was also the period of formal decolonisation of the Empire. This concealment enabled migration from former colonies to be constructed as an intrusion of 'foreigners'. Barnor Hesse and S. Sayyid highlight how dominant narra-tives of mass migration from former colonies in this period have been predominantly constructed around economic explanations of market forces without adequate attention to the historical or cultural context of (post)coloniality. Such accounts, they argue, deny the continuity 'between the imperial past and the nationalist present', creating 'a struc-tural and political separation between a racially unmarked indigenous British society and racially marked migrants'.[2] In *The Empire Strikes Back*, the Centre for Contemporary Cultural Studies' (CCCS) groundbreaking study of racism in 1970s Britain, Errol Lawrence notes how the widespread denial of the legacies of Britain's imperial past led to Black people being seen by the white population as 'importing' the 'problems' of race. Dominant narratives consistently reiterated the otherness of 'immigrants', informed by a belief in the superiority of white British culture. Cultural explanations of racial difference functioned to conceal the ways in which institutional structures and policies in fact produced inequalities. As Lawrence points out, problems such as overcrowded housing were commonly blamed on Black and Asian people themselves, who were perceived as having too many children, rather than on racist landlords and housing policies.[3]

Representing Black and Asian cultures in Britain as separate and 'other' from white English or British culture relies on a fundamentally colonial logic – an ideological construct rather than one which holds up to any scrutiny. The cultures of the colonial metropole and the colonised territories are historically intertwined and co-constituted, a truth evocatively captured by Stuart Hall when describing his migration from Jamaica to England in the 1950s: 'I was coming home. I am the sugar at the bottom of the English cup of tea. I am the sweet tooth, the sugar plantations that rotted generations of English children's teeth.'[4] Yet, the official forgetting of Empire in public discourse between the 1950s and the 1970s rendered the colonial structures of the emerging 'race relations' paradigm invisible.

The CCCS describe 1970s Britain as being in a state of 'crisis', not just economically, but also politically, culturally and ideologically. Within this context, they note how an increasingly authoritarian state 'fundamentally intertwined with the elaboration of popular racism'. The state responded to increasing numbers of Black and Asian people in Britain with increasingly strict immigration legislation and repressive social policies. Black movements organising to protect their communities were met with a violent and repressive 'crisis management' approach by state forces.[5] The CCCS highlight the sense of national existential threat which pervaded governmental (as well as popular) discourse by the late 1970s and into the 1980s, with the rise to power of Margaret Thatcher's government:

In the wake of the election of the Conservative Government in 1979 an important official debate has taken place about the position of black people in Britain. In *Hansard* one can find many humorous, and some not so humorous, attempts to produce watertight definitions of exactly who is 'British' and who 'is not'. It is important that we are clear what such debates are about: they are an aspect of a much broader attempt to bring some kind of order into a society which is widely perceived to be falling apart. They are part of a struggle to 'make sense' of a conjuncture where all that is good and wholesome seems to be under threat.[6]

This political and cultural context provides an important part of the backdrop against which women's movements of the time flourished. Alongside the rise of popular and state racism intent on excluding formerly colonised people from the national imagination and community, the 1970s were also a period of intense radical political activity and movements of different kinds. The early to mid 1970s, for instance, witnessed the height of activity of the white-dominated women's liberation movement. Feminist rebellion can be understood, alongside Black resistance, as another element of the threat to the dominant social order as perceived by the state at this time. But what is striking about many accounts of the women's liberation movement is the scant attention paid to this broader political backdrop. Writing in the early 1990s, Vron Ware suggests that this 'apparent lack of engagement' with the postcolonial backdrop of the movement was a 'symptom of feminism's uneasy awareness of its own historical context'.[7] Thus, the lack of attention to the context of state and popular racism of the 1970s within white feminist accounts should not be assumed to mean that it was insignificant. On the contrary, issues of race, whiteness and coloniality, both when they were made explicit and when they were denied, should be seen as central to the construction of feminist politics and theory at this time, as the next section will discuss.

FORGING ANTI-RACIST FEMINIST
ANALYSIS IN 1980s BRITAIN

In 'White woman listen!', another chapter in *The Empire Strikes Back*, Hazel Carby critiques white feminist theory for failing to account for the roles that slavery, colonialism and imperialism have played in structuring gender relations. Noting how white feminist theories had been developed during 'a decade in which Black women have been fighting, in the streets, in the schools, through the courts, inside and outside the wage relation', she condemns the ignorance these theories exhibited towards Black women's experiences and struggles, challenging white women's refusal to recognise their complicity in the European project of racial domination:

> White women in the British WLM [women's liberation movement] are extraordinarily reluctant to see themselves in the situation of being oppressors, as they feel that this will be at the expense of concentrating upon being oppressed. Consequently the involvement of British women in imperialism and colonialism is repressed and the benefits that they – as whites – gained from the oppression of black people ignored. Forms of imperialism are simply identified as aspects of an all embracing patriarchy rather than as sets of social relations in which white women hold positions of power by virtue of their 'race'.[8]

Carby's analysis can be located within a broader development of Black British feminist theorising and politics, which emerged from Black and Asian women's organising in postcolonial Britain. As Amrit Wilson puts it, women of colour 'suddenly became politically visible' in the mid to late 1970s. Yet, as she notes, the Black women's movement which 'moved centre-stage' at this time had a much longer history, having 'grown out of the anti-colonial struggles of the fifties', in which many women had 'long been politically active but unrecognised'.[9]

Part of this move to the 'centre-stage' for Black women's collective activism involved the creation of the Organisation of Women of Asian and African Descent (OWAAD) in 1978, a national umbrella organisation for many Black women's groups organising around the country. An autonomous Black women's movement gained momentum at this time, and the first OWAAD conference, attended by 250 women, was held in 1978.[10] In the first issue of *FOWAAD*, the organisation's newsletter, the editors highlighted the diversity of issues which had been raised at the conference:

> We discussed a wide range of topics: our immediate history, the experiences we had upon first arriving in Britain, the types of job[s] we are doing and the ways Black women are being exploited and discrim-

inated against in employment, the housing conditions we face and the education that we and our children are (not) getting, the many health issues which concern us, the different forms of State harassment we are facing daily in the guise of SUS ['suspected persons' stop and search law], passport raids and intimidation by police and immigration officers, and the situation of our sisters in the Third World.[11]

OWAAD held four annual conferences in total, connecting Black women's groups across the country. While primarily focused on issues which most immediately affected women of colour and their families, the emerging movement also provided a more prominent platform from which Black women could express their anger at the way they had been marginalised, tokenised or ignored by white women within the women's liberation movement. Ann Phoenix reflects, for instance, on the impact OWAAD had on her consciousness and confidence as a Black feminist:

> Publications from OWAAD had a direct impact on my political activity in that they partly inspired me to leave the Manchester Rape Crisis Collective, in which I had been a founding member, explaining clearly as I did so why it was untenable for me to stay in a context where there was a reluctance to address the then common interlinking of rape and 'race' and what this meant for constructions of black men as well as how it rendered black women who were raped invisible.[12]

The ways in which discussions of rape have been racialised – the 'timeworn myth of the black rapist', in Angela Davis' formulation – is a recurring point of contention and conflict within feminist politics and one which I will be returning to in Chapter 4.[13]

Reproductive rights is another key area of feminist politics which have often thrown up difficulties for cross-racial organising. The second issue of *FOWAAD* included the following statement challenging the women's liberation movement campaign against the Corrie Bill (a Parliamentary Bill which was proposing to further restrict access to abortion):

> Since black women are included in [the National Abortion Campaign's] call, we find it regrettable that once again the wider issues of abortion as it affects us have been ignored by the (mainly white) women's movement. Black women have demanded abortion, and

been forced to have sterilisations! We have demanded the right to choose, and we have been injected instead with Depo Provera against our will ... When making a demand for abortion rights, the women's movement has a duty to point out to all women that racism and impe-rialist population control programmes are also being used against black and Third World women, with genocidal implications ... [It is] high time that the women's movement recognised that 'Free Abortion on demand' can and does have grave consequences for black women, which have still to be taken up in a meaningful way.[14]

Campaigning for women's unconditional rights to abortions was a central plank of the women's liberation movement, but the fact that race and class were salient factors in determining how doctors responded to women's fertility had often not been considered by white (middle-class) feminists calling for abortion on demand. In particular, as the critique highlights, the controversial contraceptive injection, Depo Provera, was disproportionally prescribed to Black women to control their fertility, despite its documented long-term health risks, an issue which OWAAD members campaigned around extensively.[15]

It is at the same time too simplistic to suggest that no white feminists paid attention to racism before this period. Natalie Thomlinson argues that, contrary to reductive contemporary narratives of 1970s white fem-inists as universally racist and ignorant, many white women involved in the early days of the women's liberation movement had previously been active within anti-imperialist organising. She also points out that the women's movement in Britain (as well as in the US, where the links are clearer to see) was influenced by Black liberation movements. Thus, Thomlinson argues, many white feminists, particularly those who were involved in Left politics, did have some level of anti-racist analysis, as evidenced by groups such as Women Against Racism and Fascism (WARF) and Women Against Imperialism, set up by white women in the late 1970s to campaign against the National Front and popular racism. However, as Thomlinson contends, 'white feminists involved in these groups often dealt with these matters in ways that ironically reinscribed white power', organising in ways which 'excluded Black feminists and still tended to place white women centre stage as theo-rists of racism and imperialism'.[16] This is confirmed in Ware's first-hand account of her involvement with WARF at the time, in which she describes how the group always struggled to answer the questions 'What exactly has racism got to do with white women?' as well as 'How do we actually meet and work together with black women?' Ware notes how white feminists eagerly turned towards consciousness-raising strategies to address racism, yet struggled to see the links between the personal and the structural. Thus, 'the quest to uncover personal racism was frequently elevated to a supposedly political end in itself'.[17] White feminist anti-racist activism in the 1970s, to the extent that it did exist, therefore tended to focus its attention on the far right and certain forms of British imperialism without recognising the fundamentally racial structure of British society, including white women's complicity in the oppression of people of colour. It was only once Black women more collectively drew attention to white women's racism that a wider debate about it came to the fore.

Spare Rib, *racism and antisemitism*

One of the most contentious debates at this time was the extended conflict about racism, Zionism and antisemitism within the *Spare Rib* Editorial Collective in 1982–83. *Spare Rib* was the most well-known and widely read feminist magazine of the time. With the geopolitical backdrop of Israel's invasion of Lebanon, a conflict broke out within the collective over disagreements about whether to publish a number of letters which had been sent in by readers. The letters had been triggered by an article published in August 1982, titled 'Women speak out against Zionism'.[18] The letters, many of them from Jewish feminists, critiqued the article as antisemitic. An intense debate ensued within the collective, as well as within the wider feminist community, as to whether the letters were Zionist and/or racist, and whether censoring them amounted to antisemitism.[19] While the debates in the collective were not discussed on the pages of *Spare Rib* until almost a year later, some of them were documented elsewhere, such as in the pages of the weekly *London Women's Liberation Newsletter (LWLN)*.

The history of *Spare Rib* is indicative of the challenge anti-racism was posing for the women's liberation movement at this time. At the time of the magazine's tenth anniversary in 1982, of the 60 women who had been on the editorial collective, Linda Bellos, who had just joined, was the only woman of colour, and little attention had been paid to white feminist racism in the pages of the magazine up until this point.[20] In a 1989 *Feminist Review* article, Pratibha Parmar tells an anecdote from 1978, when, together with Kum-Kum Bhavnani, she had submitted an article for publication in *Spare Rib* titled 'Racism and the women's movement':

> We received a three-page letter from a member of the collective who attempted to answer our critique. 'The problem is that while *our movement* [my emphasis] is undoubtedly failing to reach large numbers of black women we have not in fact made the precise mistakes your paper describes.' Throughout, she addressed us as if we were speaking from outside of the movement and used 'we' to denote white women as being representative of the women's movement. The letter concluded by stating: 'We didn't really feel your article could form a basis for discussion inside the feminist community as it betrays so many misconceptions about the movement's history.[21]

Determined to turn the magazine in a more anti-racist direction, Bellos was instrumental in ensuring the recruitment of more women of colour onto the collective, a number of whom joined in the autumn of 1982. Yet, with the conflict around the letters brewing, power dynamics within the collective were highly racialised, and a subsequent split occurred. Bellos, among others, ended up leaving.

Although the particular intensity of the conflict in 1982–83 can in part be attributed to the volatility of politics around Israel and Palestine, it is clear that the issues were also more broadly about race and racism, including antisemitism, within the women's movement. Bellos, writing in the *LWLN* in the summer of 1983, explained how she had to leave because she did not agree that the unpublished letters were Zionist, critiquing 'the inconsistency towards Jewish women in "Spare Rib's" so-called anti-racist policy'. She criticised the other women of colour on the collective for failing to recognise her position as a Black Jewish woman. But she also pointed towards the lack of anti-racist understanding within the broader movement:

> I suspect that the reason the issue of anti-semitism/anti-zionism has split the WLM so painfully is that it has never really grasped what anti-racism really means. It is not about assimilating into white

English culture. My experience has been that many, most, white women have only paid lip service to Black women, believing that, by doing anything that Black women said, they were being anti-racist … I am deeply saddened that the work I felt I did at 'Spare Rib', in fighting those who have power – white, middle-class English women [–] has now been lost. Instead, various oppressed women are fighting each other, leaving those with power untouched. I think its [sic] called divide and rule.[22]

In analysing the way that the conflict had played out, Bellos usefully drew attention to the power dynamics which pitted differently racialised women – in this case Jewish women and non-Jewish women of colour – against each other, while the non-Jewish white, middle-class women who continued to dominate the movement became the spectators and arbiters of reason. Some of the other women of colour within the collective (who did not give their names in their published responses) did make problematic conflations between Jewish and white women – such as describing the whole conflict around the letters as a 'white women's issue'. Another comment, which expressed anger at having 'to devote most of my energy on a single group that can insist on our devotion due to the great power that they have' was certainly antisemitic, with its ambiguity as to whether it referred to white women or Jewish women or simply conflating the two. Yet, while not excusing such comments, the context of white and middle-class dominance within the movement must also be taken into account to understand why the conflict played out as it did. The fact that the women of colour on the collective so quickly became the villains in the whole debate – still largely dominated by white women – speaks to the lack of sufficiently complex race analysis within the movement. Many white feminist responses demonstrated significant ignorance and racism. In a letter published in *Spare Rib* in 1983, the Faversham Women's Group, for instance, responded to debates in an earlier issue by castigating the women of colour on the magazine's collective:

… the contributions from women of colour were particularly unhelpful. They angered us. The white women offered thoughtful accounts of how their consciousness on racism has developed. The women of colour made cryptic assertions which we found hurtful, and which were not explained. One says 'white women continue to remain the oppressors of women of colour'. Is this all white women? Are we the only oppressors? Do we oppress men of colour? What can we do about it? Anything? etc. We want to have these debates but we can't if the women of colour won't say how they came to their hate-filled positions.[23]

The group further expressed worry that the women's liberation movement was splitting 'over an issue which is not one of the seven demands, and which we do not see as a central women's issue'.[24] White women's lack of interest in racism was also evident by the decreasing support and subscriptions for the magazine following its shift towards a more anti-racist perspective.[25] There were also threats and attacks directed at the magazine's office. In an editorial in September 1983, the collective wrote of receiving phone calls saying 'Hitler' and 'Foreigners go home', as well as 'pro-Zionist slogans ... daubed on walls outside and a brick ... thrown into the office next door', noting also white women's reluctance to see such incidents as attacks against the women of colour.[26]

Yet, as a result of repeated critiques by Black feminists, white-dominated feminist groups and collectives did slowly begin to take more serious notice of racism as a structuring power of British society, including the ways in which the whiteness of the women's liberation movement excluded Black women. Amongst the more hostile letters from white feminists, there were also those declaring a commitment to change.[27] Within the *Spare Rib* Collective, a gradual change in perspective can be noted through the shift in content and analysis of women's oppression in the early 1980s. In the February issue of 1982, for instance, the editorial introduced a series of articles by Bhavnani about the racism of the 1981 Nationality Act, in which the collective state:

The British women's movement is made up of both Black and white women. We are a movement committed to fighting the oppression of all women, and this commitment must include all of us develop-ing an anti-racist and anti-imperialist perspective. It isn't enough for white British feminists to work out the ways in which they indi-vidually oppress Black people. Oppression does not spring merely from individual acts and attitudes. White feminists need to understand much more about how racism is structured into the whole of British society.[28]

Further on, the editorial explicitly links the 'institutional racism' of nationality and immigration politics to Britain's colonial history. This editorial indicates a shift towards a perspective which positioned racism as central to feminist analysis, and one which emphasised white feminists' responsibility for educating themselves about it at both an individual and a structural level. Such a shift from a majority-white feminist collective, members of which had only a few years earlier so dismissively rejected Parmar and Bhavnani's article, is clearly the result of Black feminists' interventions. There was also a long-term effect on the content of the magazine and the composition of the collective, and by 1984, half of the collective members were women of colour.[29]

Feminist Review *and academic feminism*

Black feminist theorists were also carving out space within academic discourse at this time. One strand of such work involved critical deconstructions of white feminist analytical frameworks. Carby's chapter represents one such influential intervention, and another came a couple of years later from Valerie Amos and Parmar. In 'Challenging imperial feminism' they critique 'white, mainstream feminist theory, be it from the socialist or radical feminist perspective', which they argue 'does not speak to the experiences of Black women and where it attempts to do so it is often from a racist perspective and reasoning'. Their article highlighted the limitations of white feminist analyses of the family and sexuality, pointing towards white feminist complicities in informing racist state practices which pathologised Black families, as well as in popular constructions of Black men as sexual predators. They also critiqued white feminists' desire to assimilate Black women into the white-dominated movement, noting that 'white women have condemned Black women for not engaging in the struggles they have identified as important – the colonial heritage marches on'.[30] Like Carby, Amos and Parmar argued that feminist theory must engage with the historical context of imperialism and challenge racism, and they suggested that Black feminism was meeting this challenge.

44

Amos and Parmar's article was published as part of a special issue of *Feminist Review*, titled *Many Voices, One Chant: Black Feminist Perspectives*, guest edited with 'complete editorial autonomy' by a collective of Black women, which alongside Amos and Parmar included Gail Lewis and Amina Mama.[31] *Feminist Review* had started as a socialist feminist academic journal in 1979, and had up until this point been run by an entirely white editorial collective.[32] Alongside Amos and Parmar's piece, the issue featured articles about Black women's relationship to the British state, Asian women's organising, profiles of different activist groups, a discussion among Black lesbians, as well as poetry and photography of Black women's activism.[33] The issue editors challenged the journal to continue publishing 'writings by and for Black women so that this issue does not remain a token exercise', highlighting 'an ongoing need for white women to take note of and act upon Black feminist critiques of the content and form of contemporary feminism'.[34]

Following the *Many Voices* issue, *Feminist Review* continued to host conversations about racism within feminism. The challenge to act upon Black feminist critiques was taken up in an article published the following year by white socialist feminists Michèle Barrett and Mary McIntosh, who attempted to address what they described as 'ethnocentrism' within their own earlier work and within white socialist feminism more broadly.[35] However, their article was taken to task for not going far enough. Bhavnani and Margaret Coulson critiqued Barrett and McIntosh for focusing on ethnocentrism, which they saw as an evasion of the more important topic of racism. Arguing for a more fundamental re-evaluation of socialist feminist frameworks, Bhavnani and Coulson critiqued white socialist feminism's lack of openness 'to being transformed under the impetus of black struggles'.[36] Along similar lines, Mirza criticised Barrett and McIntosh's article for participating in a 'tradition of inhibiting black women's progress by trying to accommodate an understanding of our differences within the rigid theoretical framework of socialist-feminism'.[37] A couple of years later, *Feminist Review* also published Chandra Mohanty's influential article 'Under Western eyes: feminist scholarship and colonial discourses' (previously published in a US journal), which critiques Western feminist development literature for constructing reductive and homogenising representations of Third World women.[38]

There are differing accounts and evaluations of the extent to which *Feminist Review* and socialist feminist theory transformed as a result of Black feminist interventions. Reflecting back in 1989, Parmar writes:

> while there are several problems with some of the critiques and responses that have emerged in recent years to this debate on the challenge of Black feminism to white feminist theories, the most important point has been that at least and at last white socialist-feminists are beginning to rethink their positions.[39]

Phoenix, in a more recent account, also suggests that Black feminists' interventions within the journal had significant impact, arguing that the *Many Voices* issue 'led to permanent change both to what was covered in the journal and to the composition of the collective'. She suggests that the debates which the issue generated 'contributed to the revision of feminist politics of location and positionality by heightening recognition of feminist plurality and difference'.[40] Yet, the extent to which such transformations shifted power imbalances between Black and white women was a point of contention. According to Avtar Brah, reflecting back in a 2005 discussion about the journal's first 25 years, 'nothing happened' to change the collective in the immediate aftermath of the *Many Voices* issue.[41] Brah had joined the collective a few years after the special issue, and found that the white women on the collective still 'weren't aware of their whiteness'. Lewis also reflects on this time in a recent interview, highlighting how even though a number of women of colour had been invited to join the collective, a 'thick, suffocating, fog of whiteness' remained unacknowledged, as a 'ghostly presence'.[42] This eventually led to Brah, Lewis and Bhavnani leaving the collective in 1989, stating that they would only return on condition that the white women learned to 'own' race as much as the Black women.[43]

The period which followed was a tumultuous one for the collective, and, according to Brah, a number of other members also left. The remaining members eventually wrote an editorial committing the journal to anti-racism as both a perspective and process, noting that the three women's decision to leave had 'inspired a sustained confrontation with what had been, until then, a set of working assumptions about our openness as a collective, and about precisely what was entailed in our commitment to antiracism'. The authors of the editorial admitted that

46

white collective members' approach to anti-racism up until that point
had been limited to 'bringing in more Black women', with the expectation that these Black women would do the work of anti-racism for
the whole collective. The editors described the process they were now
going through as 'leaving the home of old feminism', by recognising that
'problems of power, hierarchy and hidden agendas are no strangers to
political collectives. Nor are they ones to which there is "a solution".[44]
In resisting the possibility of easy solutions to power inequalities
between women, the collective members signalled a commitment to
staying with the difficulties of feminist racism and to anti-racist work
as a continuous process rather than as something which can be claimed
to have been achieved by writing an anti-racist policy. According to
Brah, herself, Lewis and Bhavnani rejoined the collective following this
commitment.[45] My account here is not meant to suggest a simplistic
progress narrative or successful end point to the journal's entanglement
with white feminist racism, but rather to emphasise the influence Black
feminist theorising and praxis had in deconstructing and reshaping previously white frameworks and working practices towards more critical
engagements with whiteness.

Outwrite Women's Newspaper *and anti-imperialist feminism*

As a number of white feminists committed themselves to anti-racist
work, collaborations and solidarity between Black and white women
increased. One important example of this was *Outwrite Women's
Newspaper*, published monthly between 1982 and 1988. *Outwrite* was
produced by a multiracial collective of women, with an editorial policy
that Black women (women of colour) should always make up at least
half of the group.[46] *Outwrite* as a political venture had clear links and
debts to the Black women's movement, but whereas there were divergent
opinions within the Black women's movement about whether it considered itself part of a *feminist* movement, the Black women involved
in *Outwrite* explicitly called themselves feminists. As Ranu Samantrai
writes, for the *Outwrite* Collective, 'black feminism was not a rejection
of the WLM but its placement in a properly international context'.[47]

In the first issue, the collective defined their mission as 'fight[ing]
oppression experienced by all women actively combating racism, sexism
and imperialism'.[48] *Outwrite*'s anti-imperialist and internationalist per-

spective was groundbreaking within the context of the British women's liberation movement; in the words of Shaila Shah, one of the paper's founding and long-standing collective members, the paper aimed to 'break with British insularity' which characterised the white-dominated movement.[49] Its internationalism was demonstrated through its extensive coverage of women's struggles in many countries across the global South, including in Guatemala, South Africa, Palestine, Pakistan, the Philippines, Eritrea and elsewhere.[50] The collective often voiced its criticism of dominant trends within the women's movement, and alongside coverage of international struggles, their extensive coverage of anti-racist campaigns and struggles in Britain (such as against the Nationality Act and other racist legislation) attempted to galvanise support from the wider women's movement.[51] By struggling both together and against white-dominated feminist communities, the paper provided a space within the feminist movement where white feminists were called to account for their complicities in racism and imperialism.

The paper's staunchly internationalist and anti-imperialist perspective was also coupled with a radical feminism, with extensive coverage of campaigns against violence against women, reproductive rights, lesbians' rights, as well as campaigns against pornography. There was an ongoing dialogue in its pages about disability and the way the women's liberation movement often excluded disabled women.[52] The paper also covered budget cuts affecting services such as the National Health Service (NHS), welfare, housing and education, with one well-supported campaign in the paper being the occupation of South London Women's Hospital following its closure in July 1984.[53] In linking together struggles against racism and sexism, imperialism and capitalism, *Outwrite* was instrumental in developing the practice, politics and intellectual project of a multiracial anti-racist feminism.

By foregrounding the connections between different structural oppressions, the paper was able to develop nuanced and historically contextualised analyses on a wide range of issues. Rashida Harrison notes, for instance, how *Outwrite*'s analysis of women's reproductive rights constructed 'an intentional interweaving of contraception, population control, and increased regulation of abortion' whereas elsewhere connections between these issues were often missed. Harrison's is one of the only existing in-depth analyses of *Outwrite*'s political import and legacy, specifically in terms of the development of transnational Black feminisms. As she argues, alongside its role in building bridges between Black and white feminists and bringing an internationalist perspective to feminist politics, *Outwrite*'s efforts in 'facilitat[ing] activism across geographical boundaries ... were central to the making of transnational black feminist praxis'.[54]

While Harrison's work emphasises the significance of *Outwrite*'s legacy for the development of Black feminisms, its legacy and political import in relation to the women's liberation movement specifically and for British feminisms more generally has not been adequately recognised. The paper, for instance, is much less frequently cited as part of the popular legacy of the recent British women's movement than publications such as *Spare Rib* and *Red Rag*. Yet, *Outwrite* played a significant role in carving out space for multiracial collaborative and coalitional work between Black and white feminists which was crucial to the development of broad-based anti-racist feminist politics. Part of this work involved a commitment to internal critique within the movement, and in particular holding white feminists accountable to feminists of colour, and expecting white feminists to equally own the work of challenging racism and imperialism (much like the white *Feminist Review* members were called upon to do).

Samantrai describes *Outwrite* as representing 'an important moment in the evolution of a postimperial English feminism that is the legacy of the black British women's movement'.[55] Not only can the under-explored history of the paper be used to counteract damaging whitewashed stories of British feminism, its archive provides significant insight into the development of anti-racist feminism as an intellectual project in Britain. It spearheaded anti-racist feminist analyses of the British state, linking this always to imperialism and global contexts. Also relevant for today's generation of activists, it provides a valuable archive of feminist activism in the context of a brutal Conservative government cutting back the welfare state, promoting anti-migrant policies and criminalising protest. This is not to deny that there were aspects of *Outwrite*'s politics that were contentious and controversial (e.g. its radical feminist stance on pornography and S&M, as well as its anti-Zionist position which, as with *Spare Rib*, was critiqued as antisemitic), but rather to argue that its frequent erasure from dominant histories of British feminism's recent past denies younger feminists the opportunity to learn from its rich history of anti-racist feminist theorising and praxis.[56]

BLACK AND POSTCOLONIAL FEMINISMS

Most accounts of British feminisms of the 1970s and 1980s include narratives tracing the increased fragmentation of women's concerns and organising groups, although whether this is described as having happened in the late 1970s, with the end of the women's liberation movement conferences, in the early 1980s with the demise of OWAAD, or later in the 1980s depends on which feminist activists and collectivities are foregrounded in the story. By the late 1980s, however, most seem to be in agreement that collective, public-facing grassroots feminist politics had declined significantly, and feminist activism had entered a period of lower public visibility and activity (of course, this narrative is overly simplistic and the ongoing activism of groups such as Southall Black Sisters, Women Against Fundamentalism and many organisations working to combat violence against women should be recognised).[57] The reasons for this decline are multi-faceted, including the widespread disillusionment within Left politics given the Conservative government's firm hold on power, to deep rifts and conflicts within the movement around a number of issues. Regarding the Black women's movement, Shabnam Grewal, Jackie Kay, Liliane Landor, Gail Lewis and Pratibha Parmar, editors of *Charting the Journey: Writings by Black and Third World Women*, provide an account of loss of what had earlier in the decade felt as a more forceful and organised front, consisting of 'a plethora of local Black women's groups up and down the country ... which had mushroomed in a hey day of Black political activity'. Assessing the state of the Black women's movement at the end of the decade, the editors suggested that the lack of collective ability to see the bigger picture as the movement evolved had led to irresolvable political disagreements:

In the end we generated our own internal contradictions, which it appears, we could not overcome. For we failed to notice and deal with the changes in outlook, emphasis and direction, which arose as more and more women took up the call and as the wider, social, economic and political climate changed. We failed to grow.[58]

Yet, while the extent of widespread grassroots organising may have diminished, the editors simultaneously expressed hope and investment in Black women's politics as a continuous journey, which the book set out to explore. *Charting the Journey* thus represents an increasingly reflective turn within Black feminism; an important moment of development, reflecting both forwards and back. It demonstrates how the period of intense activism, conflict and debate discussed in the previous section generated analyses and political practices which laid the foundations for the ongoing intellectual projects of Black feminisms and related theoretical and political fields, such as postcolonial, transnational, Third World, decolonial and other race-critical and anti-racist feminist projects. These intellectual fields provide much of the analytical basis for my own study, and in order to lay some of the groundwork for the critiques that I develop in Chapters 3 to 5, this section hones in on some of their key frameworks and concepts. What follows should not be read as a comprehensive theoretical review; rather I am focusing on aspects which are particularly relevant to the forthcoming analysis. In doing so, the discussion has a dual focus. Firstly, I highlight some of the theoretical innovations that Black and postcolonial feminisms have brought to the feminist project as a whole, but secondly, I also attend to some of the ways in which this work has been marginalised, as well as problematically appropriated. This latter focus comes to the fore primarily in the latter half of the second section, on intersectionality, as well as in the third section, which addresses feminists of colour's experiences of marginalisation in the academy.

Although I do not have the space to elaborate in depth, it should be noted that the politics of naming theoretical fields is complex, and the relationship and boundaries between these differently named projects are diffuse and contested. Here I refer mainly to Black and postcolonial feminisms, although it should be recognised that some theorists may locate their work differently than I do.[59] I also use the term 'race-critical feminisms' to refer more generally to all feminist work which centres the connections between racism and sexism.

Deconstructing majorities and minorities

A crucial element of invoking 'critical race/gender reflexivity into mainstream academic thinking', as Mirza describes the project of Black feminism, involves rooting gender analysis in a historically situated (post)colonial framework.[60] This, I would argue, is one of the hallmarks of Black British feminism as an intellectual project. As Razia Aziz notes, 'black women's critiques frequently have a particular vibrancy derived from an insistence on placing the question of history centre-stage.'[61] This centring of history emerges from a recognition of the persistence of the colonial in structuring contemporary race and gender relations. Historically located analysis connecting the local to the global, as Brah stresses, has been a key concern of Black feminists who, because of their 'location within diasporas formed by the history of slavery, colonialism and imperialism ... have consistently argued against parochialism and stressed the need for a feminism sensitive to the international social relations of power.'[62]

Crucially, as Suki Ali argues, a postcolonial framework has significant implications for the positioning of women of colour within Western feminist projects:

> Postcolonial approaches insist on seeing the centre as being productive of and produced by the margins or periphery, and this is a useful tool for understanding institutional contexts. The positioning of black feminism on the fringes of theory, or as critique to mainstream (represented as Anglo/Western/Northern/Imperial) feminism, in turn consolidates their centrality.[63]

A postcolonial feminist perspective thereby turns 'common sense' understandings of margins and centres on their head, emphasising the relational construction of Black/white, colonised/coloniser, and so on. Importantly, this challenges the presumed 'naturalness' of white women as the central subjects of feminism.

Lewis' analysis of the construction of people of colour as 'ethnic minorities' within British policy discourse is insightful here. Lewis argues that the shift within government policy in the 1980s from framing people of colour as 'immigrants' towards constructing them as 'ethnic minorities' was a way for the state to assert social control over communities of colour, both marginalising and pathologising them while claiming to be including them in the national imaginary. The 'ethnic minority' comes to be seen as a 'junior citizen/subject' of the nation, as someone who 'has the status of being citizen/subject whilst simultaneously being constituted as an essentialized "other" who is now a permanent figure in Britain.'[64] The construction of ethnic 'minorities' and 'majorities' naturalises the unequal power relations between them. This is a point elaborated by Brah, who highlights how 'the numerical referent of this dichotomy encourages a literal reading, reducing the problem of power relations to one of numbers, with the result that the repeated circulation of the discourse has the effect of naturalising rather than challenging the power differential.'[65] Ethnicity becomes a question of population numbers, with the term 'ethnic minority' denoting that 'non-white British' people naturally belong only in the margins of British society, because they belong to numerically smaller constituencies. In other words, or so the dominant argument goes, 'ethnic minorities' should not expect to see themselves and their interests reflected within mainstream politics and culture over and above their numerically representative status. This understanding of majority/minority underpins racist arguments that Britain is a 'white country', often thrown in the face of people of colour when they call for better representation, whether in politics, the media, higher education or elsewhere (never mind the fact that even numerically, people of colour are *under-represented* in most institutions and areas of public life).[66]

Yet, far from reflecting 'natural' relations, the construction of a majority/minority binary involves a process of *minoritisation*. Yasmin Gunaratnam suggests using this term in order to emphasise 'the active processes of racialization that are at work in designating certain attributes of groups in particular contexts as being in a "minority"'.[67] By focusing attention on minoritising as a process, this framing usefully de-naturalises the relationship between 'majorities' and 'minorities'. This highlights the role 'majorities' play in designating 'minorities' *as* 'minorities', shedding light on the political construction of a centre and a margin. Holding the colonial dimension of British nationhood in view is essential to this analysis; diasporic communities from formerly colonised countries could only be constructed as immigrants, outsiders and minorities through a disavowal of the colonial history which has intimately tied their countries of origin into an exploitative and extractive relationship with Britain for centuries. Equally, Britain can only be understood as a 'white country' through a disavowal of the fact that several hundred million 'non-white' people across the world were forcibly turned into British subjects in the colonial era.

To return to Ali's point, in drawing attention to how colonial histories shape gender relations in the present, Black and postcolonial feminist theories deconstruct the assumption of naturalised majorities and minorities in Western feminisms. As Lewis notes, reflecting back on Black British feminism in the 1970s and 1980s, 'black feminist practice, the one I knew of, was not really interested in doing minor-ness'.[68] In a critique of the use of the categories of majority/minority in a research project on European gendered citizenship, she points to the missed opportunity for engagement with 'the field of critical race and postcolonial studies that had, in an earlier moment, engaged the question of minority discourse and the notion of minoritized'.[69] This critique highlights the fact that white-centred feminist theorising too easily bypasses Black and postcolonial feminist scholarship which has long problematised ahistorical understandings of racial difference and 'ethnic minorities'.

I will return to look at how processes of minoritisation function within contemporary white-centred feminist literature in Chapter 4.

Difference and intersectionality

Black, postcolonial and race-critical feminisms have also pioneered theorising of difference and intersecting oppressions. One thing which remains consistent within these theoretical engagements is the insistence on the co-constitutive and interlocking nature of different social categories. In Brah's words, '[s]tructures of class, racism, gender and sexuality cannot be treated as "independent variables" because the oppression of each is inscribed within the other – is constituted by and is constitutive of the other'.[70] This insight lies at the root of the concept of intersectionality, which, as a term, originates from US Black feminist Kimberlé Crenshaw's work in feminist legal theory. Crenshaw first coined the term in 1989 to describe the experiences of Black women at the intersection of gender and race.[71] What the concept conveys, in Crenshaw's usage, is the impossibility for Black women of separating their experiences of oppression based on gender from that based on race and that Black women experience oppression *as Black women* (to an extent, Crenshaw also addresses class). Further, Crenshaw distinguishes between structural and political intersectionality, where structural intersectionality denotes the experience of inequality at these intersections, while political intersectionality addresses the fact that Black women's experiences are frequently erased from both feminist and anti-racist political analysis.[72]

Since Crenshaw's original formulation of intersectionality, the concept has been extensively taken up and developed within different strands and locations of feminist theory (and beyond).[73] One of the tensions which has emerged between different applications and understandings of the concept is, in Jennifer Nash's words, 'whether intersectionality is a theory of marginalized subjectivity or a generalized theory of identity'.[74] In Crenshaw's original formulation and in other scholarship which has followed, intersectionality is used specifically to locate the experiences of Black women (and often also other women of colour), i.e. intersectionality denotes a point at which different oppressive structures connect. However, other scholars, following the 'generalized theory of identity' route have taken up intersectionality as a concept which can be used to analyse all social identities as at the intersection of different structures. In Britain, Black and race-critical feminists have been at the forefront of theorising, as Brah and Phoenix conceptualise it, 'the complex, irreducible, varied, and variable effects which ensue when multiple axis of differentiation – economic, political, cultural, psychic, subjective and experiential – intersect in historically specific contexts'.[75] While this definition of intersectionality clearly indicates a multi-faceted and broad approach to the concept, with many potential points of intersection, intersectional theorising by feminists of colour usually presume gender, race and class as primary intersectional axes.

There are also debates about whether intersectionality best encapsulates the ways in which systems of domination interact with and reinforce each other, and the extent to which other analytical frameworks for analysing these interactions can be subsumed under the general banner of 'intersectional theorising'. For instance, the influential Combahee River Collective's 'Black feminist statement', written by Black socialist lesbian feminists in Boston (US) in the 1970s, argued that 'racial, sexual, heterosexual, and class oppression' constitute 'interlocking' systems of oppression.[76] This statement is often cited as 'proto-intersectional' theorising – i.e. as part of the longer lineage of Black feminist analyses of intersecting oppressions before the word intersectionality itself had been coined. Yet, the extent to which 'interlocking' and 'intersecting' are interchangeable terms is arguable. The former emphasises the fact that different systems uphold each other, in a similar way to what

Patricia Hill Collins calls a 'matrix of domination'. Collins distinguishes between intersectionality and matrices of domination, suggesting that the former 'refers to particular forms of intersecting oppressions, for example, intersections of race and gender, or of sexuality and nation', while the latter 'refers to how these intersecting oppressions are actually organized'. An analysis of matrices of domination, then, are required in order to understand how different systems of domination intersect within specific historical and social contexts. As Collins elaborates, a matrix of domination is 'an historically specific organization of power in which social groups are embedded'.[77] Sherene Razack (whose work I will return to in the concluding chapter), drawing on Collins' work, favours the framework of interlocking to intersecting oppressions because, like the concept of matrices of domination, interlocking oppressions enables us to better understand how systems of domination 'need one another'. This sheds light on the ways in which different (gendered, racialised and classed) social positions are dependent on each other. For instance, as per Razack's example, it helps us understand 'how domestic workers and professional women are produced so that neither exists without the other'.[78] In other words, this framing emphasises the ways in which members of dominant (and intersecting) social groups are implicated in the domination and exploitation of other social groups.

The emphasis on historically and socially specific locations for intersectional analysis is crucial, and there are, as Sara Salem discusses, numerous critiques of intersectional theorising for not being sufficiently grounded within the context of class exploitation and global capitalism. Salem suggests that intersectional Marxist feminist theorising provides the best tools for 'recover[ing] the critical potential of intersectionality'; through an intersectional analysis of how gender, race, class and other categories are located within the nation-state and the global division of labour, such an approach 'can be useful by showing *how* these catego- ries are created, how they exploit and not simply oppress, and *why* they intersect'. However, it should be noted that the kinds of intersectional theorising which Salem critiques are 'sanitised' versions, espoused by many liberal and academic feminists, which have travelled far from the radical roots of 'intersectionality's beginnings in Black feminist histories and Third World Liberation movements'.[79] In other words, the extent to which the concept of intersectionality can usefully shed light on how interlocking systems of domination operate depends on the lineage of intersectional theorising which one engages with.

While an in-depth examination of the trends, debates and ethics of intersectional theorising is beyond the scope of this discussion, a few key issues are important to note in order to contextualise my forth-coming analysis of how intersectionality has been taken up within white-centred theorising and debate. Primarily, it is vital to locate intersectional theorising and practice within the context of coloniality and white feminist dominance. As Salem and other scholars have high-lighted, there is a structural dimension to how this theory has travelled, which has increasingly involved it becoming disconnected from its Black feminist history and attention to women of colour's exploitation and marginalisation.[80] While, as Lewis notes, 'successful' theories gain prominence precisely because of their 'capacity to travel', it is important to not lose sight of the fact that they do so within a context of knowledge production shaped by 'inequalities of opportunity and recognition tied to structures of race, class, and gender'.

Addressing European feminist debates about the concept, Lewis uses the example of a 2009 conference in Germany to draw attention to the ways in which theoretical debates about intersectionality, while nomi-nally concerned with women's differential experiences, can take place in ways which continue to enforce domination. Lewis describes how a discussion about the relevance of race in European contexts (dominated by arguments against) was conducted at the conference as if racialised dynamics between white feminists and feminists of colour were not in fact a feature of the event itself, thereby silencing the women of colour from naming their discomfort in white-dominated feminist spaces. This lack of attention to the lived and embodied experiences of race within feminist spaces, Lewis notes, was accompanied by 'the projection of race as only meaningful in relation to women racialized as minority' while the 'racialization of whiteness and white womanhood was seem-ingly unthinkable'.[81] In these ways, race becomes particularised as only relevant for women of colour.

Both Sirma Bilge and Gloria Wekker note that intersectionality has become popular among white European feminist theorists through a re-marginalisation of race. Race has come to be seen as only one optional intersectional axis among many. Bilge theorises this as the 'whitening' of intersectionality scholarship. She describes the 'grim irony', whereby a tool elaborated by women of color to confront the racism and het-erosexism of White-dominated feminism, as well as the sexism and heterosexism of antiracist movements, becomes, in another time and place, a field of expertise overwhelmingly dominated by White disci-plinary feminists who keep race and racialized women at bay.[82]

Lewis', Bilge's and Wekker's critiques all pertain to the continental European context, in which race and feminists of colour are often per-ceived to belong mainly in the US, and to some extent also in Britain. However, it is not uncommon for white feminists in Britain to also marginalise race and the work of feminists of colour when discuss-ing intersectionality, without reflecting on the racial politics of how the concept has travelled. Sara Ahmed notes that when race becomes an optional intersectional axis, the concept of intersectionality can be mobilised to effectively halt and deflect more critical debates about racism. She describes how her talks about race and racism are often met with questions about gender, sexuality and class, highlighting how inter-sectionality can be deployed 'as a method of deflection' when 'hearing about race and racism is too difficult'.[83] Yet, as critiques such as these demonstrate, race-critical feminists have also been able to use intersec-tional analysis in order to counter and challenge these marginalising and appropriating patterns.

Black feminism and the British academy

In this section, I turn towards the structural constraints feminists of colour have faced in attempting to make space for their work in the academy. As suggested in the above discussion, questions about whose knowledge and perspectives are heard and legitimated (and by whom) are salient for examining feminism as an intellectual project. In relation to the academy, from which most of the literature that I have cited here emerges, questions of access and authority are central. In other words, who is able to gain entry *into* the academy, what positions do they gain access to, and under what kinds of conditions do they theorise? I am focusing here on the academy not because it is the only place where theorising happens (far from it!) but because it is nevertheless a signif-icant site of feminist knowledge production. Specifically, the academy serves a legitimating function whereby certain kinds of knowledge gains authority and power.

One commonplace narrative about feminism's declining radicalism from the end of the 1980s onwards is that of the movement's increasing institutionalisation into the academy.[84] White socialist feminist Lynne Segal's account of feminism's increasingly complex theorisation at the end of the 1990s provides an example of such a narrative:

> Moving on from the burning questions, bonfires and street parades, the change in the self-conception of the women's movement was the beginning of an always ambivalent slide into the cultural mainstream: goodbye to 'Women's Liberation', with its clenched fist, its militant slogans and joyful songs ('The Women's Army is Marching'); hello to 'feminism', with its diffuse theoretical underpinnings and performative uncertainties ('doing feminism', 'doing gender').[85]

Segal tells a story of feminism's shift from radical and socialist feminist analyses towards what she perceives as an over-enthusiastic enthralment with poststructuralism, thereby emphasising feminism's increasing institutionalisation within academic and highly theoretical discourse. Yet, what narratives such as this tend to elide is the fact that processes of institutionalisation also tend to be processes of 'whitening' (to borrow Bilge's phrase), at both ideological and structural levels. Segal's account of feminism's incorporation into academic poststructural theory, for instance, contrasts with that written by Lola Young around the same time. Young is similarly concerned with tracing what had happened to feminism within the academy, specifically Black British feminist theory. Turning attention to the academy both as a physical institutional space as well as a site of theorisation, she notes the low number of Black women working as academics in the British higher education sector, expressing a fear that 'black academic feminism may be severely limited before it has had a chance to evolve more fully'. Young, then, paints a different picture from Segal about the development of feminist thought and praxis as it has become institutionalised in the academy. While Segal notes (white) feminist incorporation, Young notes Black feminists' marginalisation, describing their struggles to gain a foothold within academic institutions as 'striving to embed themselves, often by stealth'. Young highlights white feminist academics' complicity in this process, noting their 'air of tentativeness, even reluctance about *fully* engaging in a *sustained* discussion/argument' about the meaning of race and power relations between differently racialised women, both 'on- and off-campus'. This was despite increased attention given to race and difference within feminist theory, as noted by both Segal and Young.

Young also addresses feminism's relationship to poststructuralism but, again in contrast to Segal, notes how Black women's marginalisation impacts on their freedom to engage with poststructural trends. Often, Young notes, Black women are forced to 'resort to the experiential' in order to have their theories about race listened to by white people:

> Thus, although the postmodern side of our brain might wish to eschew the notion of authenticity and a hierarchy of oppression, at times that is what we may invoke in order to gain some sort of acknowledgement of our predicaments and pleasures, as flawed and contradictory as that strategy may be.[86]

The structural whiteness of the academy thereby has an impact on the kinds of theorising Black feminists have the space to do. This point is also raised by Nirmal Puwar, in another article published at the turn of the century. Reflecting on South Asian women's experiences in the academy, Puwar highlights a trend of South Asian women being hired as junior researchers on race-related research projects led by white academics. This, she notes, 'allows white academics to evade the criticism that has been targeted at anthropologists', yet, she argues, 'strong traces of the anthropological relationship to the "native", be it in the metropolis or "elsewhere", are still prolific'. This included, Puwar stresses, projects led by white feminists. She emphasises the detrimental impact these structural dynamics have on South Asian women's space to theorise. Reporting on a workshop where South Asian women scholars had organised a space free of white academics and South Asian male scholars, Puwar writes:

> The space we sought to create and claim through the workshop was an attempt to facilitate an environment where we are not con- stantly having to explain and exhibit what it is like to be a South Asian woman. All too often, after this kind of experience, where we are making our 'strange lives' familiar to those around us, we are left

feeling that we ourselves have not learned something new, in other words the problems of how we theorize our situations on our own terms beyond eurocentric idioms remains very much unexplored.[87]

In both Young's and Puwar's analyses, then, a strong link is made between the structural locations women of colour find themselves in within academic institutions and their ability to develop theories which are not impelled to speak to, accommodate or otherwise engage with white-defined, including white feminist, concerns. Puwar's research on what happens when Black, Brown and female bodies enter formerly exclusively white and male elite spaces highlights how those whose bodies are not perceived to 'fit' become positioned as 'space invaders'; as outsiders within, under immense pressure to assimilate into dominant norms or risk being labelled as a problem and/or excluded again.[88] Thus their inclusion is always conditional.

The effects of diversity initiatives have also been researched by Ahmed, who observes how the language of diversity operates as a 'politics of feeling good', which allows people to relax and feel less threatened, as if we have already "solved it".[89] Ahmed points out how institutions use strategies of 'diversity pride', representing themselves as happily diverse in ways which silence any continued discussions about institutional racism.[90] She writes of the pressures Black feminists experience by 'embodying diversity' within institutions, including within feminist academic spaces:

The desire for you to embody diversity (which can feel like a desire both for you and for what you embody) comes from the right place (race needs to be made integral to women's studies, the core course should be on race). And yet it creates its sore points. If you embody race for them, then they do race through you, which can be a way of not doing race. You can also express commitment to the very idea of intersectionality. You are the point where the lines meet. A meeting point becomes a sore point.[91]

Relationships and power dynamics between white feminists and feminists of colour continue to be sources of tension within academic feminist spaces, yet these tensions are infrequently addressed by white feminists. The material conditions under which feminists of colour –

and scholars of colour more generally – operate within the academy have largely not been of concern within white-centred feminisms as intellectual projects, as I will continue to address in forthcoming chapters. The under-representation of scholars of colour has increasingly come to the fore in public debate in recent years, partly as a result of student campaigns such as 'Why is my curriculum white?', the work of networks such as Black British Academics, and calls from both students and staff to 'decolonise' universities.[92]

Despite structural constraints, feminists of colour have continued to claim space for Black and postcolonial feminist theorising and activism in the academy. In 2014, *Feminist Review* published a special issue titled *Black British Feminisms* to mark the 30-year anniversary of the 1984 *Many Voices* issue. In an interview in this issue, Mirza expresses hope about 'a new generation of black British feminists' and the continued growth of Black feminism as 'a stalwart tree with rich, deep roots, lovingly nurtured by a community of careful, critical gardeners'. Yet, the nurturing of this 'tree' comes at a cost; Mirza also speaks of the 'wearing' experience of hyper-visibility experienced by Black feminist academics '[n]avigating the gendered and classed spaces of whiteness in academia'.[93] In the same issue, Joan Anim-Addo draws attention to the disproportional absence of Black British research students, lecturers and professors within the academy, and argues that Black feminist academics must play a crucial role in supporting – '(other)mothering' – Black students and young scholars in order to cultivate Black scholarship and community in a white and hostile environment. Although her article is primarily speaking to Black feminists, she also describes it as 'an appeal to white feminist sisters ... to refuse the merely "academic" and engage with us a politics and praxis of care that seeks to counter racism, its malignant history and legacy', noting how the prevalent 'silence of white feminists resembles collusion, evoking again, this time for the twenty-first century, the question: "Am I not a woman and a sister?"'[94]

The under-representation of scholars of colour is of course not a problem exclusive to feminist academia, but rather a sector-wide indictment. And while women as a group also remain under-represented, particularly as professors and within senior management roles, as Kalwant Bhopal highlights, it is mainly white women who have benefited from initiatives such as Athena Swan, aimed at reducing gender inequality in the academy.[95] Yet, as the literature on women of colour's experiences in the academy suggest, white feminist academics have not in any sustained collective sense attempted to address the structural factors which continue to exclude and marginalise scholars of colour while benefiting white ones. The very whiteness and class-elitism of the academy in itself facilitates complacency in addressing these inequalities. This is a very different context to the activist spaces discussed in the previous section, in which whiteness was powerfully interrupted. The increasing institutionalisation of feminism into academic institutions thus clearly enabled whiteness to be better protected from further challenge. This (re-)'whitening' of feminism has also been facilitated by the marketisation of the higher education sector which has been occurring in the British context since the 1990s, and which has encouraged a neoliberal individualism and denial of systemic inequalities. This is the structural context in which the academic literature discussed in Chapters 3 and 4 has been produced.

CONCLUSION

In her analysis of the political import of Black British feminism, Ranu Samantrai argues that the movement has had significant influence on the constitution of a 'postimperial' Englishness. Foregrounding the roles that Black feminists have played as 'dissenters' within the national polity, Samantrai argues that 'the intellectual and political ferment' generated by Black feminist analyses has led to significant changes 'in the community imagined as England'. She elaborates:

> With its simultaneous interrogation of the racial and gendered subtext of Englishness, black British feminism disrupts the reference points of English majority and minority identities … [A]s black feminists negotiate the possibility of a postimperial feminism located in a First World nation, their unpredictable dissent radicalizes tensions around national inclusions and exclusions and leads to an alteration in the meaning of the nation.[96]

Samantrai argues that Black feminists' activism and theorising, in drawing attention to and speaking from the borders of national inclusions, significantly challenges the coherence of dominant ideas surrounding national belonging and citizenship. This chapter has developed a parallel argument: alongside its significance in challenging dominant *national* imaginaries, Black British feminism in the 1980s significantly impacted dominant *feminist* imaginaries. While, as stated previously, it is important not to reduce Black feminism to being a critique of white feminism, the significant role that Black feminist interventions into white-dominated feminism have played – and continue to play – in transforming hegemonic feminist frameworks and analyses must be recognised.

The three case studies of *Spare Rib*, *Feminist Review* and *Outwrite* highlight the influence that Black feminist analyses and anti-racist critiques had on white-dominated parts of the women's movement at this time. The conflict within the *Spare Rib* Collective and parts of the broader feminist community indicates the extent to which the complacent whiteness of the women's liberation movement was destabilised and challenged. Interventions by Black feminists in the pages and within the collective of *Feminist Review* eventually resulted in explicit commitments to anti-racism on the part of white collective members, and were influential in the theoretical development of race-critical (socialist) feminist analysis. The processes which both collectives went through led to a productive loss of white feminist innocence, which required white feminists to confront their investment in white supremacy and privilege to an extent that they had not had to before. *Outwrite*'s work evidences a maturation of anti-racist feminist thought and praxis, and provides evidence of some of the important multiracial coalitional work which took place at this time. Here also, white feminists were required to examine their complicities in structural racism and held to account when they failed to do so.

The work which took place in this period provided important building blocks and served as a grounding for further Black, postcolonial and race-critical feminist work, which has continued to develop and grow into the contemporary moment, as explored in the second part of the chapter. As I have argued, Black and postcolonial feminist frameworks call attention to the colonial register of gender relations and feminist politics, and emphasise the need to understand gender and race within this historical context. As such, they have called for a fundamental reconstitution of dominant white feminist understandings of gender and the movement's history. Such feminisms have continued to advance analyses which centre the connection between gender and coloniality, and it should be noted that there are of course white scholars aligned to postcolonial and race-critical feminist fields. However, as I will go on to argue, some of the key issues which were debated in the 1980s, and which many white feminists at the time were compelled to address, have since receded from view within white-centred feminist theorising and politics, particularly as these have become institutionalised within academia, popular culture and the liberal press.

3

Leaving Feminist Whiteness Behind: Narratives of Transcendence in the Era of Difference

The previous chapter highlighted significant struggles and developments which took place within British feminist politics in the 1980s, emphasising the key role Black and postcolonial feminist theorising, including critiques of white feminism, played in challenging and transforming dominant analytical and political frameworks. This destabilised, at least partially, some of the normative whiteness which had previously pervaded dominant strands of the movement. As such, this was a highly significant period for the transformation of race politics within British feminisms. Yet, this was far from the end of the story of feminist whiteness, and the following three chapters will examine how white dominance is asserted within more contemporary feminist discourse in ways which undermine, appropriate or disregard race-critical frameworks and theories developed by feminists of colour. This chapter, based on the analysis of five academic texts, draws attention to one prominent narrative often reproduced within white-centred feminist literature: namely, that while white feminists in the past were ignorant about race, their contemporary counterparts (or contemporary versions of themselves) are now attentive to race. In this narrative, feminist whiteness is situated as a problem of the past. This hinges on a transcendence of racism and whiteness for contemporary white feminists, even when racism is recognised as a significant structure in the world. Linking this back to the theme of innocence, I argue that by claiming contemporary feminist theorising, politics and classrooms as race-critical, these narratives clear renewed space for the innocent white – now anti-racist – feminist at the centre of the movement.

In the first section, I explain how I chose which books to analyse. This is followed by an introduction to the books that I discuss in this chapter, namely, *The Aftermath of Feminism: Gender, Culture and Social Change* by Angela McRobbie, *Why Feminism Matters: Feminism Lost and Found* by Kath and Sophie Woodward, *Reclaiming the F Word: The New Feminist Movement* by Catherine Redfern and Kristin Aune, *Third Wave Feminism and the Politics of Gender in Late Modernity* by Shelley Budgeon, and *The Future of Feminism* by Sylvia Walby.[1] I then move on to elaborate how feminism is portrayed within these books as having transformed from a (numerically and ideologically) white-dominated movement to a movement which is not only racially diverse but which is also knowledgeable and attentive to race and difference. In the subsequent sections I discuss two different ways in which race and racism are engaged with more generally within the texts. Firstly, I examine how the concepts of difference (Woodward and Woodward, Budgeon) and intersectionality (Walby) as well as a generic 'feminists of colour critique' (Budgeon) are mobilised in ways which displace rather than engage with race-critical analyses. Secondly, I highlight the ways in which anti-racist analysis is incorporated more substantially within McRobbie's and Redfern and Aune's texts, while racism is still situated as something largely external to feminism itself. I conclude the chapter by returning to the theme of white feminist innocence and how it is reproduced within the texts.

A NOTE ON SAMPLING

The books discussed in the next three chapters address feminism itself as a subject. These texts evaluate the current state of feminism, seeking to answer questions of what feminism is, what it was, what has happened to it, and what the authors want it to be going forward. I chose to focus on such texts because they tell us something significant about how feminist theory and politics are conceived and imagined in relation to the past, present and the future. It is instructive to analyse how and where such narratives locate racism, whiteness and anti-racism, as this illuminates the extent to which the authors conceive of race as integral to feminist theorising and politics.

The boundaries of this category are contestable and unstable, and I do not claim to have included every single book which could potentially belong within it. However, in terms of the eight texts discussed in this and the following chapter, this sample does include the majority of

UK-based academic texts (or texts based on academic research, in the case of *Reclaiming the F Word*, which is written for a broader audience) analysing feminism as a subject published between 2009 and 2017. The year 2009 became a starting point because a number of relevant books appeared around this time, suggesting a renewed academic interest in feminist theory and politics in the mid to late 2000s. The year 2017 is an arbitrary cut-off point when I stopped collecting new data. As I was particularly interested in how narratives are constructed across a whole text, I have not included edited collections, but only sole or co-authored books.

Sara Ahmed's *Living a Feminist Life*, published in 2017, also fits the selection criteria in terms of being a book which takes feminism itself as a subject. Ahmed centres critique of racism and whiteness within her analysis, and uses the term 'feminism' to signify intersectional, woman of colour-centred feminism, while 'white feminism' is particularised as that which is marginal.[2] As I focus on work which in some way reproduces whiteness, I did therefore not include Ahmed's book in the analysis. Instead, as should be apparent, I draw on and owe a great debt to Ahmed's work in the development of my own analysis. It should also be noted that, aside from focusing on books which in some way reproduce whiteness, the texts included here have not been chosen because they are *more* problematic compared to other white-centred literature published in this period. They have simply been chosen because they fit this particular category of feminist literature.

In examining the narratives about race and feminism within these books I found there to be one particularly significant distinction across them, based on which two groups emerged: one group positions racial exclusions within feminism as existing mainly in the past whereas the other group acknowledges racism within feminism as a continuing problem. These divergent narratives pave the way for some different theoretical positions on race and racism, and I therefore examine them in two separate chapters. As mentioned, this chapter discusses the books that fall into the first group, and I introduce these in the following section.

INTRODUCING THE BOOKS

The Aftermath of Feminism (2009) is the earliest book included in my analysis. McRobbie's groundbreaking critique of consumer culture's co-option of feminist politics in the service of a neoliberal 'post-feminism' (an argument originally made in article form in 2004) has been highly influential and widely cited within feminist literature.[3] In fact, all but one of the other seven books discussed in this chapter and the next cite or engage with McRobbie's argument (Walby and Woodward and Woodward somewhat critically).[4] Using examples from British and US popular culture, McRobbie argues that a combination of cultural and political forces in twenty-first-century Western society have coalesced in a complex form of backlash against feminism. Alongside a narrative of decline of activist (particularly socialist) feminist politics post-1990, McRobbie argues that a 'faux-feminism' has been 'incorporated' into mainstream politics and institutions and fed back to young women as 'empowerment' and 'choice' in order to 'ensure that a new women's movement will not re-emerge'. While a fairly gloomy account of the state of feminism, *Aftermath* does also strike a note of hope, particularly in the final chapter, in which McRobbie suggests that the feminist classroom in the 'global university', such as the one in London where she teaches, represents 'a genuinely new space' filled with both 'uncertainty and potential' for young women.[5]

Woodward and Woodward's *Why Feminism Matters* (2009) usefully contributes to debates about the complexities of and problems with feminist wave analogies – i.e. the popular narrative that feminist activity across the twentieth and twenty-first centuries can be categorised into distinct 'waves'. I will return to discuss how feminist waves are conceptualised in relation to race at various points in both this and the following chapter. For now, suffice it to say that within dominant narratives of feminism, the first wave is associated with Western (particularly British and US) suffrage movements in the early 1900s, the second wave is associated with Western women's liberation movements in the 1960s and 1970s, and the third wave is associated with younger generations of women who have grown up in Western societies after the significant cultural and legislative changes generated by the so-called second wave. Some, as will be discussed in Chapter 4, also conceptualise a distinct fourth wave of feminism, associated with the rise in social media and online activism in the last decade. Wave narratives have been critiqued and problematised from a number of perspectives, not least for their tendency to centre around white and Western – particularly Anglo-American – women's activism. As Kimberly Springer writes about the US context, successive generations of Black feminist histories have been 'drowned out by the wave'.[6]

Woodward and Woodward challenge simplistic narratives about second and third wave feminisms. They question what they see as a divisive antagonism set up between these two waves, and aim to move feminist theory forward while retaining key concepts from the past. They do so by constructing an inter-generational dialogue between themselves as mother (Kath) and daughter (Sophie), about Western feminisms past and present. They argue for the need to salvage what they consider to be key concepts from second wave feminism, which they see as at risk of being lost. They specify these key concepts as 'the feminist polemic and writing with a political agenda; an understanding of patriarchy; repoliticising the personal; and bringing back a politics of difference'.[7]

In *Reclaiming the F Word* (2010), Redfern (founder of *The F-Word* webzine in 2001) and Aune document and analyse grassroots feminist activism in Britain on the basis of a survey of over 1000 self-identified (mostly young) feminist activists. Based on academic research, the book aims to promote feminist politics to a wide audience. The results of the survey are weaved into the structure of the book, with each chapter both defining key feminist issues – such as the need for 'liberated bodies', an 'end to violence against women' and a 'popular culture free from sexism' – and highlighting feminist responses.[8] As suggested by its title, one of the key aims of the book is to wrest the representation of feminism back from negative portrayals within the media and popular culture, including claims of its death. The book and its authors gained publicity in the mainstream press at the time of publication, increasing the visibility of young feminist activists at the turn of the decade.[9] Redfern and Aune's call for a proud reclamation of feminism from tired stereotypes both foresaw and participated in the rise in activist and popular feminisms from the early 2010s onwards (as discussed further in Chapter 5), and a second edition was published in 2013.[10]

Budgeon's *Third Wave Feminism* (2011) provides a theoretically rich critique of how neoliberal individualism has permeated third wave feminist politics and theorising. Budgeon develops her argument through a textual analysis of self-proclaimed third wave feminist literature, the majority of which are edited anthologies from the US. The book provides a nuanced and detailed analysis of what Budgeon defines as the core principles of third wave feminism, identified as the valuing of differences between women, an emphasis on individualised definitions of feminism and feminist practice, and a valorisation of individual women's choices and agency. In her critical engagement with these principles, Budgeon usefully draws attention to the importance of keeping systemic power, specifically capitalism and patriarchy, in view.

Finally, Walby's *The Future of Feminism* (2011) highlights feminist struggles and achievements at a global level, assessing the challenges that contemporary transnational feminisms face. The foremost of these are identified as neoliberalism, gender mainstreaming and feminism's intersections with other social movements. Having been the UNESCO Chair in Gender Research and the recipient of an Order of the British Empire (OBE), Walby's work on patriarchy, gender and violence has long been influential within the national and transnational violence against women sectors. In a similar vein to Redfern and Aune, Walby is concerned with challenging the myth that feminism is dead.[11] Through describing a variety of activist and non-governmental organisation (NGO) projects at different levels of institutionalisation, she argues that feminism is a strong and active movement. Walby takes a different view of feminist success than McRobbie (who critiques Walby's earlier work on gender mainstreaming), seeing the institutionalisation and mainstreaming of feminism as a sign of progress rather than decline, although one which simultaneously raises significant challenges.[12] Drawing on Kimberlé Crenshaw's concept of 'political intersectionality', she argues that an intersecting feminist and social democratic movement stands the best chance in addressing global inequalities and 'environmental crisis'.[13]

There are some significant differences between these books, in terms of their aims, orientations and approaches. McRobbie's and Budgeon's texts are on the more theoretical end of the spectrum, providing sociological assessments of the state of contemporary feminism. Woodward and Woodward also evaluate theories, but with a more explicit aim of revitalising a politicised feminism. Redfern and Aune as well as Walby are more focused on contemporary activism – Redfern and Aune on the more grassroots end, and Walby on the more institutionalised NGO end – describing and analysing successes and challenges. There are also differences in how these texts approach race and its intersections with gendered oppression, as I will discuss. Yet, there are also some salient similarities, and I will begin to address these in the following section, which examines how each of the books tells the story of feminism's development in relation to race and whiteness.

BEFORE AND AFTER RACE AWARENESS

The title of this section takes its cue from Clare Hemmings' analysis of common narratives of feminism's theoretical development (see Chapter 1). In such narratives, Hemmings argues, Black feminism is often cited as a catalyst for thinking about difference, and 'fixes a before and after of racial awareness' within feminist theorising. This moment is usually located in the 1980s. When such a moment becomes fixed in time, it 'marks the work of racial critique of feminism as over and thus as able to be assumed or gestured to rather than evidenced in work after that point'.[14] Hemmings' argument is borne out in the books I discuss in this chapter. This is not to say that this story is always told in the same way or that each storyteller makes the same claims in relation to it. But there is enough commonality between them to note a trend whereby contemporary white feminists are positioned as knowledgeable about and attentive to race, implying that the problem of white feminist ignorance of racism has been left behind.

In *Reclaiming the F Word*, this narrative is constructed implicitly. Redfern and Aune state in the introduction that the book aims 'to show feminism is liberating, diverse, challenging, exciting, relevant and inclusive'.[15] The commitment to inclusivity within contemporary feminist activism is stressed throughout the book, by highlighting its diversity and attention to differences, including race, between women. Carli-Ria Rowell critiques the book for 'sidelin[ing] issues of class and ethnicity', pointing to the fact that over 90 per cent of the participants were white with a similar percentage having a university education.[16] At the same time, despite the skewed sample, the authors do attempt to approach many of the topics they discuss with at least a surface level of intersectional analysis. Among other examples, they elaborate, for instance, on how 'racist, classist and ageist beauty ideals exist alongside patriarchal ones', and map out the different ways in which the pay gap is determined not only by gender but also other structural factors.[17]

In contrast to the claimed diversity of the feminist present, *Reclaiming the F Word* implies that the British feminist past was predominantly white and exclusive of women of colour. The most explicit discussion of this appears in a section about religion, which suggests that '[j]ust as black women felt excluded by a feminism in which white women's experiences were taken as the norm, so religious feminists (many of them Asian, black and mixed ethnicities) feel that secular feminism denigrates an integral part of their identity'.[18] That Black women 'felt excluded' by a normative white feminism in the past has not been previously discussed in the book, and no details are provided here either. The use of the past tense suggests that race-based exclusions no longer occur.

At the same time, the book provides a celebratory account of this feminist past: 'Whilst recognising that second-wave feminism wasn't perfect, in our experience younger feminists are quick to acknowledge their debt to older feminists', Redfern and Aune argue, claiming that feminism 'has a proud history and we've all benefited from it'.[19] Yet, the history evoked in the book is narrow, with the women's liberation movement invoked as the only feminist activist history of the last 50 years. The book is structured into seven chapters in homage to the seven official demands of the women's liberation movement conferences, while histories of the Black women's movement and Black British feminism are not mentioned. The white-dominated women's liberation movement thus comes to stand for the universal feminist past, which all contemporary young feminists are described as indebted to.

The distinction made between a white feminist past and a diverse and inclusive present is at the same time complicated by interspersed brief references to perceptions of contemporary feminism being 'white and middle class'. For instance, one survey question asked respondents to agree or disagree with the statement 'Feminism is too white and middle class'. Although almost half of the participants agreed with the statement, this is not discussed in the book, just included as part of the quantified survey responses in an appendix. The theme of 'too white and middle class' also makes an appearance in a discussion of the potential reasons why people choose not to identify as feminist, where the authors suggest that a possible reason as to why people feel alienated may be because they 'think that feminism is only about white, middle-class women's issues'. In the final chapter on reclaiming feminism, '[r]epresentation/ inclusion of women of colour and non-Western women within mainstream Western feminism' is also listed as a bullet point among a dozen others as a concern that had been raised by survey respondents.[20] Yet, there is no reflection or analysis within the book on these perceptions and what they mean. It therefore remains unclear whether 'white and middle class' should be understood as another negative stereotype which feminism needs to be reclaimed from or whether it constitutes a continuing problem needing to be addressed. Either way, the issue is not given any further attention, and is instead glossed over by the more celebratory accounts of the movement's diversity and inclusivity.

Like *Reclaiming the F Word*, Walby's *The Future of Feminism* also stresses contemporary feminism's diversity and attention to difference, suggesting that the 'discussion of difference is a constant feature' of contemporary transnational feminist networks. Walby suggests that this attention to difference has a long history; while noting that '[s]ome early forms of feminism in the 1960s and 1970s drew on the strength of a belief in a common identity of women as women', she claims that this 'was often an aspiration of an invented tradition that was only partially achieved or constructed, given the long-standing recognition of the significance of differences and inequalities between women'.[21] In Walby's narrative, then, a past universalising (implicitly white and middle class) feminism is constructed as having been less totalising and dominant than the one alluded to by Redfern and Aune.

Despite an initially broad definition of feminism and description of its flourishing throughout the world (with a particular focus on the NGO sector and transnational networks), Walby ascribes feminism a very narrow origin point. 'Feminism develops in waves', she asserts, with each wave 'start[ing] in one location' and 'then spread[ing] out through time and space'. She goes on to state that first wave feminism started in the US and the UK before 'spread[ing[to most countries of the West' as well as becoming 'an integral part of nationalist movements seeking decolonisation'. Second wave feminism is also described as originating 'in the global North, especially in the US and the UK'. Walby goes on to describe how second wave feminism 'spread rapidly around the world', suggesting that all such activity can be traced back to an origin point in the (Anglo-American) North. The more detailed description of second wave feminist activities includes references to refuges and rape crisis centres, the Greenham Common peace camp, 'take back the night' demonstrations, and feminist bookshops – in other words, familiar white-dominated women's liberation movement reference points.[22] As with *Reclaiming the F Word*, there is no specific mention of Black and women of colour feminisms. The whiteness of this historic narrative is reinforced in a chapter titled 'What does feminism do?', which, resonating with Redfern and Aune's approach, begins to answer the question by listing the seven demands of the British women's liberation movement. Despite the book's global focus, then, this focus is tied to a colonial frame which prioritises (white) women from the global North as the leading visionaries of feminism whom women from the global South have taken inspiration from. This is reinforced by its uncritical reproduction of the wave analogy, which is a poor fit for understanding the multiple and diverse trajectories of movements for gender justice across the globe.

Both Redfern and Aune's and Walby's accounts imply that the transition from a white-dominant and Western past to a diverse, inclusive and global present have happened through an 'expanding' process whereby feminism grows outwards, reaching more and more people. These narratives of progress lack attention to the role that Black, anti-racist and anti-imperial feminist theorising and organising has played within these histories. Mary-Jo Nadeau's research on feminist narratives in the Canadian context is instructive here. Examining the self-constructed historical account of a prominent national women's organisation, Nadeau highlights how the under-representation of women of colour within the organisation during its early years is noted within the narrative, but rather than interrogating how white dominance and white feminist racism maintained their exclusion, the narrative focuses instead on women of colour's increasing involvement as 'an ongoing and progressive succession of inclusivity'. This narrative erases the histories of anti-racist challenges led by women of colour coming from both within and outside of the organisation; instead 'moments of inclusivity appear as autonomous developments'.[23] *Reclaiming the F Word* similarly promotes a story of increasing inclusivity, where histories of anti-racist critique are rendered invisible. The text lacks a narrative of how feminism has changed from being white to its contemporary diverse and inclusive manifestations. This, as Nadeau argues, reaffirms the position of white women at the centre of feminist movements, and suggests that their increasing efforts at inclusivity have been self-initiated, rather than the result of critiques by women of colour. Walby's claim that feminism's attention to 'differences and inequalities between women' has been 'long-standing', coupled with the white- and Western-centred narrative of feminism's development, similarly lacks acknowledgement of the fact that women of colour in both the global North and global South have fought long and hard to get white feminists to recognise that not all women are the same.[24] By leaving out the histories of struggle over race, difference and exclusion in the feminist past, while at the same time claiming an inclusive and diverse present, the texts lack acknowledgement of *from whom* white feminists have learned to be attentive to race and differences between women.

* * *

In contrast to *Reclaiming the F Word* and *The Future of Feminism*, the remaining three books highlight transitional moments more explicitly (although briefly), acknowledging that white feminists' increasing race awareness has been the result of critique by women of colour.

McRobbie's *The Aftermath of Feminism* constructs two quite different narratives about feminism's development in relation to anti-racism, one about socialist feminist politics and the other about feminist cultural studies. It is in fact only the latter narrative that acknowledges critique. The former places anti-racist politics as central to feminist activism from the start of the second wave. Tracing post-war feminist activism as emerging from the left, McRobbie suggests that feminist politics in Britain in the 1970s – at least the socialist strand – were much more deeply intertwined with anti-racist and class struggles than contemporary depictions of the movement allow for. She suggests that 'these intersections have shaped the field of feminist scholarship and also women's and gender studies courses'. While McRobbie acknowledges that feminism's intersections with other movements have always been 'fragile and seemingly torn apart by internal conflict', she argues that feminist politics in the 1970s and 1980s 'did nevertheless constitute a terrain of radical political articulations, comprising groups who perceived inequities and oppressions across the boundaries of sex, race and class'. She argues that a backlash against feminism has since taken place, which has involved a 'process of undoing' the connections between different radical movements, forcing apart 'cross-border solidarities' between, among others, 'black and white feminist and anti-racist struggles'.[25] This narrative, then, suggests that previously vibrant – if precarious – anti-racist, socialist feminist politics have been torn apart by the assault of neoliberalism.

In a separate discussion about academic feminism, McRobbie constructs a different narrative at odds with the depiction of the second wave as having always been concerned with the intersections of gender, race and class. Here, early feminist cultural studies research (where McRobbie situates her own past work) is described as having originally been ignorant of differences of race, class and sexuality:

> Looking back we can see how heavily utilised [the binary opposition of femininity and feminism] was, and also how particular it was to gender arrangements for largely white and relatively affluent (i.e. housewifely) heterosexual women. While at the time both categories [of the 'housewife' and the 'ordinary woman'] had a kind of transparency, by the late 1980s these came under scrutiny ... The concept of the housewife in effect facilitated a certain mode of feminist inquiry, but we were at the time inattentive to the partial and exclusive nature of this couplet.

As a result of these exclusions coming under scrutiny, McRobbie suggests that academic feminism found it 'necessary to dismantle itself'. 'For the sake of periodisation', she argues, 'we could say that 1990 marks a turning point, the moment of definitive self-critique in feminist theory. At this time the representational claims of second wave feminism come to be fully interrogated by post-colonialist feminists like Spivak, Trinh and Mohanty among others.'[26] Here white feminist ignorance of race is stressed, painting a different picture of feminism's relationship to anti-racism than that discussed above. By denoting a 'turning point', this latter narrative constructs a clear before and after race awareness.

The contradiction between McRobbie's two narratives is not elaborated upon within the text, but it can be resolved by understanding the former as addressing activist socialist feminism and the latter as addressing academic feminism. However, the claim that 1970s British socialist feminism was already anti-racist obscures the whiteness of the dominant strands of this movement. As discussed in Chapter 2, white socialist feminism came under significant critique in the 1970s and 1980s for its failure to fully incorporate racism into its analysis.[27] A *Scarlet Woman* report from a national socialist feminist conference in 1979, for instance, highlights how 'the fact that the conference had very little discussion on anti-racist, anti-fascist and anti-imperialist work was strongly criticised'.[28] Yet, in McRobbie's narrative, these debates, which took place at the movement's height, find no acknowledgement; all socialist feminists are positioned as having always had an anti-racist analysis. Whiteness within dominant strands of socialist feminist politics is thereby obscured.

In the feminist cultural studies narrative, on the other hand, whiteness is recognised, but as soon as it is brought into view, it is immediately positioned as having been transcended in more contemporary times. Critiques by scholars such as Gayatri Spivak, Chandra Mohanty and Trinh T. Minh-ha (US-based feminists of colour associated with postcolonial theory) are recognised as having initiated a process of dismantling 'the representational claims of second wave feminism' – in other words, claims by white, middle-class feminists to represent all women.[29] The description of these claims as having been 'fully interrogated' suggests that this process has been completed once and for all. There is even a precise point in time when this interrogation is presumed to have been completed. After this point, white feminists are implicitly 'fully' aware of their own white specificity, and of postcolonial feminism. Early academic feminism also becomes identified as white: when claiming that categories such as the 'ordinary woman' and the 'housewife' originally seemed transparent, McRobbie is clearly writing from a white perspective, as for feminists of colour, the category of the 'housewife' was never transparent in the way that she suggests. As Hazel Carby highlighted in 1982, pointing to white feminists' ignorance of Black women's experiences, '[i]n concentrating solely upon the isolated position of white women in the Western nuclear family structure, [white] feminist theory has necessarily neglected the very strong female support networks that existed in many black sex/gender systems'.[30] The continuity of the 'we' through the paragraph is revealing, with the 'we' at the beginning of the paragraph who are looking back, the same 'we' towards the end of the paragraph who were 'inattentive' to race and class exclusion in the 1970s – in other words, white and middle-class feminists. The continuity of this 'we' indicates these feminists as the central subjects of the book's narrative, both then and now.

Woodward and Woodward also identify the role critiques of whiteness have played in the transformation of feminist theorising. Their narrative of the feminist past focuses mostly on academic feminism and education. The dominant sentiment they convey is that of feminism as a site of affirmation for (all) women, describing the women's studies courses which were formed in the 1970s and 1980s as 'often life-transforming, through their validation of women's experiences and intimate and private social worlds'. They also critique what they see as a third wave feminists' contempt for second wave feminists, pointing out that 'the third wave often defines itself as pro-sex and multi-ethnic, as a critique of the perceived whiteness of the second wave'. They challenge this critique through an anecdote about Sophie's surprise when, 'well versed in the critiques of the second wave', she first came across her mother's old *Spare Rib* magazines 'and noted how prominent the discussion of race and accusations of racism were in these magazines'.[31]

At the same time, Woodward and Woodward acknowledge that women's studies and second wave feminism have been subject to critique, noting that they do not wish to 'overstate the achievements of feminist politics or to underplay the persistence of patriarchal and post-colonial practices of exclusion'. In a discussion of the place of feminist theories in contemporary higher education, they point out that '[s]ome of the criticisms of women's studies in the academy have been framed by its ethnocentrism in relation to the politics of race'. They argue, though, that important 'theoretical shifts' have taken place, which 'have been very productive, especially in their engagement with questioning ethnocentricity and interrogating whiteness, and an acknowledgement of intersectionality'. In a similar vein to McRobbie, the narrative here marks a 'shift' within feminist theory which suggests ethnocentricity and whiteness are now productively engaged with. The argument suggests that feminism's continued relevance requires its theories to 'remain dynamic and responsive to social transformations, by acknowledging and seeking to make sense of the lived experiences of difference'.[32] Yet, while this suggests an ongoing process, no further attention is given to feminist ethnocentrism and whiteness within the book after this point. The book thereby partakes in the practice of 'gestur[ing] to rather than evidence[ing]' continued critical engagement with race, to return to Hemmings' characterisation of 'before and after' narratives.[33]

Budgeon also problematises simplistic distinctions between second and third wave feminisms, noting that a 'language of inclusivity … represents one of [the third wave's] defining rhetorical devices and it is used, often controversially, to define its establishment as separate from second wave feminism'. Third wave feminists, Budgeon argues, emphasise their difference by 'representing second wave feminism as ethnocentric and overly concerned with imposing similarity upon women's difference'. Although she critically analyses such claims by third wave texts, she does at the same time accept the focus on difference as being at the core of what distinguishes the third wave from the '[w]hite solipsism and ethnocentric tendencies' of 'some second wave approaches'. On several occasions, she draws attention to feminists of colour's central role in this transformation, describing the 'complex character' of third wave feminism as owing 'a large debt to the critiques of feminists of colour'.[34] However, there is very little engagement with the specific content of any such critiques.

Across McRobbie's, Woodward and Woodward's and Budgeon's accounts, then, critiques by feminists of colour are acknowledged as playing a pivotal role in the transformation of dominant (i.e. white-authored) theoretical frameworks. What is notable across all these accounts, though, is the brevity of attention afforded to these processes of transformation, given their acknowledged significance. In *Aftermath*, the 'exclusive nature' of white feminists' theorising is made visible very briefly and positioned in the past, with a definitive break being inserted between an 'inattentive' (white) feminist theory to one which critically engages with its own founding assumptions and concepts. White feminists' prior ignorance is implied to have been fully (self) interrogated by the fact that whiteness within feminism is not referred to any further within the book. Similarly, ethnocentrism and whiteness within feminism are briefly brought into view in *Why Feminism Matters*, but then lost sight of again. *Third Wave Feminism* describes critiques by feminists of colour as signifying an important moment in the development of feminist theory, yet few specific theorists of colour are named, with 'feminist of colour critique' coming to signify a generic critique of whiteness. The texts which Budgeon engages with most extensively on this point are evaluative accounts of the development of feminist theory, not the actual critiques by feminists of colour which are gestured towards. While US Black feminists Patricia Hill Collins and bell hooks are cited in passing in relation to this debate, it is notable that their work is not quoted, nor engaged with at any other point in the book.[35] Similarly, Woodward and Woodward reference Black British feminists Avtar Brah and Ann Phoenix, as well as race-critical feminist scholar Nira Yuval-Davis, but without further engaging with their work.[36]

*   *   *

Whether the moment of transformation from a white and ignorant past to a race-critical and diverse present is narrated implicitly or explicitly, all five texts indicate that such a transformation has occurred. To an extent this reflects an accurate change within hegemonic feminism: there *is* undoubtedly more attention given to these questions within white-authored theory and white-led politics today than there used to be. What matters, however, is how this narrative is framed and what it enables. When racism and whiteness within feminism are framed as belonging only to the past, this suggests that there is no need to continue to discuss them in the present. Contemporary white feminists are thus implied to have transcended the need to continue to address race and whiteness within their theorising and praxis.

DISPLACING RACE ANALYSIS

In this section, which focuses on Woodward and Woodward's, Budgeon's and Walby's work, I examine some ways in which the assertion that white feminists are now race aware can lead to the reproduction of white-centred theoretical perspectives, through a displacement of actual race analysis.

Woodward and Woodward's and Budgeon's texts both raise concerns which can be summarised as 'difference politics gone too far'. While Woodward and Woodward, as discussed in the previous section, suggest that the theoretical interrogation of ethnocentricity and whiteness is necessary, they simultaneously question the extent to which differences between women should be foregrounded within feminist theorising. As a response, they advocate a 'grown-up politics of difference', expressing a concern that 'the primacy of sexual difference' is not being adequately recognised within contemporary feminist theory. In their view, the critique of binary sex/gender categories and sexual difference feminisms, while useful to an extent, has gone too far the other way, and there is now a need to 'reclaim the lost category "woman"'.[37] They suggest that there is a need to be able to speak and write of women's experiences as *women*, something which they feel has been lost by the mainstreaming of poststructuralist theory and an increased focus on differences.

Woodward and Woodward describe difference as having been 'central to feminism in the 1980s' and admonish third wave feminists for 'underestimating the extent of second-wave engagement' with issues related to difference. This can only be assumed to be an implicit reference to race and other differences such as class, disability and sexuality, given the centrality of these categories in debates about difference in the 1980s (see Chapter 2). Yet, despite alluding to these debates, the chapter focuses on sexual difference only. Woodward and Woodward write that 'a politics of difference can be reconstituted through an exchange between different versions of feminism and different feminist voices', and the chapter is described as a dialogue between feminist theory from both the second and third wave. However, the discussion completely excludes the work of feminists of colour. And despite suggesting that their chapter attends to conversations between 'postcolonialism' and feminism in relation to 'difference and inequalities', there is not actually any engagement with (post)coloniality in the discussion. In fact, after postcolonialism's mention in the chapter's introduction, it immediately recedes from view. Instead, the chapter's call for a 'grown-up' politics of difference acts as a call for a return to white feminist scholarship on sexual difference in its imagined isolated form. The sense of dismissal of women of colour's feminist theories becomes complete in the book's final chapter, which presents an all-white list of 'key thinkers'.[38]

In order to understand Woodward and Woodward's claimed attention to ethnocentrism and whiteness and simultaneous reinforcement of both, it is instructive to look at where in the book feminists of colour *are* cited. In doing so, it becomes clear that, with the exception of Rebecca Walker (founder of the Third Wave Foundation and one of the most well-known feminists associated with the third wave), whose work is referenced several times across the book, literature by feminists of colour is mainly cited on the few occasions when the topic of race comes to the fore.[39] The most extended of these discussions appears in a chapter exploring young women's relationship to feminism. Here, Woodward and Woodward discuss a Black female student, who they describe as having become interested in feminism while doing a dissertation on hip-hop and youth culture. In the discussion of this student, a number of US feminists of colour are cited in quick succession.[40] Considering the lack of engagement with scholarship by feminists of colour in most other parts of the book, such scholarship is thereby positioned as relevant mainly when it pertains to race, and mainly to explain women of colour's experiences.

Returning to Aileen Moreton-Robinson's work on feminist whiteness (see Chapter 1) is instructive for illuminating the logic at work here. Moreton-Robinson observes that white feminist academics tend to locate race as belonging to people of colour, while situating themselves as 'non-racialised disembodied subject[s]'. As she argues, this framing refuses to recognise whiteness itself as a racialised position. This resonates with Woodward and Woodward's positioning of race as a topic which belongs mainly to people of colour and, conversely, their use of scholars of colour's theory mainly when it pertains to race. As Moreton-Robinson argues, framing racism as 'a people of colour issue fails to interrogate and locate white complicity'.[41] When ethnocentrism and whiteness are only brought to the fore when analysing women of colour's experiences, white women's experiences remain 'non-racialised'. While the authors mention 'obvious similarities between us, especially of class and ethnicity', there is no reflection on how this similarity may influence the perspectives taken in the book.[42] Despite a claimed interrogation of whiteness, then, *Why Feminism Matters* in fact pays very little attention to it.

* * *

For Budgeon, the rise of neoliberalism – i.e. the dominance of free market values like individualism and competition within economic, social and cultural life – is the main culprit for an excessive politics of difference. Neoliberalism, she argues, has coalesced with the third wave's emphasis on difference in enabling a feminist politics prioritising women's individual differences from each other. While she recognises the value of multiplicity, Budgeon argues that third wave feminists must more critically interrogate the influence of neoliberal individualism on third wave theorising. Budgeon's critique usefully calls attention to the ways in which individualistic analyses of difference can become divorced from attention to systemic inequalities, and she calls for renewed attention to structural inequalities. Yet, her critique of these systems notably only extends to 'the operation of patriarchy and capitalism', not racism or white supremacy.[43]

Rebecca Clark Mane's critique of the 'grammars of whiteness' which underpin some prominent US self-proclaimed third wave texts is helpful in pinpointing why the lack of attention to race in Budgeon's analysis is problematic. In her reading of a number of third wave anthologies (all of which also feature in Budgeon's analysis, and the majority of which are edited by white women), Clark Mane notes how anti-racist critiques by Black feminists and feminists of colour are 'often afforded a place of honor or veneration in the third-wave narrative', as marking its starting point, and a moment of transformation after which feminist theory attends to differences between women.[44] Such a gesture of 'veneration' is present in Budgeon's work, through her nod to the 'large debt' third wave feminism owes to 'critiques of feminists of colour'.[45] Yet, as Clark Mane suggests, a 'post-modern abstraction and appropriation of women-of-color feminist theorizing' pervades such narratives. Theories and concepts developed by feminists of colour are often 'abstracted and decontextualized' from the context of racism and interlocking oppressions in which they were developed. This process of abstraction enables an endlessly proliferating politics of difference through which race becomes merely one in a multitude of other differences. Yet, Clark Mane points out, an understanding of the work of bell hooks, Audre Lorde, Patricia Hill Collins and other feminists of colour frequently cited in white, third wave literature should not lead to an uncritical embrace of an abstract concept called difference. Instead, it should lead to 'recognition of the importance of race as a historically specific, structural, and relational category that is coconstitutive of gender'. What is particularly ironic, Clark Mane notes, is that the endless proliferation of difference 'is named as women of color's primary contribution to third-wave feminism'.[46]

Budgeon, like Clark Mane, critiques the lack of attention to systemic oppression in third wave feminist literature, but unlike Clark Mane, focuses only on patriarchy and capitalism, with whiteness remaining invisible. This is particularly problematic considering the book's rehearsal of the story that critiques by feminists of colour were foundational to the third wave.[47] This narrative implies that it was feminists of colour's anti-racist critiques which inaugurated a shift away from analysing structural power relations. The race analysis foregrounded by 'critiques of feminists of colour' is, in Budgeon's account, in conjunction with neoliberal individualism, implicated in the fragmentation of the (white) feminist focus on gendered oppression.

Budgeon's work in fact demonstrates a lack of engagement with the actual theories, including critiques, of the 'feminists of colour' who are vaguely evoked. As I highlighted above, only a few specific – and only US-based – texts by feminists of colour are actually referenced when this 'large debt' is acknowledged, but none of them are discussed with any depth. As a result, the significance of race as a structural category is lost within the book's analysis. Avtar Brah's theorisation of difference in *Cartographies of Diaspora*, for instance, provides in-depth insight on race and gender's co-constitutional, structural, historical and relational qualities. Distinguishing 'difference as a marker of the distinctiveness of our collective "histories" from difference as personal experience inscribing individual biography', Brah emphasises that while they are connected, these 'cannot be "read off" from each other'.[48] Brah's multi-layered conceptualising of difference as experience, social relation, subjectivity and identity grapples, as does Budgeon, with questions of how to think about difference without subsuming individual experience into structural position or group identity, and vice versa. Yet, Budgeon does not engage with any of the significant theorising (some of which is discussed in Chapter 2) on the complexities of difference by Black (British) and race-critical feminists, such as Brah. My point is not that Budgeon should have engaged with one particular theorist or another, but rather that a whole field of race-critical feminist scholarship on difference is markedly absent when it is clearly relevant to the kinds of questions the book is attempting to address. The lack of engagement with race-critical feminist scholarship indicates a lack of sustained attention to race. As with the third wave literature the book critiques, this analysis contributes to the continuity of whiteness which troubles such literature, and thus fails to address the relevance of structural racism for understanding gender in late modernity.

*   *   *

Walby is less preoccupied with the risks of difference. While she raises some concerns about the danger of difference being foregrounded at the expense of equality, she nevertheless positions an understanding of women's differences as central to feminism. She emphasises the importance of 'networks, alliances and coalitions' which 'foreground the practice of recognising differences and commonalities simultaneously', and argues that the 'use of coalitions as a method of organising feminism across difference is now taken for granted' within transnational feminist work. While describing the 'intersection of gender inequality with other inequalities' as a challenge for feminism, Walby argues that intersectional organising is crucial for feminist movements.[49] It is her engagement with the concept of intersectionality that I will explore here, as despite this concept originating from Black feminists' analyses of the intersections of gender, race and class, Walby deploys it in a way which effectively displaces anti-racism.

In line with her emphasis on the importance of mainstreaming gender analysis into existing institutions and political structures, Walby argues that feminism has the best chance of influencing change when it politically intersects with other social movements and progressive forces. She begins her chapter on 'Feminist intersections' by outlining a history of the concept as originating from Black women's experiences of exclusion. Walby describes Crenshaw's original work (see Chapter 2) as 'highly critical of the way in which Black women can be rendered invisible at the intersection of "race" and gender projects' and as 'offer[ing] a critique of identity politics that obscures groups at such points of intersection'. However, after this initial discussion of Crenshaw's work, race and anti-racism start to disappear from view. In turn, the chapter considers the usefulness and possibilities of 'politically intersecting' feminism with other progressive movements, specifically environmentalism, human rights and social democracy. Walby concludes that a 'social democratic project ... infused with feminism' contains the possibility of including all other progressive struggles within it, and constitutes the best hope for meeting present global challenges. She concludes the book by stating that

> [i]f there is an effective synthesis between social democracy and feminism, then the majority of the population would be engaged in a democratic project that stood some chance of success in reforming capitalism and in tackling the environmental crisis, as well as in reducing gender and other forms of inequality.[50]

Here, racism is no longer acknowledged explicitly, but is implicitly contained amongst 'other forms of inequality'.

While Walby writes of systemic 'gender regimes', there is little attention to systemic racial power regimes within the book.[51] In fact, apart from the discussion of Crenshaw's work, race is rarely mentioned. The term 'ethnicity' is more frequently used, in a way which elides discussion of structural racism. For instance, in relation to feminist politics, the issue of differences between women is described as having 'been formulated most sharply in relation to ethnicity', and debates about intersectionality are described as having 'prioritised the relationship between gender and ethnicity'.[52] Racism within feminism is thereby reframed as differences of ethnicity. As Sara Salem and Vanessa Thompson note, drawing on Melissa Weiner's work, European scholars (as opposed to North American ones) tend to prefer 'to speak of "ethnicity" in discussions that are essentially about race'.[53] Weiner argues that policymakers and scholars prefer this term, because it 'evokes notions of culture but fails to account for hierarchical power and value implications central to racial identities and racialization processes'.[54] Salem and Thompson suggest that this substitution forms part of broader patterns of erasure whereby European societies displace racism as something which 'happens "over there" – in the United States or in other non-European contexts'.[55] *The Future of Feminism* reproduces such a race-evasive framing of Europe. This is particularly evident in Walby's faith in the EU to deliver gender equality on a global level. Writing in the wake of the 2008 financial crash (and pre-Brexit), Walby argues that the EU could potentially overtake the US as 'the leading global hegemon'. She frames this as a battle between neoliberalism (US) and social democracy (EU) and argues that the 'balancing of forces in favour of the EU over the US ... would create quite a different context, much more benign and open to the further development of feminist projects'.[56]

While it is unarguably true that the EU has a better record on gender equality than the US, Walby's characterisation of the EU project as 'much more benign' fails to account for its deep investment in global inequalities. Her description of the EU as having been 'founded with a mission to prevent war and the holocaust from ever happening again in Europe' erases the colonial dimensions of the Union's origins.[57] As Gurminder Bhambra points out, drawing on the work of Peo Hansen and Stefan Jonsson, the post-war European integration project was as much about consolidating European geopolitical power and ensuring the continued access to African natural resources in the wake of decolonisation as it was about ensuring peace on the continent of Europe. As Bhambra writes,

> [t]o the extent that peaceful coexistence was an aim of the architects of Europe, it was one to be bought at the cost of African lives, labour and land; a cost that the architects of the time did not see as a cost and the apologists for Europe today fail even to acknowledge.[58]

Uncritical support for the EU as a peaceful project participates in what Hansen and Jonsson call Europe's 'self-legitimising myth'.[59] Europe's power is not only enacted through trade, but also through migration control policies which have ensured a lack of safe routes into the continent, with well-known devastating consequences in the Mediterranean and beyond.[60] The argument that intersecting feminist movements with a social democratic EU can reduce all forms of inequality fails to acknowledge and address the ways in which the EU has always been and continues to be a racialised project.

The Future of Feminism's engagement with the concept of intersectionality, then, suggests a reckoning with race which is in fact not really there. In considering the different possibilities of intersecting feminism with other social movements, anti-racism is not even on the list of options. Subsuming race under 'other inequalities' minimises the significance of coloniality and systemic racism within the global structures, movements and institutions that the book is concerned with. While it gestures towards white feminists' exclusion of women of colour in the brief discussion of Crenshaw's work, this is not discussed further. Usefully, Walby acknowledges inequalities in access to resources between feminists in the global North and South, and also rejects the phrase 'global feminism' for its tendency to 'make less visible important distinctions' and to 'elevate inappropriately the practices of those in dominant countries'.[61] Yet, the analysis evades direct attention to the ways in which coloniality and racism fundamentally structure the relationship between women in the global South and North. Instead, it is implied that contemporary transnational feminism, with its close attention to difference, no longer needs to explicitly address racism as a structural axis of inequality, nor anti-racism as a necessary political project.

* * *

Despite a claimed race awareness, then, there is a lack of attention to structural racism in these three books. The suggestion that white feminists have successfully incorporated anti-racism into their work functions to displace the need for actual race-critical analyses. Structural racism is not considered on a par with structural sexism, and instead, anti-racist analysis appears as an optional extra, brought in when convenient. The occasional engagement with race or ethnicity contributes to the appearance of race awareness, but makes very little difference to the analyses presented, which continue to be rooted in white-centred frameworks.

RACISM: 'OUT THERE', BUT NOT 'IN HERE'

In contrast to the three books discussed above, *The Aftermath of Feminism* and *Reclaiming the F Word* incorporate race into their analyses to a much greater extent. McRobbie's book is the most thorough in analysing racism as a structuring power within contemporary Western society, and she engages in depth with race-critical and postcolonial scholarship. She positions anti-racism as a parallel movement to feminism, and as a politics which has similarly been attacked and 'undone' by the media and politics. Her analysis consistently holds gender, race and class in view, such as in her discussion of how young women are stratified by class and race in terms of access to educational and professional success and how the cultural 'post-feminist masquerade' of the 'fashion-beauty complex' has 're-instat[ed] whiteness as a cultural dominant'. Through a discussion of reality television shows, the book also highlights the continued existence of a relationship of unequal power between white and Black and Asian women in contemporary British society.[62] In fact, McRobbie's book is the only one of the five which specifically engages with whiteness as an analytical concept. Although they do not engage with whiteness in the same way, as mentioned above, Redfern and Aune do highlight that women's experiences are structured not only by gender but also by other social divisions, including racism.

There is one significant area, however, where both books overlook the significance of how racism operates, and that is within feminist politics and spaces themselves. This can be seen in Redfern and Aune's articulation of one of their central arguments, namely, that feminism needs to be 'reclaimed'. By outlining the multitude of ways in which women are still oppressed, they make a convincing case for the need to strengthen collective organising against gender-based oppression. In fact, the book's seventh demand is 'also [their] suggestion for a solution – a feminist revival, or an end to the backlash against feminism'. This demand, they explain, came from analysing the survey results and finding that 'the state of feminism' emerged as a concern among many of the respondents:

> [T]heir comments can be summarised as a desire for a larger, more visible, diverse and inclusive feminist movement, and an eagerness to ensure that more people – especially young people – are attracted to and empowered by it. In short, for even more of us to reclaim feminism. To a large extent, we believe that a feminist resurgence is occurring, and we've hopefully given a taste of the movement's passion and vibrancy. But we want to build on what's already there and spread feminism to more people.[63]

The 'spreading' of feminism is posited here as automatically having a beneficial effect for all women. The narrative of feminism as an inspirational and wholly positive movement to end women's oppression makes such suggestions sound like common sense; i.e. if everyone embraced feminism, then this would end gendered oppression. This argument builds on the narrative of increasing inclusivity central to the book's account of feminism's development. Feminism becomes an all-encompassing solution.

However, proposing feminism as an all-encompassing solution only makes sense when based on an assumption that feminist politics have always had positive effects for *all* women. Yet, of course histories of feminist movements are much more complicated than that, and there are very good reasons – prime among these being racism within white-dominated movements – as to why many people do not wish to identify with them. As Valerie Wagner argues, the logic that everyone must claim a feminist identity in order to end gender oppression prioritises the maintenance of feminism as a recognisable movement and an identity-based community. As Wagner suggests, such claims can in fact stall meaningful activism, as a feminist discourse centred on the need for stable feminist identities limits the developments of localised movements. In Wagner's words, this stops them from 'tak[ing] forms unrecognizable to each other', which, she argues, they inevitably must do in order to address the different challenges different communities of women face.[64] We can see this happening in *Reclaiming the F Word*: by focusing on the need to reclaim a feminism which already exists, a limit is placed on what feminism is and can be in the future. As the book presents a white feminist history, and portrays contemporary feminism as a (now more diverse, but still quite white and middle-class) continuation of that movement, it grants authority to those forms of activism which are recognised as feminist by normative standards. At the same time, it erases 'unrecognizable' forms from the narrative. In this case, this results in the erasure of Black British feminism, past and present.

The desire to 'spread' feminism outwards correlates closely to what Ien Ang calls a 'politics of inclusion'. Writing within the Australian context in the mid 1990s, Ang highlights how white feminists responded to women of colour's critiques by inviting them *in*. 'As a woman of Chinese descent', Ang writes, 'I suddenly find myself in a position in which I can turn my "difference" into intellectual and political capital, where "white" feminists invite me to raise my "voice", qua a non-white woman, and make myself heard.' Yet, as Ang argues, this response to critique on the part of white feminists does not adequately question the foundations of feminist politics and communities:

> [T]oo often the need to deal with difference is seen in the light of the greater need to save, expand and improve or enrich feminism as a political home which would ideally represent all women. In this way, the ultimate rationale of the politics of difference is cast in terms of an overall politics of *inclusion*: the desire for an overarching feminism to construct a pluralist sisterhood which can accommodate all differences and inequalities between women.[65]

Ang critiques this approach, as it fails to alter power relations between differently positioned feminists. Premised on the notion of a centre and a periphery, the most powerful members remain at the centre, inviting others in towards themselves. This approach is illustrated in Redfern and Aune's introductory chapter, which they end with an explicit invitation to the reader: 'Welcome to the new feminist movement'.[66] Yet, inviting *inwards* does not interrogate historical or current processes of exclusion. It does not question how whiteness and racism alienate many women of colour from white-dominated feminist communities. As Ang writes, it 'should come as no surprise that such a desire is being expressed largely by white, Western, middle-class women'.[67]

* * *

For McRobbie, whiteness – specifically *feminist* whiteness – similarly drops out of view when the focus turns towards the 'feminist academy' in the final chapter. In this chapter, McRobbie argues that 'the feminist post-colonial classroom' within the 'global university' constitutes a site of possibility for revitalising feminist politics. Each year, she explains, 200 students – predominantly young women from outside the UK – enter her lecture theatre to study postgraduate optional modules 'reading feminist and post-colonial theory'. McRobbie describes such classrooms as constituting 'a genuinely new space ... fraught with uncertainty and potential'. She acknowledges that they are 'marked by transparent differences of power', but that they also provide 'a "hospitable" cosmopolitan setting' where 'there is a prevailing ethos of radical multiculturalism and classroom democracy'. She suggests that paying attention to such spaces provides a way of 'pondering not just the passage for these young women in and out of the feminist academy, but also the post-colonial politics that are played out through these encounters'.[68] McRobbie engages with Spivak's work in this discussion, setting her own argument about the significance of this space in a hypothetical dialogue with Spivak, whom she suggests would argue against its significance because of its focus on a global elite in an imperial, capitalist centre, rather than on those who are excluded.

Despite the naming of power differences, there is no explicit discussion of race or whiteness here. Race differences are implied by the fact that the majority of the students are described as being from overseas, yet not engaged with in terms of how this affects the classroom as a feminist space. The recognition of power asymmetries is also tempered by the description of the space as one characterised by a 'radical multiculturalism'. This description suggests that this classroom is an anti-racist space, yet it does so without making race explicit.

As McRobbie does acknowledge the existence of power differences in her classroom, it may seem unwarranted to critique her analysis of it. Yet, I believe that the silence about the whiteness of the 'feminist academy' is worth reflecting on. As a fellow white feminist scholar who has attempted to create anti-racist feminist classrooms, I am intimately familiar with the difficulties of actually creating and maintaining such spaces within the institutional whiteness of the academy. Just because we may teach postcolonial feminist theories does not mean we know how to create anti-racist pedagogical environments. In my own experience, conversations about race, coloniality and capitalism with groups of students of different racial, class and national backgrounds can certainly be 'fraught with uncertainty and potential', but also with difficulty and risk, particularly in relation to ensuring a non-oppressive and non-othering environment for students of colour. Such conversations must engage with the context of the inherent inequalities in which they take place, i.e. the institutional whiteness and racism of the Northern neoliberal academy. This work requires white scholars to reflect on their own roles and complicities in reproducing the (feminist) academy's whiteness. But this is what is so often lacking. To bring it back to McRobbie's discussion, what is missing from it is any acknowledgement of the fact that the global postcolonial feminist classroom in Britain exists in the context of an institutionally white academy where scholars of colour are under-represented, subject to racist discrimination, over-scrutiny and micro-aggressions, and where students of colour are subject to a so-called 'attainment gap'.[69]

Heidi Mirza writes how in the 'brave new world of globalization and internationalization in higher education, academia in post-colonial and now so-called "post-race" Britain still remains hideously White and still not a place you expect to find many Black bodies'.[70] *Feminist* academia – if we take this to mean spaces where academic feminists work and teach – are certainly no exception to this hideous whiteness. While I am not suggesting that McRobbie is unaware of these inequalities, the fact that they are not acknowledged within the book's discussion of the 'feminist academy' functions to obscure critiques which have been made of its complicity in reproducing racism. In Chapter 2, I discussed feminists of colour's accounts of their experiences within the academy, highlighting white feminists' complicities and sometimes active roles in maintaining white dominance within these institutional spaces. As

Joan Anim-Addo writes, white feminists' silence about 'Black absence' in the academy 'resembles collusion, evoking again, this time for the twenty-first century, the question: "Am I not a woman and a sister?"'.[71] Anim-Addo's comments point towards the dearth of white feminist attention towards addressing the material, structural exclusion and marginalisation of women of colour in the academy. In the contemporary context, this often coexists with an increased attention to women of colour's scholarship. As Suki Ali observes, '[w]hile scholars of colour are underrepresented, underpaid and under-promoted in the academy, white academics continue to aver their commitments to anti-racism while paying little attention to the impact these shifting fields have upon minority ethnic colleagues'.[72]

What does it mean that the 'feminist academy' now (sometimes) teaches postcolonial and women of colour's feminist theories, but that the vast majority of those who teach it are still white? This is a crucial question, yet one which often remains unspoken. The silence around feminist academia's collusions and investments in the white academy functions as a form of distancing, which Aída Hurtado and Abigail Stewart describe as one of five 'mechanisms of power employed in the exercise of whiteness'.[73] Gail Lewis highlights the displacement which often occurs within academic feminist spaces when it comes to the topic of racism. As she points out, racism is always situated elsewhere; 'what you're not allowed to do is to say "these issues are right in our front yard", they are "our"' (as in feminists') issues'.[74] These strategies of distancing ensure that accountability and requirements for action on the part of white feminists are continually deferred.

* * *

In both *Reclaiming the F Word* and *The Aftermath of Feminism* there is a mismatch between the analyses the books present of the world 'out there' (intersecting structural inequalities and post-feminist neoliberalism) and the one they present of the world 'in here' (the inclusive and diverse feminist movement and the radically democratic, postcolonial feminist classroom). Whiteness disappears from view in the latter. In McRobbie's case, this disappearance is enabled via the narrative that white feminist academics have, since the early 1990s, taken anti-racist and postcolonial critiques of whiteness on board. By positioning white feminist exclusions as belonging in the past, there is no need to account for feminist whiteness in the academy in the present. The white feminist academic can thus retain her position at the centre of the 'feminist academy' without having to account for this positioning or the absences which continue to pervade this space. In Redfern and Aune's case, the promotion of a politics of inclusion, coupled with a narrative which emphasises feminism's transition from an innocent white past to an innocent diverse present, leaves whiteness intact at the centre, erasing both racism and anti-racist critiques from the story of feminism.

CONCLUSION: TRANSCENDING FEMINIST WHITENESS

This chapter has examined different versions of the story that while feminism used to be white and ignorant about race in the past, contemporary white feminists are knowledgeable about race and incorporate this knowledge into their theorising. Although versions of this story vary in their emphases, explanations and turning points, what they all have in common is a sense that the shift towards a race-critical feminism has occurred. Through the positioning of contemporary white feminists as well versed in race analysis, and through the descriptions of contemporary feminist politics as inclusive, diverse and attentive to difference, white feminist racism becomes history. Such narratives are misleading, given that racism within feminism is clearly *not* history. The relegation of racism within feminism to the past legitimates a lack of attention to these issues in the present.

In positioning feminism's race problems in the past, the stories which have been explored in this chapter gesture towards white feminists having gone through a process of accountability, whereby they have listened to critiques by feminists of colour and transformed their praxis and theorising. Yet, this process of transformation is given very brief attention. Why is this discussed so cursorily, given its claimed significance for feminism's theoretical and political development? Why is the language used to discuss it often so oblique and euphemistic, with the word racism all but absent? The answers to these questions signal our return to the theme of white innocence. All the stories told across the books are strongly guided by the need to retain, or reclaim, an innocent position for white feminists. Varying levels of acknowledgement that they used to be ignorant or 'ethnocentric' are conceded, yet through leaving this complicity with racism behind, a new space for innocent white feminists is cleared.

The acknowledgement of past white feminist ignorance functions as a 'non-performative' declaration. Ahmed argues that when white people 'declare' their whiteness and (past) ignorance, this is often primarily done as a way of proclaiming their anti-racist credentials. Thus, as Ahmed writes, when 'institutions as well as individuals "admit" to forms of bad practice ... the "admission" itself becomes seen as good practice'. However, such declarations do not in themselves challenge racism. Instead, as Ahmed argues, they reveal a desire for transcendence from being a racist subject.[75] In relation to white-centred feminism, the acknowledgement of past white ignorance, accompanied by a claimed race awareness in the present, functions to declare the transcendence of the white feminist: from ignorant to knowledgeable about racism, and thus as having transcended the position of racist subject. This transcendence reaffirms her innocence. As critiques of her racism, ethnocentrism and/or ignorance can be seen to destabilise her perceived 'natural' place at the centre of feminist movements, the re-establishment of her innocence is crucial for this place to be reaffirmed. There is thus a constant push to *move on* from confronting evidence of racism and whiteness as something which continues to exist within feminist theorising and politics. I will return to consider the importance of resisting this repeated moving on and its associated desire for transcendence in the final chapter.

4

Inevitable Whiteness?
Absolving White Feminist Dominance

As I outlined at the beginning of Chapter 3, the academic books which I analyse fall into two different categories when it comes to their approach to racism and whiteness within feminism. One set of books, discussed in the previous chapter, constructs problems related to racism and white ignorance within feminism as existing mainly in the past (when they are acknowledged at all). The other set, which I now turn to, recognises these as ongoing issues. Only three of the eight books fall into this category, namely, *The Politics of Third Wave Feminism: Neoliberalism, Intersectionality, and the State in Britain and the US* by Elizabeth Evans (2015), *Radical Feminism: Feminist Activism in Movement* by Finn Mackay (2015) and *The Feminist Fourth Wave: Affective Temporality* by Prudence Chamberlain (2017).[1]

All of these books pay substantial attention to issues related to racism and women of colour's marginalisation within feminism. It is not coincidental that they also represent the latest published books in my sample; I suggest that their more concerted focus on these issues is a response to the more prominent discussions about racism within feminism which have taken place within activist communities, on social media and within the liberal press in recent years (as I will discuss in Chapter 5). The widespread uptake of intersectional analysis among feminist activists in the last few years is recognised within the books, all of which emphasise the concept as a key organising principle for contemporary feminists. Yet, as I will demonstrate, the recognition of ongoing problems of whiteness within feminist politics can be incorporated into white-centred feminist theorising in ways which still reproduce white dominance and which evade serious attention to what white feminist accountability and commitment to change might look like. This is partly achieved by the continued marginalisation of women of colour's involvement and labour within the contemporary feminist communities and 'moments' that the three books examine, and also through a lack of attention to white feminists' complicity in racism.

I will begin the next section by introducing the books. After this, I trace the stories which each of the books tell about feminism's development in relation to race and racism. I highlight how these books trouble simplistic narratives of 'before and after' race awareness, instead foregrounding the continuity of both racism and women of colour's anti-racist activism and intersectional frameworks within feminist movements. However, while such accounts are more realistic and honest, one of their potential pitfalls, and one which I argue these texts fall into, is that they can lead to a sense of inevitability about racism and whiteness which can end up perpetuating the problem. I address this in the subsequent two sections. Firstly, I outline some of the ways in which Evans and Chamberlain, despite attempts to address the marginalisation of women of colour within feminism, simultaneously reproduce this marginalisation. Here I argue that one way in which whiteness becomes reproduced is through a presumption that white dominance is inevitable within the British national context. A complacency about the inevitably of whiteness leads to it becoming (re-)naturalised. Secondly, I examine how racism's presumed inevitability leads Mackay to prioritise the exoneration of white feminists from anti-racist critique over and above challenging racism. In all these accounts, then, as I will conclude, white feminists' accountability for and capacity to challenge racism are minimised.

INTRODUCING THE TEXTS

Evans' *The Politics of Third Wave Feminism* is a comparative analysis of feminist politics in Britain and the US. Based on interviews with activists in six locations across the two countries, Evans examines the effects of neoliberalism on feminism, how the concept of intersectionality is used by feminists, their attitudes and relationship to the state, as well as the relevance and usefulness of the term 'Anglo-American' feminism. Evans is particularly interested in the relationship *between* neoliberalism and intersectionality, raising concerns that the two have dovetailed to promote an increased individualism within feminism, at the expense of a more collective political agenda.[2]

Mackay's *Radical Feminism* focuses on the self-defined radical strand of feminist activism, specifically on Reclaim the Night (RTN) marches in the UK. The earliest of these marches were organised in 1977 in Leeds. A more recent revival of annual marches, spearheaded by the London Feminist Network (founded by Mackay), has been taking place around the country since 2004. Mackay's research is based on interviews with self-identified radical feminist activists, alongside other documentary sources. As well as providing a history and analysis of the organising of RTN marches past and present, Mackay analyses contentious debates in which radical feminists are centrally involved, namely, in her words, 'the role of men in feminism; the inclusion of transgender, transsexual or self-identified gender-queer people in feminism; and also the long-running divisions between feminists positive about the so-called sex industry – namely, prostitution and pornography – and those feminists who include these institutions in their definitions of male violence against women.'[3] While examining different sides of these conflicts with some nuance, unsurprisingly Mackay's text aims to strengthen the credibility of radical feminist positions. For instance, in her discussion of trans inclusion, she denies the existence of transphobia within radical feminist communities, despite the extensive evidence to the contrary.[4]

In *The Feminist Fourth Wave*, Chamberlain analyses five case studies of feminist activism, using affect and queer theories to reconceptualise feminist waves as 'affective temporalities' – i.e. as intense moments of collective feminist 'feelings' and activity. Her aim in doing so is to challenge exclusive wave narratives tied to 'generation and identity' which tend to privilege the activities of white, middle-class, non-disabled and straight women. Reframing waves as affective temporalities, Chamberlain argues, highlights that such moments do not represent the entirety of feminist movements, but rather times characterised by 'exceptional surges of energy'. She suggests that such surges occur 'in response to changing socio-political cultures', gaining 'momentum and strength as certain campaigns or issues capture public imagination'. Waves are then 'sustained through a number of activists becoming visibly involved in what appear to be the central concerns of the movement'. Chamberlain suggests that reconceptualising waves in this way can usefully 'address feminism's exclusions and difficult history', because it clarifies that surges of intensity emerge from 'a wider sea of feminism' which both enables them to take place and outlives these moments.[5]

All three authors raise concerns about ongoing racial exclusions within feminist activist communities. Evans is upfront about the fact that structural inequalities, including racism, continue to be a feature of feminist communities. She notes that 'adequate recognition of the multiple inequalities facing women, who are not white, middle-class, heterosexual, and able-bodied, is yet to be fully realised' and that 'the exclusion and marginalisation of specific groups of women remains a salient problem for feminist activists'. She dedicates a chapter to the topic of 'feminist inclusivity' which focuses on how inclusions and exclusions related to a number of axes of structural oppression, including race, play out within contemporary activism.[6]

Mackay's introduction includes an entire section on positionality in which she identifies herself as white, among other categories, asserting that 'it is important to be transparent about our identities and understand how they act upon our lives and the lives of others'. When introducing the activists interviewed for the book, she acknowledges that most of them were white, noting that this 'does raise a significant absence in this book'. She acknowledges that 'as a White feminist, working in a sector dominated by White women, it is possible that my own profile discouraged Black women from taking part in my research'. She stresses that the relative lack of feminists of colour in her sample is 'by no means representative of the diversity of women involved in feminism today and in the past'. While noting this absence does not resolve the fact that her book then becomes about white radical feminists, Mackay is at least transparent in recognising that whiteness has shaped and limited the research. Her book, as I will discuss, also engages with anti-racist critiques of RTN in a very direct way, and she acknowledges that 'racism and ethnocentrism [are] still troubling notions of sisterhood and solidarity'.[7]

Chamberlain's aim to reconceptualise wave narratives engages with critiques of the whiteness such narratives tend to engender, acknowledging that 'BME [Black and minority ethnic] activists and WoC [women of colour] have a history of being marginalised within the lit-up moments of feminist history'. It is precisely for this reason, she argues, that 'feminism needs to reimagine its time keeping, in order to achieve true intersectionality'. She is also explicit about the fact that 'in spite of continuing attempts at intersectionality, there are still ongoing exclusions'.[8]

All of these books, then, demonstrate an awareness of and engagement with critiques of whiteness within contemporary feminist communities, and these issues are given significant attention. In the remainder of this chapter, I will examine this attentiveness more closely. In the following section, I start by looking at the stories these texts construct about race and intersectional analysis within feminist communities, with particular attention to their engagement with wave narratives.

RACE, INTERSECTIONALITY AND WAVE NARRATIVES

One aspect of feminist storytelling which has garnered significant attention and debate within feminist theorising is the prevalent use of the wave metaphor: the division and labelling of feminist activity across time, generations and, according to some definitions, ideological strands into distinct waves (first, second, third and fourth).[9] This is true also for the books I examine in this and the previous chapter, with a number of them centrally concerned with analysing the activities and meanings of particular so-called waves of feminism. As is clear from their titles, both Evans' and Chamberlain's books are invested in the explanatory and conceptual power of waves. At the same time, they both approach wave narratives with caution, engaging with debates about their problems, exclusions and complexities. They both, for instance, cite Kimberly Springer's critique of how women of colour's activist histories are 'drowned out by the wave' because of the way in which wave narratives tend to centre the activities of white women.[10] Chamberlain emphasises how intense moments of women of colour's activism are often temporally different to those of white women, with 'periods of feminist history that are often perceived as silent' sometimes being periods of 'a significant amount of activism by [women of colour]'.[11] Still, both Evans and Chamberlain use the wave metaphor as a key conceptual lens for understanding contemporary feminism, partly because of a sense of inevitability (as does, it should be noted, Springer). As Evans writes, 'whilst some feminists reject the idea of belonging to a wave, and its use as a framing metaphor, all are (ultimately) compelled to engage with it, even if to repudiate its legitimacy'. She suggests that engaging with the metaphor therefore 'provides an opportunity for us to confront our understanding of feminist subjectivities and to better understand why and how some feminists choose to engage with it'. Although she develops a multi-faceted theorising of the third wave, Evans primarily uses it to describe feminist activism from the early

1990s until the early 2010s.[12] Chamberlain similarly describes the wave narrative as 'inescapable' because 'it seems impossible to articulate a different position without invoking the wave'. Noting that 'each wave as it is popularly understood has a periphery that is badly represented', she argues that ultimately this is because 'the way its stories are told need to be reworked' rather than a problem with the metaphor itself.[13]

Both Evans and Chamberlain critically consider the place of race and intersectional analysis in relation to wave narratives, critiquing accounts which over-identify the emergence of intersectional thinking with the advent of the third wave. As Chamberlain notes, '[c]riticism of the wave and historical revisionism has demonstrated the ways in which certain "concepts", such as intersectionality, have existed long before they are named as specific to a third wave'. While she notes that self-proclaimed fourth wave literature positions intersectionality as a key concept and practice, Chamberlain herself is critical of this claim, citing Evans to point out that 'intersectionality has been discussed within feminism since the 1980s'.[14] And while Evans describes intersectionality as having become the 'theoretical approach *de jour* for many gender scholars over the past two decades', she points out that the concept's genealogy dates back to earlier discussions about 'divisions of class and race'. She notes that 'it became a central debate among US and British black feminists in the 1970s/1980s who felt that their interests as black women were marginalised' (notably none of the citations here are to Black British feminists, a point I will pick up again below).[15] At the same time, both books emphasise the intensification and more widespread uptake of intersectional analysis within third and fourth wave feminisms. Thus, the books centre intersectionality as a key concept for third and fourth wave feminisms while also acknowledging the longer genealogy of (proto-)intersectional thought. In doing so, they emphasise that feminists (of colour) have long been theorising the ways in which gender, race and class intersect, and that such theorising is not limited to any one particular wave.

Mackay has less patience for conceptualising or categorising (radical) feminist activism in relation to particular waves. Suggesting that a 'resurgence of feminism has been sweeping our shores since the early 2000s', Mackay is not so concerned about '[w]hether we term this a new wave of feminism or not'. She is critical of narratives which position second wave feminism as history, arguing that 'it is as relevant today as it ever was'.[16] In terms of race and whiteness, Mackay is also critical of narratives that suggest women of colour have not always been part of feminism:

> It is a shame that the received wisdom about not only RTN, but the movement as a whole, is that it is a movement for White women. There is an important difference between stating that feminism is a movement for White women and pointing out that it is White domi-nated. It has been, and is still the latter here in the UK, but that does not mean Black women have not been active in feminist struggles for centuries or that Black feminists did not play a key role during the Second Wave here in the UK …[17]

Mackay's account of women's activism in the 1970s highlights Black women's activism more explicitly than any of the other books discussed in this and the previous chapter. In her chapter narrating the emer-gence of second wave feminism, after discussing the development of the women's liberation movement and its national conferences in some depth, Mackay acknowledges that these conferences 'were by no means the only large-scale events of the period', noting among other events OWAAD conferences (see Chapter 2) and Black feminist groups and organisations such as Southall Black Sisters, the Brixton Black Women's Group and the London Black Women's Centre, as well as the activism of Olive Morris.[18]

Mackay, like Evans and Chamberlain, also foregrounds intersectional analysis as a key concept for contemporary feminism, although she does not associate it with a particular wave. Describing it as 'a special term used in feminism to describe the fact of multiple and intersect-ing identities and the structural power relations between them', Mackay outlines Crenshaw's original argument (see Chapter 2) in some depth. She suggests that an intersectional approach 'has become central to contemporary feminist activism' and emphasises the importance of understanding one's social position and identity in relation to both priv-ilege and oppression, a point returned to a number of times throughout the book, and one which Mackay clearly tries to practise.[19]

All three books, then, tell stories of British feminism's increased attention to racism and intersectionality in recent times, while simul-taneously acknowledging that feminists of colour have long been developing intersectional analyses of gendered oppression, as well as critiquing white feminist exclusions. Importantly, increased attention to race and difference is not taken as a sign that white dominance within feminism has been overcome, but rather that there is more attention given to them by white feminists. These narratives, in contrast to those discussed in Chapter 3, thus emphasise continuity rather than transformation in terms of the existence of racism within feminist theories and communities. By resisting simplistic progress narratives regarding (white) feminists' uptake of intersectionality, they enable a more complex and honest approach to considering white dominance within feminism in the present. However, and as I will explore in the following two sections, one of the risks of framing white dominance within feminism as a constant feature is that it becomes understood as inevitable. This in turn can encourage complacency in terms of actually challenging racism.

NATURALISING FEMINIST MAJORITIES AND MINORITIES

Here I will explore some of the contradictory ways in which white dominance can be simultaneously problematised and reproduced. I will examine how, in the case of *The Politics of Third Wave Feminism* and *Feminism's Fourth Wave*, a normative whiteness becomes reproduced through a process of *minoritising* women of colour's experiences and concerns. While these books both discuss women of colour's involvement within feminist knowledge production and activism, there is at the same time an assumption that feminist politics are majority-white and that this is inevitable and, in a sense, natural. This sense of inevitability thereby reproduces itself; as Sara Ahmed observes, '[t]he belief that racism is inevitable is how racism becomes inevitable'.[20] This resignation to inevitable whiteness, I argue, results from an uncritical investment in 'common sense' national imaginaries which construct people of colour as minorities, and white people as the majority. In articulating this argument, I am drawing on Avtar Brah's, Gail Lewis' and Yasmin Gunaratnam's work interrogating the normalising function of majority/minority narratives.[21] As discussed in Chapter 2, their work draws attention to the ways in which the construction of people of colour in Britain as 'ethnic minorities' in the post-war era erased the fact that they belonged in/to Britain just as much as white people. This positioning of people of colour as outsiders to the nation is enabled through an erasure of Britain's colonial history.

Stressing third wave feminism's diversity, Evans specifies that she took due care 'to ensure that the interviewees were not just white, middle-class, heterosexual, and able-bodied women'. At the same time, it is clear from the book's findings and discussion that the majority of the participants were white (a breakdown is not provided for reasons of anonymity).[22] This in itself is not that surprising, assuming the research aimed for some resemblance of proportional representation based on demographic statistics. But while analysing data from a majority-white sample of feminists will of course produce a particular white-centred slant, the implications of this are not critically interrogated within the book. Instead, a numerical dominance of white women within the feminist communities Evans approached or was granted access to translates into a *normalising* whiteness within the analysis. In other words, the analysis does not address what the predominant whiteness of the sample means and does to the data. This becomes a problem when the book generalises – as it frequently does – about what 'feminists' think, who they are and what they do. For instance, when discussing multiculturalism, Evans describes feminists' 'ideological uncertainty' in taking positions on issues such as 'the wearing of the veil' for fear of 'being accused of cultural insensitivity or of neo-colonial tendencies'.[23] This framing, supported with citations from mainly white non-Muslim theorists, clearly presumes a non-veil wearing, non-Muslim feminist subject, and participates in the construction of the veiled Muslim woman as a silent 'other'.

The presumed white norm becomes particularly acute in the book's discussion of British feminism, which is constructed as less immersed in anti-racist and intersectional perspectives than US feminism. This is despite the fact that Evans usefully argues against the commonly expressed view that race is more significant to American than to British society and politics. Pointing out the lack of popular books about feminism written by British feminists of colour, she notes:

Of course, one could argue that race and the specific historical legacy of slavery is such that US feminists would be more aware of the need to address the issue; however, Britain also has its own particular history when it comes to race, immigration, and the legacy of empire. It would be incorrect to suggest that there were no active black women's groups in Britain; therefore, the high-profile feminist campaigners that typically produce popular books are self-evidently a narrow demographic that is unreflective of the feminist movement in Britain.[24]

Yet, Evans' analysis does simultaneously suggest that race is *seen by feminists* as less significant in the British context than the US one, and that there has therefore been less discussion of race within British feminism. This again presumes the perspective of white feminists as the norm. Such a perspective is clear, for instance, in the suggestion that feminist organisations in Britain 'are aware of the need to, as one interviewee put it, "look less white"', something which would clearly not be the case for those organisations and groups that are led by women of colour.[25] And while the importance of the 'legacy of empire' for Britain is mentioned here, this legacy is not explored within the book.

A normatively white perspective is also centred in the book's discussion of intersectionality. While emphasising some of the values of intersectional analysis, Evans simultaneously frames it as introducing a number of problems for feminism. These issues are approached with some nuance, yet they are clearly addressed from a perspective of privilege and dominance. For instance, claims that it is 'not clear how or whether the term can be operationalised or included as part of feminist praxis', nor 'what an intersectional feminism looks like' are at odds with long histories of intersectional organising.[26] While I do not wish to deny that there are real challenges inherent in doing intersectional work, as Sirma Bilge notes, there is a tendency within white-dominated feminist scholarly communities to over-complicate intersectionality; to conduct 'metatheoretical musings' about its usefulness as a concept with little reference to how it *is* being used in practice.[27] As Sumi Cho, Kimberlé Crenshaw and Leslie McCall write, 'we think answers to questions about what intersectional analysis is have been amply demonstrated by what people are deploying it to do'.[28] Evans' work is grounded in empirical research and thus does not rely on the level of abstraction that Bilge as well as Cho, Crenshaw and McCall critique, but the fact that her data suggests that it is not clear what intersectional organising might look like belies its whiteness. This is compounded by the description of intersectionality as a challenge 'presented to feminists', as well as by '[f]eminist responses to intersectionality' being discussed as if the concept has emerged from outside of the collective, which again indicates a white perspective.[29]

Evans raises concerns about the politics of intersectionality which echo those raised by Budgeon and Woodward and Woodward in relation to the politics difference (see Chapter 3). While Evans describes intersectional theory as offering 'the chance to undertake radical and complex analysis of power', citing Crenshaw's original work, she simultaneously suggests that intersectional analysis poses a threat to collective activism and 'the sustainability of this third wave'.[30] Describing intersectionality as 'a framework that seeks to emphasise difference amongst and between women', she argues that it poses a 'danger of reducing levels of analysis to an individual rather than collective level'.[31] This danger is described as particularly heightened in the context of neoliberalism's emphasis on individualism.

Evans certainly makes a salient point about how the neoliberal context encourages individualistic politics in the name of intersectionality. But a fuller understanding of this process requires an analysis of whiteness and white feminist appropriation of the concept of intersectionality, something which is missing from the book. As Bilge argues, the concept of intersectionality has been 'systematically depoliticized' within white-dominated academic discourse. Bilge, like Evans, sees neoliberalism as central to this process, arguing that 'neoliberal assumptions' have created the conditions whereby the social justice-oriented roots of intersectionality have become 'diluted' and 'disciplined'. She argues that the concept has become 'commodified and colonized', and turned into 'a tool that certain feminist scholars can invoke to demonstrate "marketable expertise" in managing potentially problematic kinds of diversity'.[32] In other words, according to Bilge, among others (see Chapter 2), intersectionality has been incorporated into white-dominated feminist discourse in order for its radical anti-racist potential to be contained and neutralised. In this depoliticised version of intersectionality, the work of feminists of colour is often marginalised and white feminist work centred. Race becomes an optional intersectional axis, as discussed in relation to Walby's work in Chapter 3. The erasure of the racialised power dynamics inherent in the circulation of the concept contributes to what Bilge describes as intersectionality's 'whitening'.

As Bilge's analysis shows, to understand the effects inherent to inter-sectionality's collision with neoliberalism requires an understanding of whiteness. However, Evans' discussion of intersectionality does not account for whiteness or attend to the racial power dynamics in terms of who engages with the concept and how. Instead, only the concept's 'popularisation' is noted.[33] Yet, intersectionality's 'popularisation' could be seen as synonymous with its 'whitening'. The description of inter-sectionality as seeking 'to emphasise difference' relies on a depoliticised understanding of what intersectional theorising and practice aims to do. This framing removes intersectional theorising from the history and context central to its emergence within Black feminist thought, i.e. the structural location of oppression and discrimination experienced by Black women at the intersection of white supremacy, patriarchy and capitalism. Cho, Crenshaw and McCall draw attention to this, noting that the early development of the concept 'was not located somewhere outside the field of race and gender power but was an active and direct engagement with issues and dynamics that embodied such power'. As the concept has become increasingly popular within academic theoris-ing, they stress the importance of remembering that it 'neither travels outside nor is unmediated by the very field of race and gender power that it interrogates'.[34]

That the type of intersectionality engaged with in *The Politics of Third Wave Feminism* is itself largely a whitened and neoliberal version can be explained by the fact that, apart from some initial discussion of Crenshaw's early work, the book engages with very little Black feminist literature on the topic. In a two-and-a-half-page literature review of theories on intersectionality, a number of predominantly North American feminists of colour are referenced, alongside white ones (including British and Europe-based scholars).[35] But aside from this, there is surprisingly little engagement with literature on intersection-ality, despite the term being in the book's title. There is no discussion of how the unequal 'playing field' of women's and gender studies and feminist activism has led to intersectionality being re-theorised in white-centred ways. Instead, the book's rather pessimistic assessment of intersectionality chimes along the lines of arguments discussed in the previous chapter of the politics of difference having 'gone too far'.

The erasure of *British* feminists of colour is particularly problematic given the specific focus on comparing the US and the UK. As the book itself notes, there is a tendency to speak uncritically of an Anglo-American feminism without distinguishing the particularities of the two national locations. But repeatedly, when it comes to discussing Black feminism, there is a complete lack of engagement with any work by Black feminists based in Britain. In a five-page section on race and inclusion, the opening paragraph begins by stating that 'Black feminists have long documented racism within the women's and feminist movement, illustrating the various formal and informal ways in which women of color have been excluded, marginalised, or discriminated against by white women.' Yet, the references here are only to US feminists of colour. This absence becomes even more striking when the book is specifically discussing race in the British context. 'Whilst there is a strong history of black feminism within Britain, the popular feminist books that have been published in recent years have not included any written by or specifically directed at black or ethnic minority women', Evans notes, but there are no citations. Instead, the only references contained in the paragraph which follows are to the aforementioned popular feminist books by white authors. A few paragraphs later, British 'women's groups dedicated to BME women' are mentioned, namely, the Iranian and Kurdish Women's Rights Organisation, Muslim Women's Network UK and Southall Black Sisters.[36] However, there is no specific discussion of their work. By rendering much scholarship and activism by British feminists of colour invisible, the book legitimates its own argument that race is a more prominent issue in US feminist politics than in Britain. It overstates the whiteness of British feminism through its erasure of most Black British feminist scholarship and activism.

* * *

Chamberlain's account of fourth wave feminism houses some similar contradictions. Despite the book's express aim of reconceptualising the wave metaphor in order to address the marginalisation of the work of feminists of colour, four out of five of its case studies focus on, in Chamberlain's own words, 'campaigns and organisations that are for the most part run and faced by white women'.[37] These include Slutwalks (with a specific focus on the London march), the *Everyday Sexism* project, campaigns against misogynistic Facebook pages, the campaign for a woman to feature on the new £5 note, and the use of irony in student activist Bahar Mustafa's alleged tweet #killallwhitemen. Chamberlain's discussion of these case studies focuses not only on the work of the activists themselves, but also on the backlash and some of the points of contention around them. In relation to Slutwalks, for instance, this includes a discussion of the Black Women's Blueprint open letter critiquing (North American) Slutwalks organisers for not taking account of the more deeply stigmatising connotations of the word 'slut' for Black women.[38]

By focusing on both the activism itself and the public debate and response to it, Chamberlain suggests that these case studies constitute moments of increased intensity within feminism. Yet, who defines and judges what constitutes a surge in intensity? This question is not adequately addressed in the book. One of the problems with determining what truly belongs within an 'affective surge' is that such a determination relies also on our own affective responses. It does not appear as though the case studies were chosen because of some kind of 'objective' measurement of intensity, but rather because these moments seemed most obviously intense to the author. My own affective response and reading of feminist activism in the five or so years prior to the book's publication is quite different. While my account would of course be no more objective than Chamberlain's, this highlights the subjective nature of our affective attention, i.e. what pulls us in certain directions to notice particular actors and activities. Ultimately, choices were made about which examples of activism to focus on within the book, with white women's activism foregrounded. This in itself over-determines the whiteness of the fourth wave the book constructs. It is notable, in particular, that the Black Feminists UK group, which was very active during the time period of the book's case studies, is absent from the analysis. Considering that the book defines social media use and discussions of intersectionality as key elements of the fourth wave, this is a significant absence. Transnationally, creators and users of hashtags such as #solidarityisforwhitewomen and #thistweetcalledmyback have called attention to women of colour's labour in spearheading intersectional feminist analysis online; labour which goes unrecognised while the analysis itself is appropriated by more institutionally supported white feminists.[39] As I will discuss in Chapter 5, this was particularly the case in relation to the rapid spread in activist and mainstream media engagement with the concept of intersectionality. Okolosie, in her analysis of Black Feminists UK's online activism, points out how feminists of colour have been repeatedly expected to '"teach" intersectionality' to white feminists.[40] However, the influential role that members of the Black Feminists group played in shaping feminist debates around this time is not considered in *The Feminist Fourth Wave*.

At the same time, feminists of colour are not wholly absent from the book's account of the fourth wave. The case of Bahar Mustafa's tweet, Chamberlain explains, is included in order to explore how 'linguistic strategies', particularly irony, are used by feminists.[41] Mustafa's work as a diversity officer at Goldsmiths College's students' union became the subject of mass scrutiny and online attacks when her attempt to organise an event exclusively for people of colour caught right-wing media attention and outraged claims of 'reverse racism'. Shortly afterwards, Mustafa was reported to the police and charged for allegedly tweeting '#killall-whitemen', although charges were later dropped.[42] Chamberlain draws attention to the fact that white Hollywood actor Emma Thompson made a similar joke about killing old white men at the 2016 Academy Awards, yet did not receive the kind of backlash which Mustafa did. Chamberlain usefully highlights that women of colour's and white women's experiences within feminist activism are not the same, with women of colour's actions and words being much more intensely scrutinised and resisted:

> Mustafa's case surrounding irony demonstrates that some bodies are still at greater risk, even if they seem to have found a home within feminism. White, able-bodied and middle-class women are still at less risk in certain forms of protest, while BME activists are taking on far greater difficulties. Both Mustafa's experience, and the race reading of the Slut Walk in America show that in spite of this contemporary's aspiration to intersectionality and equality, there are still great lacks and absences.[43]

Chamberlain goes on to directly address the relative absence of women of colour within her case studies in a later chapter, via a discussion of the work of Nimco Ali and her organisation Daughters of Eve, which campaigns to end female genital mutilation (FGM). Here, Chamberlain suggests that campaigns such as this 'importantly situate themselves outside of the timeframes of feminist waves, ensuring that work continues on a grassroots level in order to effect long-term cultural and social change'. Describing Daughters of Eve as 'central to raising awareness of true intersectional feminism', Chamberlain argues that their work, while resonating with aspects of the fourth wave, and contributing to the intensity of the fourth wave moment, is at the same time different because it 'has a much longer future', tackling issues which have not been previously addressed in Britain. This work is described as different from projects such as *Everyday Sexism* which, Chamberlain argues, 'gained popularity on account of its "universality"'. In contrast, Ali's work is described as having 'been hindered by the "uniqueness" of her experience', thus having garnered less widespread attention.[44]

The inclusion of one case study which focuses on a woman of colour, the discussion of Daughters of Eve's work, as well as some critical discussion of the whiteness of the other four case studies, indicates *The Feminist Fourth Wave*'s attention to race and intersectionality. Yet, by prioritising predominantly white women's activism in the first four case studies, and then discussing Daughters of Eve as an example of activism which does not quite fit into the wave model that the book constructs, the latter's position at the edges of more mainstream (i.e. white) feminism is reaffirmed. The description of Ali's struggle as 'unique' in contrast to the concerns of white women contributes to the idea that women of colour's issues, while important, are 'minority' concerns.

The choice to focus only on Daughters of Eve's work also has essentialising effects. Chamberlain explains this choice by emphasising that the organisation 'very much participated within, impacted upon and resonated with this fourth wave affectivity', due to their extensive use of online campaigning methods.[45] However, with this being the only woman of colour-led activist group discussed in the book, it effectively comes to represent women of colour's activism more broadly. Given the long imperial feminist history, critiqued by Uma Narayan and Chandra Mohanty among others, of women of colour and 'Third World' women being constructed as uniquely oppressed by 'their culture', the exclusive focus on an organisation campaigning on FGM risks reinforcing this construction.[46] While Chamberlain does not blame the practice of FGM on 'minority cultures', it is still notable that the issue is framed as tied to questions raised by British multicultural society in a way that white women's issues are not. The work of Daughters of Eve is described as 'demanding that multicultural Britain respond to a specific and urgent issue', whereas none of the other case studies are described as existing within the context of multiculturalism. This distinction is emphasised further when the book describes 'feminism's difficulty with practising total intersectionality' as 'drawing attention to multicultural issues as opposed to those of white British women', as if white British women do not exist within a culture, nor are shaped by living within a multicultural context.[47] Multiculturalism is framed as only relevant to the discussion when women of colour's 'issues' are being addressed, which makes the particularities of 'white' and 'British' dominant cultures invisible.

Multiculturalism becomes further problematised and associated with people of colour and migrants when, in the concluding paragraphs of the discussion of Daughters of Eve, the focus moves suddenly onto the topics of 'extremism', Islam and migration politics:

> The rise of extremism, as well as discussions of FGM, require the UK to address multiculturalism in ways that are neither culturally deterministic, nor racist. While there have been numerous feminist debates about Islam and the veil within this fourth wave moment, the difficulty of Britain's multicultural society has been inflamed and exacerbated by Europe's wider migrant crisis. This is not to say that these issues will not impact upon women, but that there are issues at stake here that have wider scope than feminism. It is likely that practices such as FGM as well as a rise in racism within the UK itself will require particular attention to be paid to the way in which the country can address its range of cultures and religions.

An extended footnote accompanies this paragraph. This starts by pointing out that the 'relationship between Islam and feminism' and 'the migrant crisis' are 'different issues, even though they are often conflated by the mainstream press'. Chamberlain goes on to highlight right-wing media constructions of 'an influx of non-refugees' bringing 'religions and cultures that marginalise and subordinate women'. Chamberlain problematises such constructions, but then brings in the issues of 'forced marriage and honour-based abuse' and describes the 'problematic of gender, religion and culture' as having been 'exarcerbated by incidents of mass sexual assault in European cities as well as reports of abuse in migrant centres, allegedly perpetuated by migrants'. The footnote concludes by pointing out that such incidents have led to 'right-wing politicians using feminism as a means by which to justify xenophobia and exclusionary politics'.[48]

These two paragraphs take the reader through a whirlwind of complex and contentious topics, none of which are fully elaborated. While the discussion importantly signals concern with how racism shapes public debates about migration, 'Islam and feminism', and sexual assault, and while it draws attention to problematic conflations between these various topics, the quick gallop through them creates its own conflations and slippages. For one, there is an assumption that there is an obvious relationship between these various issues that does not need to be explained. This reproduces what Ahmed describes as a 'stickiness' between them. In analysing the proximity constructed between 'the figures of the asylum seeker and the international terrorist' within government discourse, Ahmed draws attention to the way 'emotions work by sticking figures together (adherence), a sticking that creates the very effect of a collective (coherence)' (Chamberlain herself draws on this concept in other parts of the book).[49] According to Ahmed, the frequent 'sticking' of words such as 'Islam' and 'terrorist' and 'asylum seeker' in close proximity naturalises a connection between them, creating a figure of collective fear. She notes that this connection does not have to be explicitly made; it is rather the repeated proximity of certain signs, words and objects that creates the links.

In relation to gender, Naaz Rashid's research on policy discourse about Muslim women similarly highlights how topics such as veiling, forced marriage and FGM are frequently positioned on a continuum with 'extremism' and terrorism within Muslim communities, despite the connection between such topics being unclear and unevidenced. She ascribes this 'conflation of what are conceptually distinctive policy concerns' to the 'securitisation of the policy landscape', which folds all 'social problems' associated with Muslims together in highly problematic and reductive ways.[50] The fact that Chamberlain simultaneously highlights increased levels of racism, then, does not undo the affective lumping together of the topics of 'extremism', 'FGM', 'Islam', 'the veil', 'migrant crisis' and 'mass sexual assault'. These all become potent signifiers for what is referred to as 'the difficulty of Britain's multicultural society'. This framing relies on the dominant contemporary public discourse which repeatedly constructs 'Muslims' as a problem for Europe and 'the West'.[51] While framing the discussion around the need to challenge anti-Muslim racism, this brief interlude and footnote simultaneously reinforce it by linking the different topics together in the first place. The seemingly commonsensical connection between them is in fact the *effect* of Islamophobia and anti-Muslim racism.

The terms used also do political work. The term 'extremism', for instance, is closely associated with the UK and US governments' so-called 'War on Terror'. It is a highly problematic term which, as Arun Kundnani argues, decontextualises 'so-called jihadist terrorism' from 'Western state violence', labelling only the former as extreme. In Kundnani's words, '[w]hat governments call extremism is to a large degree a product of their own wars'.[52] In the UK, the government's counter-terrorism strategy, in particular the 'Prevent' strand, requires public bodies to monitor their service users (patients, students, social service clients, etc.) for signs of 'extremism' and 'radicalisation'.[53] Prevent is highly controversial and has come under significant critique for targeting Muslim communities for surveillance and criminalisation.[54] As Rashid argues, 'despite the government's vociferous denunciation of "Islamophobia" and frequent assertions that far-right extremism is also being targeted by the Prevent agenda, the focus remains on Muslims who continue to be regarded as collectively responsible for terrorism'.[55] In Chamberlain's passing reference, 'extremism' 'sticks' to the other signifiers to indicate 'Muslim' without this even being stated. Neither is the validity of the term addressed. Similarly, the description of 'Britain's multicultural society' as a 'difficulty' which has 'been inflamed and exacerbated by Europe's wider migrant crisis' needs significant unpacking to undo the racist logic that it draws on. The 'common sense' dominant reading of this is that migrants have caused a crisis in Europe, and that this has contributed to Britain's multicultural difficulty (it is unclear what the 'difficulty' refers to). I do not believe this is Chamberlain's intention, yet this framing indicates a lack of attention to how racist discourse functions, and thereby participates in the colonial construction of mass migration – rather than European coloniality and racism – as the cause of societal crises in Britain and Europe.[56]

In the book's account, then, feminists of colour become intimately tied with 'multicultural Britain' and its perceived challenge of integrating racialised others (predominantly figured as Muslim), whereas white feminists are not seen as connected to these issues or in any way implicated in these debates. Similarly, intersectionality is mainly discussed in relation to feminists of colour. White women are thus positioned at the centre and as representing the culturally unmarked norm within feminist activism, and women of colour's experiences are positioned as particular, marked by intersectionality and multiculturalism. In this way, whiteness becomes (re-)normalised despite the simultaneous attention given to it in other parts of the book.

*   *   *

While I do not doubt that both Evans and Chamberlain are genuinely concerned with challenging racism, their books both frame the relationship between white women and women of colour via an assumption that women of colour constitute a minority interest group within feminism. This is not about the precise terminology used (all terms come with varying sets of problems) but the processes of minoritisation by which women of colour are constructed as a smaller and separate group from white women. White women's centring within feminism is perceived as natural and inevitable, given white people's numerical majority within Britain, Europe and the West more broadly. Yet, the construction of people of colour as minority constituents can only be done from an ahistorical perspective which does not consider the country's colonial history and the central role race has played in shaping national imaginaries of inclusion and exclusion. By the same token, framing women of colour as a minority constituency within feminism evades an examination of the power relations between the centre and the margins. The construction of 'majorities' and 'minorities' within feminism needs to be critically interrogated in order to be deconstructed. As bell hooks' argues, feminist theorising which begins from the margins – i.e. which centres those who are most oppressed – much more effectively illuminates the structures which oppress women (all women, but in different ways) than theorising done from the 'centre'.[57] The centring of white feminists due to their numeric majority results in the reproduction of white dominance within the movement, one often at odds with expressed commitments to challenging it.

JUDGE AND JURY: WHITE FEMINIST ACQUITTALS

While most white-centred feminist literature evades direct confrontation with anti-racist critique, Mackay's *Radical Feminism* stands out in contrast by attempting to address such critiques head on. Although it breaks with dominant patterns of evasion, *Radical Feminism* still ultimately emphasises white innocence, however, through a concerted attempt to absolve white feminists from responsibility for racism.

In a chapter outlining the history of RTN marches, Mackay dedicates two sections to discussing racism and anti-racist critiques that have been made of the marches. While these sections both highlight structural racism in Britain and also within feminism, Mackay is simultaneously keen to clear the record of early RTN marches, in particular the original march in Leeds in 1977, which she describes as having been 'publicly accused of racism; a charge which has frequently been applied to RTN generally and which has become widely accepted as a truism ever since'. Mackay describes how the march was criticised for its choice of route through Chapeltown, an area of Leeds with a large Black community. While this was seen by some Black feminists to have racist effects, colluding with the racist perception that Black men are more likely to be perpetrators of sexual violence (particularly against white women), Mackay painstakingly explains why such perceptions are based on incorrect information. She explains that there were two marches on the night, and the reason one went through Chapeltown was because the body of one of the victims of the so-called 'Yorkshire ripper' had recently been found there. Neither did the march call for increased policing; Mackay quotes one of the original organisers as saying that working with the police 'would have been an anathema' to them.[58]

Despite such clarifications having been offered by the organisers at the time, Mackay laments that the 'charge of racism is one that appears to have stuck to RTN and which surfaces fairly frequently'.[59] She cites Kum-Kum Bhavnani and Margaret Coulson's 1986 article in *Feminist Review* (see Chapter 2), which, alongside its critique of white socialist feminism, criticised 'the failure of anti-rape campaigns to challenge racist stereotypes of the sexuality of black men'. Bhavnani and Coulson criticise RTN organisers for having 'not taken up racism as an issue, nor seen how their campaigns against male violence are complicated in the context of racism'. They argue that the organisers had instead 'affirmed racist ideas by marching through Black areas and calling for greater policing'.[60] Mackay demonstrates how several other articles repeat similar critiques, citing Bhavnani and Coulson's article as the source, while reiterating the point that the Leeds RTN march never called for increased policing. She states that '[w]hether all such references could be traced back to 30 women marching through Chapeltown in Leeds in 1977 is unknown'.[61] Mackay's research found no evidence that calls for increased policing were ever made by any RTN organisers. It should be noted, however, that even on her own measure of what counts as 'proof', there *is* evidence to be found in the archives: a press release for a march in Hackney in 1982 called for 'improved back-street policing', although organisers subsequently withdrew this, claiming in the *London Women's Liberation Newsletter* that the demand had been 'passed by mistake'. There is further discussion within this issue about the politics of the proposed Hackney march, the planning of which had coincided with the release of police statistics on street crime 'broken down in a racist manner', fuelling anti-Black racism.[62]

Mackay is sympathetic to anti-racist critiques of RTN and treads a very careful line between wishing to absolve the early marches from blame while simultaneously recognising their validity within the larger context of structural racism. She quotes Hazel Carby's 1982 essay on white feminist racism (see Chapter 2), and points out that second wave feminism 'is often critiqued for lacking in intersectional analysis and for overlooking race and racism'. She concludes:

> When RTN first emerged in the UK, it was therefore just one element of a wider WLM which had already long been justly critiqued for historic and ongoing racism and ethnocentrism. It is perhaps then unsurprising that RTN, as one highly visible and well-publicised aspect of that movement, also became subject to these valid and still pressing critiques. However, the specific charges being investigated here made against the original RTN rely on claims that the early marches called explicitly for increased policing and that they cynically targeted their protests in predominantly Black and global majority ethnic communities. I have endeavoured to highlight in this chapter that these particular charges are unfounded; while acknowledging the context in which they were made.[63]

While recognising the validity of anti-racist critiques, the main point and purpose of this account is clearly to discredit the 'specific charges' against the Leeds RTN. In her analysis of these debates, Mackay draws attention to 'gaps between intent and reception', arguing that 'it is the job of political organisers to attempt to predict and traverse these'. However, when she highlights 'the history of racist stereotypes linking Black men with criminality and sexual aggression', she immediately absolves white feminists from participation in this history, arguing that this link 'was not a construct of feminists however, let alone those organising RTN in Leeds in 1977'.[64]

The suggestion that this racist history can be so easily discarded as nothing to do with white feminists evades the significant entanglement of discourses around rape with racism. In *Women, Race and Class*, Angela Davis highlights white women's complicity in the creation of 'the myth of the black rapist', and their active involvement in the lynchings of Black men following the abolition of slavery. As Davis documents, 'the rape charge turned out to be the most powerful of several attempts to justify the lynching of Black people'.[65] Davis, Hazel Carby and Vron Ware all highlight the crucial work of Ida B. Wells, the African-American journalist whose investigations into lynchings found that, in Ware's words, 'in every incident in which white women were said to have been assaulted, the facts had actually been distorted out of recognition', with 'almost no evidence to support the rape theory, except that in each case there was a white woman who had been found to have been associating with a black man of her own free will'.[66] Through her research and campaigning, Wells developed a crucial analysis of the interlocking systems of white supremacy and patriarchy. As Carby writes, 'Wells was able to demonstrate how a patriarchal system, which had lost its total ownership over black male bodies, used its control over women to attempt to completely circumscribe the actions of black males.' Yet, although Black women were central to the anti-lynching movement, there was from the white women's movement a 'resounding silence about – and therefore complicity in – the attempt to eliminate black people politically, economically, and, indeed, physically'.[67]

While the history of lynching is particularly tied to the Southern United States, the broader themes pertaining to race and sexuality are deeply embedded within coloniality. As Ware's research on the British Empire highlights, white women 'provided a symbol of the most valuable property known to white man and it was to be protected from the ever-encroaching and disrespectful black man at all costs'.[68] In more recent times, Davis highlights how a number of white feminists writing about rape in the 1970s and 1980s 'facilitated the resurrection of the

timeworn myth of the Black rapist'. Davis analyses, among other literature, Susan Brownmiller's well-known book *Against Our Will: Men,
Women and Rape*, describing arguments within it as 'pervaded with
racist ideas' of Black men as prone towards sexual violence.[69] Notably,
Mackay draws on Brownmiller's book, and describes it as one which
was 'significant' in influencing second wave feminists in Britain, and
particularly radical feminist activism against violence against women,
such as that of RTN.[70]

Rather than dismissing the racist association between Black men and
rape as 'not a construct of feminists', a more accountable approach, then,
would be to attend closely to the connections between white feminism
and the continued prevalence of this racist stereotype, in order to challenge white women's collusion with racism. As Amos and Parmar wrote
in 1984:

> [T]he compliance of many white feminists with the racist media
> and the police is shown in their silence when public hysteria is peri-
> odically whipped up through images of white women as innocent
> victims of black rapists and muggers. When white feminists have
> called for safer streets, and curfew of men at nights they have not
> distanced themselves from the link that exists in common sense racist
> thinking between street crime and Black people. Again, when women
> marched through Black inner city areas to 'Reclaim the Night' they
> played into the hands of the racist media and the fascist organiza-
> tions, some of whom immediately formed vigilante groups patrolling
> the streets 'protecting' innocent white women by beating up black
> men. Therefore we would agree that 'any talk of male violence that
> does not emphatically reject the idea that race or colour is relevant
> automatically reinforces these racist images'.[71]

There is no reference here to white feminists calling for increased
policing; rather, Amos and Parmar's critique focuses on the material
effects of white women marching through predominantly Black areas,
and emphasises the need for white feminists to actively take a stance
against the prevalent stereotyping of Black men as sexual aggressors
in order to challenge racism. These issues are also raised in Bhavnani's
account of being involved in feminist communities in Leeds at the time

of the original marches, published in a 1985 issue of *Spare Rib*. Her words are worth quoting at length:

> During the time I spent in Leeds, I became closely involved in women's groups around the Women's Movement, and also in black anti-racist and trade union politics. But it was the events of Bonfire Night in Leeds when a number of disturbances occurred in Chapeltown as a result of which approximately a dozen young black men were arrested on a range of charges, that helped to shift my political priorities away from the Working Women's Charter group, and the Socialist Feminist group and more towards black and anti-racist politics. I became involved in a number of defence initiatives around these Chapeltown trials, and also attended large chunks of the trial in order to watch 'British' injustice operate.
>
> But many of the women whom I knew through the women's groups were not as involved or as present in these meetings. The unease which resulted from the realisation that my white 'sisters' did not see anti-racist activity as relevant for their brand of feminism became sharper when, some time later, a Reclaim the Night march was organised, whose route went through Chapeltown, a predominantly black area of Leeds. I refused to go on the march because of its racism, this refusal being clearer in my mind when issues such as 'better' policing were discussed as a strategy to keep the streets safe for women. But the streets were never safe for any black person, and the presence of the police on the streets only seemed to be a guarantee that black people would be more likely to be harassed.
>
> And what about the implications that it was black areas which were unsafe for women? (Which women?) All this meant a lot of heated discussions with a number of white people, including some white 'feminists'. The latter also seemed to get upset every time I asserted I was a black feminist socialist and so involved in a different type of politics. I was creating differences, they said, and not understanding that we were all women. But where was their solidarity with me as a black woman? Why was it that I always seemed to be able to see the white perspective on feminism, but they never even acknowledged that there could be a black perspective?[72]

Neither Bhavnani's nor Amos and Parmar's critiques are cited by Mackay. Neither of these assert that the Leeds marches demanded increased policing, but Bhavnani's account points out that 'better' policing was an issue discussed in organising meetings at the time. Her account highlights the fact that such discussions – even if not everyone agreed – produced an environment where she felt marginalised and unheard. White feminists' inaction, silence on issues of racism and lack of solidarity with anti-racist campaigns are foregrounded here, and these relate specifically to the context of the Leeds RTN march. Yet, Mackay's evidence-seeking is limited to speaking to white feminists involved with the march, not with Black feminists who felt unable to take part in it.

The language of charges and accusations also has particular effects. As Ahmed points out, the 'hearing' of anti-racist critique as 'accusation' is a 'subtle but effective' strategy used by white people to reframe the subject of the critique as the victim. As she points out, 'the two words "racism" and "accusation," when stuck together, tend to conjure up a scene of an individual subject who is under attack by a collective'.[73] This reframing shifts the focus towards the perceived injury caused to the 'victim', prioritising white reality and white comfort over people of colour's experiences of racism. The language of accusations – and the description of Mackay's research as an investigation into these, carries connotations of a legal process, requiring certain types of evidence as proof.[74] However, this approach in itself reinforces the power inequalities which are inherent within a society where people of colour's accounts of racism are always questioned and frequently disbelieved. As Philomena Essed's research into 'everyday racism' establishes, it is precisely the everydayness of racism which makes it difficult to prove: when a person of colour names an incident as racist, a white person can easily deny it is so, by refusing to see how it fits into broader repetitive racialised patterns. The demand for certain kinds of documented evidence is used to dismiss people of colour's accounts. The demand for evidence perceptible to white people thus in itself reproduces whiteness; in Essed's words, '[t]he presupposition that those exposed to discrimination are not competent enough to make sound judgment about the situation is a powerful tool of everyday racism'.[75]

Mackay's insistence on the need to reclaim an innocent narrative for RTN exemplifies an assertion of white authority and the belief that white feminists are best placed to provide the most accurate account of the 'truth' of the matter. Despite acknowledging the existence of structural racism, the account provided is primarily concerned with absolving white feminists of responsibility for the racist construction of Black men as rapists. While it is acknowledged that racism and ethnocentrism have shaped British feminist communities, both past and present, this is explained by the fact that feminist politics are not immune from the ideas and structures of wider racist society. Thus, it is seen as inevitable that white feminists do participate in racism (although the original RTN organisers, it is claimed, did not). At the same time, this framing implies that because racism is not of their own making, there is little that white feminists can do about it. This reproduces a colonial representation of white femininity as powerless. As discussed in Chapter 1, Mary Louise Fellows and Sherene Razack describe how, when called to account for power inequalities between women, feminists often make claims to their own perceived marginality, participating in a 'race to innocence'.[76] Mackay's analysis of all women's oppression under a racist patriarchy not of their own making participates precisely in the kind of 'race to innocence' which Fellows and Razack identify. By focusing attention on clearing the RTN name from 'accusations', Mackay's account also reorients the discussion away from women of colour's experiences of racism. As a result, white feminist innocence is prioritised over and above a concern with how racism affects women of colour's experiences within feminist movements, and the effects white feminists' actions have on communities of colour.

The preoccupation with innocence, then, gets in the way of considering the ways in which white women have historically been and continue to be complicit in the construction of men of colour as sexual predators, and what can be done to tackle its harmful – sometimes lethal – effects. Such an 'investigation' would be much more productive; it would enable white feminists to better understand how whiteness works to maintain hierarchical relations between differently racialised groups of men and women, and equip them to challenge such dynamics. This is much more likely to be conducive to building relationships of trust between differently racialised women, and to contribute towards the undoing of relations of domination between them. As I will return to in Chapter 6, feminist arguments which are not also anti-racist easily become co-opted by far right politics and movements, as has been demonstrated again in recent years by the rise in far right mobilisations which construct Muslim men as sexual predators of white women.[77] As Amos and Parmar's and Bhavnani's accounts highlight, when white feminists remain silent on these matters, it reveals a lack of understanding and care about how racism functions in gendered and sexualised ways.

CONCLUSION: THE POLITICS OF INEVITABILITY

In different ways, all the books discussed in this chapter attempt to address questions related to racism and women of colour's marginalisation within feminism. Yet, they simultaneously exhibit complacency about the fact of continued white dominance. In *The Politics of Third Wave Feminism* and *The Feminist Fourth Wave*, the fact of white numerical majorities is translated into the framing of white women's campaigns and concerns as representing a normative perspective. In Evans' book in particular, white feminist perspectives remain unacknowledged at the centre of the book's analysis. Chamberlain is more explicit about the centring of white women's activism within her account of the fourth wave, and aims, through attending to 'the margins', to also highlight women of colour's activism. However, this raises the question as to why the wave narrative is emphasised in the first place, if it is already given that its reconceptualisation will continue to mainly shine a light on white women's work. There is a presumption about the narrative's inevitability, but this in itself speaks to a white-centred perspective. Much Black British feminist literature does not in fact engage with wave narratives to any great extent. For instance, only one chapter in the edited collection *Black British Feminism* refers to Black feminism as part of a wave.[78] Black British feminism's relative lack of engagement with wave narratives is reflected on by Heidi Mirza when she comments: 'Black British feminism for me is not so much a riding of the progressive "waves" of Western feminist narratives, but rather something more akin to what Sara Ahmed … has imagined as "lifelines" that are thrown to successive generations.'[79]

Mackay is also explicit about the whiteness of her interview sample, stressing that this should not be taken to reflect a lack of diversity in the broader (radical) feminist movement. However, in discussing relationships and tensions between white feminists and feminists of colour, she prioritises the 'truths' of white feminists over and above those of feminists of colour, giving white voices and perspectives authority in determining what racism within feminism looks like and what it does not. This reaffirms the perceived legitimacy of a white-defined narrative of British feminism.

Ultimately, then, while highlighting ongoing race problems within feminist communities, none of the books address the need for white feminists' accountability in relation to racism. Women of colour are framed, in *The Politics of Third Wave Feminism* and *The Feminist Fourth Wave*, as facing additional barriers and issues to those faced by white women, but white women's roles in perpetuating racism and whiteness within feminist communities are not addressed. While *Radical Feminism* acknowledges racism as a problem among feminists, the focus on absolving a specific group of white feminists is a distancing tactic which continuously defers accountability towards some other unspecified time and place. This prioritises white innocence over actually tackling racism. In a similar vein, *The Feminist Fourth Wave* prioritises saving the wave narrative, despite acknowledging and reproducing women of colour's marginalisation within it. And *The Politics of Third Wave Feminism* prioritises the sustainability of white-dominated feminist groups by framing intersectionality as a bigger threat to their continuity than the racist exclusions they engender. In common with the books discussed in Chapter 3, these texts are underpinned by an assumption that white women are rightly at the centre of British feminist theorising and politics. Processes of inclusion and minoritisation enable white-centred scholarship to demonstrate awareness of racism and acknowledge the existence of feminists of colour, while simultaneously retaining an unquestioned central – and innocent – position for white women within feminist theorising and spaces.

5

Liberal Whiteness and the 'New' Feminism

This chapter examines the representation of a 'new feminism' in popular publishing and the liberal press since the late 1990s. The 1990s was generally a decade of low visibility of feminist content within the British public sphere. There was, of course, ongoing grassroots and academic feminist work, but, as Angela McRobbie highlights, the rise of 'post-feminist' popular culture forcefully delivered the message to the mainstream that feminism had become irrelevant and outdated.[1] Towards the end of the decade and into the 2000s, however, a so-called 'new' or 'young' feminism started to become increasingly visible within the liberal public sphere. This mirrored and was formed in interaction with increased levels of grassroots activism by a younger generation of feminists, as outlined by Catherine Redfern and Kristin Aune.[2] This chapter traces how this so-called 'new feminism' has been promoted and represented within mainstream liberal feminist discourse in the last two decades. Specifically, the chapter analyses the representation of feminism within three popular books as well as in the *Guardian* and its Sunday paper the *Observer*, the UK's main liberal-left broadsheet newspapers (all general references to the *Guardian* below should be presumed to also include the *Observer*).

The idea of a 'new feminism' was explicitly articulated in Natasha Walter's book of the same name, published in 1998. I will discuss her book alongside two others, published about a decade later, which also claim to represent a 'new' kind of feminist: Ellie Levenson's *The Noughtie Girl's Guide to Feminism* (2009) and Caitlin Moran's *How to Be a Woman* (2011).[3] While a number of other feminist books have been published in the mainstream UK publishing market – particularly since 2010, reflecting the rising popularity of (some types of) feminism among the liberal public – I chose to focus on Walter's, Levenson's and Moran's books in my analysis because they have similar aims to those discussed in Chapters 3 and 4, in that they take feminism itself as a subject, make claims about what it is and should be, and what contemporary feminists are like.[4]

I chose to focus on feminist content in the *Guardian* because it has a history of positive coverage of feminist politics since the late 1960s.[5] Out of all British newspapers, as Kaitlynn Mendes writes, it is 'undoubtedly the most sympathetic to feminism', and it regularly documents feminist activism.[6] The paper counts a number of self-defined feminist journalists and columnists among its staff, and also commissions feminist content written by freelance journalists, bloggers and activists. Its extensive feminist content means it plays a key role in representing feminism to mainstream liberal audiences in Britain. The *Guardian* has documented what it often describes as a 'new' feminist movement since the mid 2000s onwards.

As I will argue, the narratives and representations of feminism within these books and newspapers converge to produce a depiction of 'new' feminist subjects and a 'new' feminist movement with some problematic consequences in terms of race. Some parts of this discourse, particularly that of the three books, promote a much more aggressive whiteness than other parts, such as more recent *Guardian* content. However, both ends of the spectrum work together to maintain a consistent underlying white liberal framework. Charles Mills describes liberalism – a political ideology championing 'individual rights and freedoms' – as the 'globally triumphant ... dominant political outlook of the modern age'.[7] Liberal feminism developed out of liberalism as a political framework organised around the notion that women should have equality with men in being able to exercise their individual rights and freedoms. Although its boundaries and scope are contentious, on a basic level liberal feminism tends to prioritise campaigns for equal rights, making reformist demands for redistribution of power between women and men in the public sphere. As Loretta Kensinger suggests, alongside equality, the core themes which tend to be emphasised in definitions of liberal feminism are 'rationality, rights, self-development, and self-fulfillment'.[8]

Despite its lofty premise of equality between all persons, liberalism was founded upon what Mills conceptualises as a 'racial contract', in which white people (historically, white men) 'contract to regard one another as moral equals who are superior to nonwhites and who create, accordingly, governments, legal systems, and economic structures that privilege them at the expense of people of color'.[9] Similarly, Carole Pateman identifies a 'sexual contract' through which (white) men have contracted to rule over women.[10] Proponents of liberalism tend to argue that these exclusions were anomalies in the system which have since been rectified, yet, according to Mills, this argument underestimates the extent to which a racial logic continues to underpin liberal societies. As bell hooks argues, 'systems of domination' – white supremacy, capitalism and patriarchy – are inherent within liberalism. She critiques liberal feminism for buying into these structures, describing it as rooted in the 'belief that women can achieve equality with men of their class without challenging and changing the cultural basis of oppression'.[11]

Suggestions that all individuals within a liberal society have access to the same rights – to freedom of speech, for instance – often fail to account for the structural factors which impinge on the ability of members of oppressed social groups to actually exercise such rights without disciplinary consequences.[12] 'Freedom of speech' also implies that everyone is equally listened to when they express their views, without recognition that race, gender, class and other identity markers of the speaker significantly impact on how they are heard. This is particularly so when the speaker is a member of an oppressed social group speaking to someone who is part of the oppressor group. Reni Eddo-Lodge writes of an 'emotional disconnect' on the part of white people when people of colour speak about racism: 'Even if they can hear you, they're not really listening. It's like something happens to the words as they leave our mouths and reach their ears. The words hit a barrier of denial and they don't get any further.'[13] Considering liberal ideology within the context of coloniality, then, it is clear that what may be constructed as universal rights and freedoms are rarely experienced or protected as such. The chapter highlights how this unacknowledged racial logic of liberalism underpins the representation of feminism in the books and newspapers in question.

The first section below contextualises the forthcoming analysis, by considering the relationship between popular and activist feminist discourses. By 'popular feminism', I am referring to feminist content aimed at mainstream audiences, rather than at activists or academics. The following section introduces the books and the newspapers, and examines the narratives these texts contain about feminism past and present, noting how a distinctly white lineage and heritage of British activism and thought from the 1970s to the present day is constructed via an erasure of Black feminism and anti-racist feminist histories. In the next section, I then consider how these white histories enable the construction of a 'new' white, imperial feminism in the three books; one which remains oblivious to multiplicity within feminism and critiques of whiteness by feminists of colour. I highlight how the books construct their 'new' feminist subjects through a racialised process of othering of Black women, Muslim women and women from the global South, and how they advocate a 'power feminism' which relies on an imperial and nationalistic discourse. In the subsequent section, I discuss how the *Guardian* coverage has participated in the promotion of a small group of white and middle-class women as the intellectual leaders of twenty-first-century feminism, drawing attention to the ways in which the depictions of these individuals reproduce colonial ideals of a noble and selfless – innocent – white femininity. It would at the same time be inaccurate to describe the *Guardian*'s feminist coverage as just 'white', as from around 2010, it is clear that the paper has attempted to diversify its coverage. The final part of the chapter examines this transformation, with a focus on debates about intersectionality and privilege, and finds that while a more diverse range of voices and writers are now given space within the paper, the liberal framework which underpins this public sphere of debate co-opts and depoliticises anti-racist critiques while appearing to have taken them on board.

INTERACTIONS OF POPULAR AND ACTIVIST FEMINISMS

The primary focus of this chapter is the representation of feminism in popular publishing and the liberal press, but it is important to understand how these representations interact with activist feminist politics. While many feminist activists and academics wish to distance their work from the mainstream, as Joanne Hollows and Rachel Moseley argue, it is necessary to understand feminist politics and popular culture as deeply intertwined, as most people first encounter feminist ideas (whether depicted positively or negatively) *through* popular culture.[14] In more recent years, the prominence of social media has led to activist and popular feminist discourses becoming increasingly interactive, and online activism has played a crucial role in bringing more overt feminist politics into the mainstream (the #metoo movement being a prime example).[15] At the time of writing, feminism is in fact having a very popular moment, with, as Rosalind Gill notes, increased visibility and attention across mainstream media to *some* forms of feminist activism and *some* types of feminist issues, alongside the popularity of 'corporate, neoliberal feminism' and 'celebrity and style feminism'.[16] Feminist arguments have become more visible than ever, even if still frequently contested and ridiculed.[17]

Activist feminist debates and communities have transformed significantly – and continuously – since the early 2000s. As Redfern and Aune evidence, a renewed interest in feminist politics among young people led grassroots feminist networks and communities in the UK, both on- and offline, to grow exponentially in the first decade of the century.[18] With the emergence of social media from the mid to late 2000s onwards, the intensity and visibility of feminist debates has continued to grow. This activity has included intense and repetitive struggles over racism. In the US-centred feminist blogosphere of the mid 2000s, radical women of colour such as brownfemipower, BlackAmazon (Sydette Harry) and Sudy (Lisa Factora-Borchers) developed pioneering intersectional analyses on issues such as immigration and sexual violence while also calling on white feminists with bigger online platforms to be accountable for the ways in which they both marginalised and appropriated the knowledge that women of colour were creating.[19] US popular feminist books such as Jessica Valenti's *Full Frontal Feminism* (2007) and Amanda Marcotte's *It's a Jungle Out There* (2008) were critiqued by many women of colour bloggers for universalising from a white, class-privileged perspective while marginalising feminists of colour's work (and, in the case of Marcotte, for using racist imagery on the book sleeve).[20]

Some of the US-centred debates were also picked up and discussed on British-based blogs, influencing white feminists to take on more intersectional analyses. Posts from the most widely read British blog, *The F-Word*, provide interesting evidence as to how the hegemonic activist discourse has transformed over the years. The first five years following its 2001 launch saw *The F-Word*'s content written primarily through a gender-only, white and otherwise privileged lens. This slowly began to shift from 2006 onwards, with an increased awareness of racism and white privilege and a much more explicitly intersectional approach becoming predominant on the site from 2009.[21]

British-centred debates about race developed with more intensity following the formation of the Black Feminists UK activist group in 2010.
Both on- and offline, the group created a space for the reinvigoration
and increased visibility of a collective Black British feminist politics,
with a younger generation of women of colour keen to draw inspiration
and learn from earlier eras of Black feminist activism in Britain.[22] On
the group's blog (unfortunately no longer in existence), members wrote
about topics such as the 2011 London riots, police racism, and government discourse on multiculturalism and terrorism – topics which were
not often covered on other feminist blogs.[23] It was also a space from
which members could critique racism and whiteness within the liberal
feminist public sphere.[24] As the platform grew, members of the group
significantly influenced discussions about race and intersectionality
within online feminist discourse.

One of the most heated and extended conflicts around this time
took place following a comment made by author and columnist Caitlin
Moran on Twitter. In response to a question about the lack of representation of people of colour in the US TV programme *Girls* (written by
and starring American white feminist Lena Dunham), Moran tweeted
that she 'literally could not give a shit about it'.[25] Unsurprisingly, many
anti-racist feminists took Moran to task for her comment, and a larger
debate about racism within feminism ensued. The *Black Feminists* blog
hosted a series of posts addressing not only the specific incident but
also the long history of Black women's struggles against white feminist
racism.[26] As Stephanie Phillips wrote, 'Moran's dismissive comment
blew up because it represented how women of colour felt mainstream
feminists thought and we've had enough of it'.[27]

As the concepts of intersectionality and privilege became introduced
into mainstream liberal debate, they became subject to intense backlash,
not just among feminists on social media, but also within both the
right-wing and liberal press.[28] Lola Okolosie highlights how Black feminists' attempts to centre intersectionality as 'normative practice for the
wider movement' were met with resistance from many white feminists,
including high-profile columnists, variously dismissing it as 'alienating
and academic' and a 'cloak for abuse'. Such debates have been painfully
played out online, with Black feminists being repeatedly drawn into the
position of having to, in Okolosie's words, '"teach" intersectionality ....
[and] "explain" ourselves'.[29] In a particularly controversial article in the

liberal magazine *New Statesman*, regular columnists Rhiannon Lucy Cosslett and Holly Baxter argued that the conflict following Moran's comments exposed class differences within the movement more than anything else, describing intersectionality as 'esoteric theory' and as espoused only by 'those armed with an MA in Gender Studies and a large vocabulary to match'. They claimed that '[g]oing into certain state comps and discussing the nuances of intersectionality isn't going to have much dice if some of the teenage girls in the audience are pregnant, or hungry, or at risk of abuse'.[30] Their argument conveniently ignored the fact that many of those teenage girls would not only be at the sharp end of class and gender oppression, but also racism, and were therefore likely to already have a lived understanding of how different forms of oppression interact to cause them harm. As Lianne pointed out, in a response on the *Black Feminists* blog, 'obsessing over the use of one word' appeared to be a strategy on the part of 'big name feminists' to 'avoid talking about intersectionality itself and dealing with how it affects people'.[31]

There are resonances in Cosslett and Baxter's piece (and others of a similar ilk) to the broader discourse blaming a multicultural so-called 'metropolitan elite' for the deteriorating conditions of a 'white working class' which became so prominent in the lead-up to Brexit.[32] Eddo-Lodge makes the connection between white feminist rejections of race analysis and right-wing racist arguments very clear. She observes how Black feminism has been repeatedly reduced to 'nothing more than a disruptive force, upsetting sweet, polite, palatable white feminism':

> British feminism was characterised as a movement where everything was peaceful until the angry black people turned up. The white feminist's characterisation of black feminists as disruptive aggressors was not so different from broader stereotyping of black communities by the press. Women of colour were positioned as the immigrants of feminism, unwelcome but tolerated – a reluctantly dealt-with social problem ... It is important to see the white feminist push-back against intersectionality not in isolation, but rather in the historical context of establishment clampdowns on the black struggle.[33]

Although the *Guardian* has on balance been more sympathetic to intersectional feminism than other publications, it has still played an instrumental role in neutralising threats to the white liberal status quo. This is something which I will explore in the final section of the chapter. Here, my point is to emphasise how activist feminist debates significantly impact the ways in which feminist politics are represented and debated within the mainstream public sphere. Analysing media representations of feminism enables us to see how meanings of feminism are struggled over across and within activist and popular feminist discourses.

While many (particularly young) people may now be more likely to encounter feminist ideas on social media, it is important to pay attention to how feminism is articulated and represented within the mainstream press and publishing, because these institutionalised and commercialised sites still have significant power to shape debates and 'package' them for broader audiences. This commodification of feminist ideas must be understood in the context of whiteness. To put it bluntly, both the books and the newspapers that I analyse in this chapter are aimed to appeal to white – and middle-class – people. As will be clear from my discussion of the books, their address to white people is evident from the conspicuous absence of feminists of colour within the narratives they present. In relation to the *Guardian*, with page clicks and papers sold constituting the ultimate endorsement of content, the main purpose of its coverage can be understood as aiming to make feminist ideas, debate and activism interesting and palatable to its readers. Statistics suggest that 75 per cent of the *Guardian*'s core readership is middle class, with a fairly even gender split, and about two-thirds are over 35 years old.[34] Although figures on ethnicity are not available, as will be evident from the forthcoming analysis, the typical white, middle-class *Guardian* reader is clearly the primary target of much of its content. In the next section, I begin by looking at the narratives which the books and papers construct about feminism's transformation from the past to the present.

FROM 'OLD' TO 'NEW' FEMINISMS

Proclamations of the dawn of a 'new' feminism rest on assumptions about an 'old' one. The relationship between these 'old' and 'new' feminisms is described in different ways across the books and newspapers. In *The New Feminism*, Walter argues passionately that a new incarnation of feminism is thriving in the UK. While she acknowledges it to be heavily indebted to the battles won by the women's liberation movement, Walter claims that the 'new feminism' is in most respects very different. The old feminism, Walter argues, became preoccupied with 'identity politics', and lost its way by shifting its gaze inwards, policing women's private lives. The new feminism, on the other hand, Walter suggests, must and does 'look outward again', and 'must reconstitute itself as a straightforward argument for political, social and economic equality'. 'Everywhere you go', she writes, 'you see women flexing their muscles and demanding equality', going on to argue that feminism's battle can be won as long as feminists stop being dogged by the old movement's 'political correctness' and instead 'join hands with one another, and with men, in order to create a more equal society in Britain'.[35]

Walter draws extensively on the work of 'older' feminists in constructing her arguments. While she often does so in order to disagree with their analysis, who and what theories she uses to represent feminism's past is significant, as she would not be able to advocate her feminist politics in the way that she does without repeatedly referencing that which, according to her narrative, came before. She engages frequently with the work of white feminists from both Britain and elsewhere, including Germaine Greer, Lynne Segal, Catherine McKinnon, Andrea Dworkin, Mary Daly, Sandra McNeill and Gloria Steinem, among others. Yet, the book does not engage with any scholarship by feminists of colour. One of the few times it even mentions Black women's involvement in the feminist past is in a passing criticism of identity politics, which is described as having 'robbed feminism of much of its potential for concrete, collective change'. Here, in criticising the 'old' feminism's perceived exclusion of men, Walter compares this to how feminists 'began to argue that no white woman could understand a black woman's weight of oppression, and that every white woman had to accept guilt for that oppression'.[36] This, Walter argues, is part of the problems of 'old' feminism. Thus, Black women are made briefly visible only to (poorly) illustrate a problem, and to argue for men's inclusion. The only feminist of colour quoted is Hannana Siddiqui (once) of Southall Black Sisters (who are mentioned twice more). Both are framed as grassroots activists only, not as feminist thinkers, despite the fact that several past and present members of Southall Black Sisters are published authors.[37] As Heidi Mirza wrote in a *Guardian* comment piece around the time of the book's publication (notably one year after the publication of Mirza's edited collection *Black British Feminism*), '[t]he debate surrounding the state of New British Feminism makes me aware that one thing has not changed: new or not, British feminism is still self-confidently all white'.[38]

Levenson's *The Noughtie Girl's Guide to Feminism*, although markedly different in tone, in many ways resonates with Walter's book, which Levenson cites as one of her influences. Marketed as a 'witty and intelligent new look at the F-word' and complete with a 'chick-lit' inspired cover, it is framed as a humorous and light-hearted text. 'Noughties girls', Levenson describes, are women born after the 1960s, 'who were children or not even born when the UK had its first female Prime Minister, women who have always known they could access legal abortion should they want it', likely to have careers and financial independence and generally reaping the rewards of feminism, but unlikely to call themselves feminists.[39] Levenson presents herself as an ambitious professional woman with a love for gossip magazines and fashion – the typical 'noughties girl' – and argues that noughties feminism is irrevocably a mass of contradictions, but one which should be embraced. Her polemic reproduces the well-worn neoliberal argument that feminism is all about women having the *choice* to do whatever they want – whether the issue at hand is abortion or wearing high heels – as well as about having equality with men.

Similar to Walter, Levenson is disdainful of '1970s feminists'. Taking a step further, Levenson even renounces the need to know about feminist history, arguing that younger feminists 'don't need to know what steps we have made towards equality – you just need to know that we're not there yet'. At the same time, Levenson repeatedly makes claims about 'traditional' feminism. For example, in the concluding chapter, Levenson writes: 'One of the problems with feminism of previous generations is that there seemed to be an insistence that women embrace every aspect of the movement in an all or nothing kind of way. But noughtie girl feminists reject this idea of being told what to think, whoever it is by.'[40] Such generalisations of what feminism was in the past paint a similar picture of a restrictive, prescriptive and homogeneous feminist movement as that of Walter's 'old' feminism. Again, Black feminism and feminists of colour are absent from Levenson's narrative.

Moran's book is a more personal tract than Levenson's and Walter's, part memoir and part feminist manifesto. At the same time, at the time of its publication, it was widely promoted and hailed as a book about modern feminism.[41] The description of the book on the back cover is indicative of this framing: '1913: Suffragette throws herself under the King's horse. 1970: Feminists storm Miss World. Now: Caitlin Moran rewrites *The Female Eunuch* from a bar stool and demands to know why pants are getting smaller.' Moran, clearly, believes the best resistance to sexism is through the use of humour. Moran's working-class background, as well as her own sense of always doing things wrong, is a repeated source of humour and central to her personal narrative. In this sense, her story of the modern British feminist, which includes overcoming class barriers, is different from that of Levenson and Walter. However, given her teenage career success in television and journalism, Moran's personal experience is hardly ordinary, and her anecdotes about modern womanhood in Britain are often similar to those presented by Levenson and Walter. The book does not present class inequality as a structural issue to be addressed in conjunction with gender inequality, but rather as a personal struggle which Moran has overcome.

Moran is critical of what feminism as a movement has become – lamenting how what was once 'the one most exciting, incendiary and effective revolution of all time' has 'shrunk down into a couple of increasingly small arguments, carried out among a couple of dozen feminist academics'. But what is notably different in Moran's version of the feminist past, compared to Walter and Levenson, is her wish to reclaim the spirit of an earlier feminism, rather than reject it as prescriptive and irrelevant. This is typified in her adoration of her 'heroine' Germaine Greer, whose writing in *The Female Eunuch* she describes as having been '[n]ew; fast; free'.[42] Contrasted to Levenson's description of Greer as 'a stereotypical man-hating feminist' whom younger women cannot relate to, it is clear that Moran's representation of the recent feminist past is much more positive than that of Levenson and Walter, who are both keen to distance themselves from anything which could potentially be understood as offending men.[43] Moran even jokes that 'feminist' on its own does not seem enough, and that she prefers it pre-fixed with the adjective 'strident'.[44] Aside from references to Greer, though, Moran does not explicitly draw on writings or thinking by other feminists.

As the *Guardian*'s coverage of feminism is produced by numerous journalists and editors, it of course does not construct one singular narrative in the way that each of the books does. At the same time, there is a notable coherence in how the feminist past and the feminist present are constructed. Articles published in the early 2000s tended to focus predominantly on older white feminists who were active in the women's liberation movement, often with a retrospective approach. In particular, these articles profile individual well-known writers and academics, such as Greer, Segal and Sheila Rowbotham, emphasising their ongoing influence on British feminist politics.[45] These articles construct feminist activism as having been at its peak in the 1970s. Greer is repeatedly positioned as the central personality and thinker of the movement, alongside a limited repertoire of references to other individuals and books. References to *Spare Rib*, *The Female Eunuch*, the feminist peace camp at Greenham Common, and women's liberation movement conferences and marches come to symbolise the familiar landmarks of recent feminist history – as is more stereotypical imagery, often invoked ironically, such as that of dungarees and bra-burning.[46]

While the whiteness inherent in these references is unlikely to be surprising to anyone, it is worth stressing the ideological character of it, rather than presuming it to be inevitable. For instance, comparing the visibility of the women's liberation movement and the Organisation of Women of Asian and African Descent (OWAAD) conferences within this coverage is telling. Each time these conferences were held, several hundred women attended. Yet, while the former are frequently mentioned as landmarks of feminist history (including in more in-depth retrospective pieces), the OWAAD conferences were only mentioned three times across the articles in my sample: twice in comment pieces by feminists of colour (Diane Abbott and Amrit Wilson) and once in a 2015 retrospective piece about *Spare Rib*, in which an OWAAD conference report is featured from the magazine's archive.[47] This more recent visibility reflects the overall increased attention to Black feminism in later years, which I discuss further below. But on the whole, across almost two decades of coverage, an overwhelmingly white feminist past is constructed as the main cultural archive and lineage of contemporary feminists.

This white archive is the backdrop which contextualises the emergence of a 'new' movement. From 2006 onwards, an increasing number of articles started announcing the arrival of a new generation of feminist activists, asserting that, despite a constant barrage of claims that feminism was dead and/or irrelevant, there was in fact an increasing interest in feminism among young politicised women. Coverage of this 'new' feminist activism has continued fairly consistently since this time, with news and feature articles repeatedly announcing the arrival, burgeoning and rise of a young and passionate movement. The cheer-leading style of some of these headlines gives an indication of the tone: 'Marching to freedom', 'Let's make some noise', 'Feminism is not finished', 'Feminism is back and we want to finish the revolution, say activists', 'Feminists hail explosion in new grassroots groups', 'The fourth wave of feminism: meet the rebel women', 'The great feminist revival', and 'A year of brave, inspiring, young feminists'.[48]

The construction of this 'new' or 'revived' movement sets up a relationship between these young feminists and an 'old' movement. This relationship is constructed through statements which indirectly reference the past (e.g. feminism is 'not finished' or 'back'), as well as through more explicit connections to the past: new feminist publications are compared to women's liberation magazines *Spare Rib*, *Shrew* and *Red Rag*; a new feminist network is described 'as a natural extension of the consciousness-raising groups [of] the 1970s and 1980s'; a new burst of feminist publishing 'repackages longstanding arguments'; the 'feminist resurgence' is described as 'following the trajectory that the second wave took'; an activist is quoted as saying that 'the fundamentals of feminist activism remain the same'; and young feminists are described as 'building on the walls left by those who came before'.[49] The reference points which constitute what 'came before' within these narratives is the same women's liberation movement history; consciousness-raising groups, 'landmark' books authored by white women, women's liberation protests and conferences stand in as short-hand for a universal feminist past, without reference to the whiteness inscribed within these.

The three books and the *Guardian*'s coverage, then, construct the relationship between 'old' and 'new' feminisms in different ways. For Walter and Levenson, the new feminism and the new feminist is constructed in opposition to the old. This is not the case for Moran, whose 'strident feminist' strives to recapture the radicalism of older feminists such as Greer. And the *Guardian*'s coverage of the 'new' feminism emphasises continuity with earlier forms of feminism, with the 'newness' of the movement hinging primarily on the fact that it is being led by a younger generation. Yet, while the relationship differs, what is consistent across the texts is how the 'old' feminism is represented. Resonant with the academic books discussed in Chapter 3, the feminist past is constructed as consisting solely of white women's activism within the women's liberation movement, with women of colour's activism and intellectual contributions rendered invisible. Whether this narrowly conceived white feminist past is referred to positively or negatively, what matters is that this representation of the past distorts and erases the diverse histories of feminist thought and activism, and limits the imagination of what feminism is and can be.

The relevance of anti-racism to the development of British feminist politics, then, is obscured across all these texts; they exhibit the same lack of race awareness as that of the 1970s white feminists they draw on. Yet, a crucial difference is of course that, in contrast to some of the white feminist ignorance of race displayed in the 1970s, there is a much more established tradition of Black feminist thought and anti-racist feminist theorising in Britain now. The ignorance, evasion and/or disinterest exhibited in these narratives must therefore be understood as an implicit refusal to learn about Black feminism and the significance of race for feminism. As outlined in Chapter 1, 'white ignorance', according to Mills, is not simply an 'absence of true knowledge' – it is a wilful ignorance about racism which 'fights back' in order to maintain a privileged white position, 'protecting those who for "racial" reasons have needed not to know'.[50] 'White ignorance' is a crucial part of the racial contract of liberalism, whereby people of colour's knowledge and theorising about racism and white supremacy is repeatedly erased from the white liberal 'common sense'. The following two sections consider how this white ignorance of anti-racist feminist theorising and activism enables the reproduction of imperial feminist arguments and representations.

THE NEW IMPERIAL FEMINISM

Critiquing the whiteness of the three books is not hard, because it is so glaring. Drawing on and reproducing a simplistic white feminism, the books, for instance, present arguments about 'equality' through a gender-only lens which has long been critiqued and debunked as unworkable for women who are not white, middle class and generally privileged.[51] Differences between women are constructed as irrelevant to feminist goals. For instance, Walter describes her visit to Siddiqui in the 'small, frayed office' of Southall Black Sisters, contrasting it to 'the vast, echoing tearoom of the Institute of Directors in Pall Mall' where she visits the head of the City Women's Network. Walter concludes that while the two women 'wouldn't have much to say to one another' and probably would not 'be able to run a conference that both women would feel easy attending', what matters is that 'they are working for the same end: equality for the sexes; power and self-respect for women'.[52] Missing is any examination of the inequality of power *between* the two women, including the relational aspect of their respective positions. In other words, to what extent have the advances of professional middle- and upper-class (predominantly white) women working in the City been made at the expense of working-class Black and Asian women such as those supported by Southall Black Sisters? Levenson also rejects the idea that feminism should take on board intersecting axes of inequality. Describing a straw poll conducted among her friends to find a more palatable word than 'feminism', she explains that 'the only alternative ... which came up were variants on the word equal'. She goes on to argue against adopting such a variant because it 'suggests a concern with discrimination against all types of social group – age, sexuality and race as well as gender'. This is a problem according to Levenson, who suggests that '[i]f we bind [feminism] up with other forms of discrimination then we lose sight of the specific fight for women's equality'.[53] Yet, of course it is only white and otherwise privileged women who can see such a fight in isolation.

What is perhaps more insidious than such simplistic arguments about equality, though, is the uncritical ways in which the authors tap into deeply colonial discourses, as well as the problematic ways in which they make women of colour *visible* at certain moments, reproducing objectifying and orientalist stereotypes. As Valerie Amos and Pratibha Parmar noted in 1984, challenging 'imperial feminism' requires attention not only to the lack of anti-racist analysis, but also to the ways in which 'Black women have been made "visible" in such writings and the terms in which [their] experiences have been explained'.[54]

While insights and acknowledgements of women of colour feminisms are wholly absent from all three texts, it is clear that the authors wish to include women of colour implicitly in their generic construction of the modern feminist. For example, although she explicitly notes that she has 'not attempted to cover' 'many of the issues specifically concerning lesbians' in her chapters on sex and marriage, Levenson adds that aside from this omission, she hopes 'that this book is interesting for all women', implying a universal appeal across other differences.[55] Walter's text makes passing comments such as 'visiting salons where women young and old, white and black, preen in front of mirrors' which equally illuminate an implied inclusion: racial differences are casually remarked upon, but only to indicate that they do not matter. At other times, racialised depictions of women of colour make it clear that whiteness is in fact central within these texts' constructions of the modern feminist. Walter writes, for example, that 'white women may have much to learn from Black British culture, which seems to be more upfront about celebrating women's sexual allure alongside their power, and not getting bogged down in waif-like images'.[56] Her description of Black British culture as 'seeming' to be this way reveals a lack of research and interest about the experiences of Black women, underscoring that *The New Feminism* is clearly aimed at white women. This othering process incorporates aspects of both race and class. Walter claims that working-class women are included in her vision of the new feminism, yet simultaneously positions them as 'other': 'less glamorous', less 'smart', less 'articulate' and more 'extraordinary' than the professional middle-class woman we tend to associate with feminism.[57]

Moran also makes comments which reveal her unfamiliarity with anti-racism. She suggests, for instance, that women reclaiming the phrase 'strident feminism' is similar to the way that 'the black community has reclaimed the [n-word], a statement disturbing on several levels. Not only is the comparison a very poor one, but the claim that the latter term has been universally reclaimed by Black people reveals an obvious lack of knowledge about Black politics. In fact, Moran only brings up the topic of racism in order to make comparisons to sexism: in arguing that women should proudly declare themselves feminists, she suggests that not doing so is as non-sensical as if 'in the 1960s, it had become fashionable for Black people to say they "weren't into" civil rights'.[58] These flippant comic statements powerfully indicate a lack of care about Black people's experiences.

The texts casually invoke women from the global South in similar ways. In making a point about the role 'nineteenth-century feminists' played in liberating women by breaking open 'the doors of schools and universities for young women', Walter makes a passing comment that 'women in the developing world [do] not use reliable contraception even when it is available to them' because of their lack of access to education.[59] Here, women from the global South are used as props to make an argument about women's liberated status in the global North. This kind of framing has long been critiqued within postcolonial feminist theorising. As Chandra Mohanty argues in 'Under Western eyes', Western feminist research which produces homogenising, ahistorical representations of the 'oppressed third-world woman' participates in a form of 'discursive colonisation'. This, Mohanty argues, is part of the process by which the Western feminist constitutes herself as a subject: 'By contrasting the representation of women in the third world with ... western feminism's self-presentation in the same context, we see how western feminists alone become the true "subjects" of this counter-history', while Third World women 'never rise above the debilitating generality of their "object" status'.[60] Walter's argument illustrates this process well: women outside the West are portrayed as universally uneducated and incapable of making decisions about their lives, positioned as voiceless victims of patriarchy with which the modern Western woman is contrasted. The so-called 'developing world' is constructed as inherently 'behind' the West in terms of women's rights, feeding into colonial and liberal notions of human progress and development.

In a similar vein, in a section titled 'What about foreign women?', Levenson claims that '[c]ompared to women elsewhere in the world, we have fantastically free lives, though this should not be used as an argument to stop us getting complete equality in the West'. She thereby establishes a sharp distinction between Western women and those 'elsewhere', continuing:

> ... as feminists is it essential that we are aware of and attempt to change the lot of women elsewhere in the world? Should there be a sense of international sisterhood? ... We can apply the sisterhood on two levels – both the need to improve women's lives around the world at a human rights level, and the push for greater equality in our own lives ...[61]

Women from the global South are included in an imagined 'international sisterhood', yet the agency sits firmly with Western women only, who could potentially use their relative 'freedom' to 'change the lot of women elsewhere', women who clearly do not have any ability to change their lot themselves. This othering of 'foreign women' is repeated when Levenson tells an anecdote about a woman she knows who had promised to obey her husband. She wonders if the reader will assume this woman is old, or 'a foreign woman from a country less enlightened than ours', before revealing that this woman was British like herself, then going on to chide women like this, for not only letting themselves down 'but their whole gender'.[62] Again, the colonial underpinnings are clear, with Western liberalism constructed as the pinnacle of progress, from which Western women can look 'back' in horror at the experience of powerless women from 'less enlightened' lands, to remind themselves that in comparison, they have freedom and control over their lives.

Moran also others racialised women – in this case Muslim women who wear burqas. This is done in the context of explaining how she decides whether something is sexist, which she calls 'are the boys doing it?' test. 'It was the "Are the boys doing it?" basis on which I finally decided I was against women wearing burkas', she writes. She describes burqas as a response to 'quite a man-based problem', concluding that 'I don't know why *we're* suddenly having to put things on our heads'.[63] Although Moran has presumably never considered or been told to wear a burqa, she presumes that the reasons why women do so are transparent to her. Her use of 'we' positions her and women who wear burqas as the same. As with Levenson's description of a global sisterhood, Moran's argument erases power differences between women and reinvigorates an imperial feminist 'saviour' gaze, erasing the agency of women who wear burqas.[64]

In a later discussion, Moran argues for the need for women to claim worldly power in distinctly imperial terms. As part of this argument she suggests that women need to accept the lack of powerful female figures from history:

Let's stop exhaustingly pretending that there is a parallel history of women being victorious and creative, on an equal with men, that's just been comprehensively covered up by The Man. There isn't. Our empires, armies, cities, artworks, philosophers, philanthropists, inventors, scientists, astronauts, explorers, politicians and icons could all fit, comfortably, into one of the private karaoke booths in SingStar. We have no Mozart; no Einstein; no Galileo; no Gandhi. No Beatles, no Churchill, no Hawking, no Columbus. It just didn't happen.[65]

Moran goes on to ask 'Why wasn't it a woman who discovered the Americas, in 1492?', and explains how women have not achieved these kinds of milestones because '[w]e're not as good at hefting stones, killing mammoths and rowing boats ... In addition, sex often had the added complication of getting us pregnant, and leaving us feeling "too fat" to lead an army into India.'[66] At yet another point, railing against the shrinking size of women's underwear, Moran jokes:

> ... as a country, our power has waned in synchronicity with the waning of our pants. When women wore undergarments that extended from chin to toe, the sun never set on the British Empire. Now the average British woman could pack a week's worth of pants into a matchbox, we have little more than dominion over the Bailiwick of Jersey, and the Isle of Man ... How can 52 per cent of the population expect to win the War on Terror, if it can't even sit down without wincing?[67]

References to colonial conquest and the British Empire, armies and the 'War on Terror' are, in Moran's comedy arsenal, references to what makes Britain great. The imperial legacy of Britain is also uncritically evoked by Walter and Levenson in their lauding of Margaret Thatcher as a feminist icon, whom Walter describes as 'the great unsung heroine of British feminism'.[68] Making the imperial connection more explicit, Walter interprets Thatcher's 'constant references to "Victorian values"' as evidence that she liked to be able to use 'examples of other ages when Britain was ruled by women'.[69] Yet, Walter does not acknowledge that Thatcher's references to Victorian Britain were also references to the high period of the British Empire. This connection was undeniably embedded in Thatcher's image, and formed part and parcel of her anti-Black, anti-immigrant agenda, which Black and anti-racist feminists campaigned extensively against.[70] As Amos and Parmar wrote at the time, questioning some white feminists' celebration of Thatcher: 'Such uncritical acceptance of the virtues of strong female images serves only to further alienate Black women whose experience at the hands of the British state demands a more responsible political response.'[71]

As Amos and Parmar's and Mohanty's work highlight, imperial white and Western feminisms construct a binary between white/Northern feminists and Black/Southern women; a construction which rests on a simultaneous absence and presence of racialised women within their analysis. True to form, these books fail to engage with the scholarship of feminists of colour, and draw attention to women of colour mainly as a point of comparison – a point of 'difference' from the books' main protagonists. Women from the global South, women of colour, Muslim women, and the topic of race and racism appear in these books simply as rhetorical props, emphasising the inherent whiteness of the 'new', 'strident' feminists and 'noughtie girls'. They also buy into and reproduce dominant imperial narratives of Britain's past and what made it 'great'. These books, then, promote a 'new' popular feminism employing a decidedly *old* imperial perspective.

CLASS, RACE, MORALITY AND THE REPRESENTATION OF FEMINIST 'LEADERS'

Walter's, Levenson's and Moran's 'new feminists', 'noughtie girls' and 'strident feminists' resonate with the *Guardian*'s representations of individual feminist campaigners and writers. Despite portraying feminism as a collective movement to a greater extent than other newspapers, the *Guardian* simultaneously elevates the leadership of particular individuals within the movement. And although there have been clear attempts to diversify the representation of activists in more recent years, when it comes to in-depth profile pieces, regular coverage, and the representation of expertise in relation to *British* feminism specifically, the individuals who have had the largest presence within the paper and who have been described as the most influential and important voices within the movement are predominantly white, as well as fitting a middle-class, heterosexual and non-disabled feminine ideal. As the focus shifted from the 'old' to the 'new' feminists, Walter was frequently positioned as the key thinker of this new movement in the mid to late 2000s. In the period around 2010 to 2013, this mantle shifted towards Kat Banyard, the author of *The Equality Illusion* (2010) and founder of the activist organisation UK Feminista. From 2013 onwards, Caroline Criado-Perez, founder of the Women's Room media directory, who successfully campaigned to get a woman featured on a British banknote, and Laura Bates, founder of the website *Everyday Sexism*, have increasingly become the most prominently cited spokeswomen for British feminist activism.[72] Walter and Bates regularly write for the paper, and Banyard and Criado-Perez have been occasional contributors. Moran has also enjoyed a high profile within the paper, but is less associated with activism and more embedded within the world of celebrity and media culture.[73]

In addition to these individuals often being asked to provide comments for articles about feminism more broadly, all have been the subjects of longer individual feature pieces. These in-depth 'character pieces', based on interviews with the subjects in question, alongside the requisite photoshoot, provide much insight into how intellectual 'leaders' of feminism are conceived within the paper. In particular, these articles blatantly ascribe class and race privilege with positive value, emphasising characteristics of selflessness and sacrifice as central to their subjects' feminist identity. A piece about Walter in 2010, who is described as 'one of Britain's foremost feminist voices for more than a decade' is framed around the fact that Walter rarely gets angry, describing her in terms such as 'intellectual' and 'refined'. Written by the (then) women's editor Kira Cochrane, the article describes Walter as having 'written rationally, often compellingly, on everything from prostitution to parental leave and pornography to equal pay', and commends the fact that, despite these being 'subjects that can provoke real fury', 'Walter's approach to them tends to be calm, sane, straightforward'. Cochrane highlights how the negative reactions *The New Feminism* received from some prominent feminist writers (such as Greer) led Walter to lose confidence and 'faith' in feminism. The narrative arc subsequently hinges on Walter's rediscovery of her sense of purpose through her work setting up the charity Women for Refugee Women in 2006. Cochrane describes this as work that Walter 'is clearly passionate about, and which has inspired some of her best journalism', and Walter is quoted as saying that the work has led her to experience 'so much … sisterhood … it's real, and it's hugely sustaining'. The article concludes by returning to the question of anger, and quotes Walter on why she does not write from a place of rage:

> I haven't suffered in that way. I just haven't. I don't have that personal weight of rage that some inspirational feminists have. And I'm not going to pretend that I do. It's maddening when you feel a comfortable, middle class feminist trying to take the weight of the world's sorrows on her shoulders.

Cochrane frames and interprets this comment as follows:

> Instead, she says, what she does is 'to put the argument in place and think about it', to act as a conduit for the stories of women who have suffered, whether it's a rape victim seeking refuge, or a young lap dancer in London. In some ways, her lack of intrinsic rage makes Walter's writing even more admirable, particularly considering the opprobrium she's faced. She does it out of a social conscience, 'out of solidarity', she says. What better reason is there?[74]

Echoes of an imperial 'white woman's burden' come through strongly in this portrayal.[75] Walter's work is implied to be selfless, motivated only by her desire to help more oppressed women than herself. The description of her work with refugee women as having 'inspired some of her best journalism' resonates with the colonial trope of privileged white women finding their inspiration and purpose through helping and uplifting powerless 'others'. Morality is also inscribed with privilege: the assertion that Walter's commitment is 'even more admirable' because she has not herself suffered, positions her as an inherently more moral person precisely because of her privileged life experience. This description implies that Walter does not gain anything herself from this work, despite the paycheques, high public profile and esteem that the liberal media has rewarded her with. The public profile is instead described more as another burden she bears, leading her to face 'opprobrium' from other feminists. Equally problematic, describing Walter's role 'as a conduit' implies she transparently represents other women's experiences without altering them through her own position and interpretation. This suggests that privileged women like Walter are needed to speak up for those powerless women who cannot speak for themselves, yet the unequal power relationships between Walter and the women she represents are ignored. The praise for her lack of anger simultaneously reinforces classed and racialised idealised qualities of the intellectual and appropriately *feminine* (i.e. white and middle-class) feminist campaigner.

An interview with Kat Banyard (also written by Cochrane in 2010), described as 'the most influential young feminist in the country', emphasises Banyard's demeanour in similar terms, describing her as 'modest, mild mannered, quiet, with just a subtle edge of intensity when she speaks'. Cochrane continues:

> I ask where her incredible drive comes from – the motivation that has led her to pursue full-time feminist activism, without pay, while many of her peers are (often understandably) forging careers based on the size of their salaries. Is she driven by anger? No again. 'I think I just like seeing the best in humanity. If you believe in the inherent dignity of people, in justice and human rights, then feminism is for you.'[76]

Moral uprightness again looms large in this depiction. The emphasis on Banyard's lack of interest in money constructs a portrait of a self-sacrificing – and thus admirable – individual. The classed implications of whether one can afford to be unconcerned with money remain unaddressed. The description of Banyard's 'modest' and 'mild mannered' personal characteristics completes the picture of the noble, respectable, white, middle-class woman. Similarly, a feature piece about Bates, described as 'a leading figure' of "fourth wave" feminism', notes how Bates' 'verbal poise and crisp articulacy make her a compelling advocate'.[77] The classed and raced nature of the dominant representation of white, middle-class feminists as morally upright and selfless campaigners is also reinforced through the types of feminist issues which tend to be given coverage. In particular, prominent publicity has consistently been given to anti-porn and anti-sex work activism, which is often represented as hegemonic within contemporary feminism with little recognition of the highly contested – and classed – nature of feminist debates on these issues (note, for instance, how the 'young lap dancer' is positioned as a victim in Cochrane's feature about Walter, discussed above).[78]

Continuing along the themes of innocence and sacrifice, a number of features and interviews with Criado-Perez are titled using interview quotes which emphasise Criado-Perez's experience as a victim of online abuse (following her successful banknote campaign): 'Twitter has enabled people to behave in a way they wouldn't face to face', 'I speak as someone psychologically scarred', 'What happened to me was a wake-up call for society'.[79] While I have no wish to minimise the harm Criado-Perez has suffered as a result of the abuse she has received, it is important to question who gets to be recognised as victims in discussions of online abuse, something which women of colour have repeatedly drawn attention to on social media, but which has often been ignored within mainstream media coverage. In 2014, a collective of (mostly US-based) online organisers of colour created the Twitter hashtag #thistweetcalledmyback to draw attention to women of colour's unrecognised labour in developing anti-racist feminist analysis online, as well as the abuse they face as a result:

> The response has been sometimes loving, but in most cases we've faced nothing but pushback in the form of trolls, stalking. We've, at separate turns, been stopped and detained crossing international borders and questioned about our work, been tailed and targeted by police, had our livelihoods threatened with calls to our job, been threatened with rape on Twitter itself, faced triggering PTSD, and trudged the physical burden of all of this abuse. This has all occurred while we see our work take wings and inform an entire movement. A movement that also refuses to make space for us while frequently joining in the naming of us as 'Toxic Twitter.'[80]

The media and white feminists are both implicated here and I will be returning to the liberal white feminist framing of women of colour's anti-racist critique in the following section. For now, the point bears stressing, as blogger Izzi I. writes in the US context, that the mainstream media has been 'much quicker to sympathize with victims of harassment who are white, middle-class women', despite the fact that feminists of colour have been more heavily targeted by organised white supremacist and misogynistic online communities.[81] A similar trend has been evident also in the UK, with the mainstream media only starting to acknowledge intersections of racism and sexism when Azmina Dhrodia's research for Amnesty International revealed that Diane Abbott received almost half of all abusive tweets sent to female MPs in the run-up to the 2017 election. Dhrodia found that even after excluding Abbott, Black and Asian women MPs received 35 per cent more Twitter abuse than white women MPs.[82] Who gets to occupy and speak from the position of innocent victim, then, is racialised. The speaking part is, of course, key: Criado-Perez has been frequently interviewed, in the *Guardian* and elsewhere, about her experiences of online abuse, thus she is not the silent, objectified victim mobilised in some of the imperial arguments discussed in relation to the books above.[83]

The representations of these high-profile white feminists in the *Guardian* emphasise both their status as self-empowered female subjects of the twenty-first century, but also, through their ascribed selflessness and sense of moral duty, their vulnerability. This vulnerability is recognisable as a hallmark of the familiar colonial and heteropatriarchal construction of white, middle-class – and innocent – femininity. Such depictions again erase the positions of power that white middle-class feminists hold in relation to less privileged women, instead emphasising their activism as a form of *sacrifice* in order to save 'other' women.

INTERSECTIONALITY, *GUARDIAN* STYLE: DEPOLITICISING ANTI-RACISM

In more recent years, the *Guardian*'s representation of feminist politics has transformed significantly in relation to race, moving towards a more diverse depiction of contemporary feminists, as well as more sustained debates about differences between women. In this section, I examine this shift with a critical eye to the process of containment and commodification of anti-racist feminist politics. Jonathan Dean argues that feminism in the broadsheet press has been 'domesticated', with certain formations of feminism (liberal, individualistic, reformist) affirmed in order to disavow other versions (those perceived as 'man-hating' or too radical).[84] While Dean's analysis, which included the *Guardian* and was published in 2010, does not pay significant attention to race, his argument is relevant in considering how concepts used by anti-racist feminists, such as intersectionality and privilege, have been taken up in the paper and debated in ways which 'domesticate' and contain the threat which they pose to the paper's liberal white status quo.

An article by Cochrane published towards the end of 2013, titled 'The fourth wave of feminism: meet the rebel women' illustrates the transition within the paper's representation of activists, and in particular, a shift towards a language of intersectionality.[85] The article represents a racially diverse constituency of feminists tackling a broad range of issues, including state racism, and claims that the majority of feminist activists today 'define themselves as intersectional feminists'. The article is based on extracts from a short book on the 'rise of fourth wave feminism' by Cochrane, published by the *Guardian* around this time, in which intersectionality is described as the fourth wave's 'defining framework'.[86] Although still lacking in attention to power differences between women, feminists of colour are here described as more central in terms of intellectually leading the movement.

Changes in the *Guardian*'s representation of feminism, as discussed above, have taken place in response to an increasingly visible debate about racism in online and activist feminist communities. In a sense, then, this article is reporting accurately on an increased attention to intersectionality within activist communities, including among white feminists. But it is important to pay attention to the power struggles which lie beneath the surface of these shifting representations. For one, social media has enabled anti-racist feminists to hold editors and journalists to account for lack of representation in a much more visible way. We must also consider the relationship between the paper's news and feature content and that of its comment sections. Alongside the multitude of regular columns by regular columnists which appear both in the paper edition and online each week, the *Guardian*'s website also hosts feminist debate on its 'Comment is Free' blog, where a wider range of writers can pitch or are invited to contribute commentary. Some of these comment pieces may be published in the printed paper, but most are only published online.

While few comment pieces in the early 2000s highlighted the significance that differences between women have played within feminist politics, from 2010 onwards, there has been a marked increase in pieces directly addressing differences and inequalities between women. A number of these have presented direct challenges to the whiteness of the movement as represented in the paper. In one of the earliest articles of this kind, published in 2008, MP Diane Abbott writes that 'most black women feel excluded' from the feminist movement and that the 'unrelentingly white and middle-class nature of the modern women's movement has repelled many of us'.[87] She writes about OWAAD and 'the many clever and charismatic black female activists' she worked with in the 1980s, presenting a historical narrative sharply at odds with the regular feminist content at the time. Another piece challenging the dominant white narrative was written by Chitra Nagarajan and Okolosie in 2012, in which they responded to white feminists' defences of Caitlin Moran, noting that '[t]he feminist story belongs to all women everywhere but that is not the impression you would receive from the mainstream media'.[88]

Comment pieces such as these represent a counter-discourse to the dominant feminist frames constructed in the *Guardian* – one which has long been established within anti-racist feminist politics, but which had seldom been heard within the mainstream press before this time (with infrequent exceptions, such as Mirza's *Guardian* comment piece in 1998, cited above). The increasing presence of such arguments within the *Guardian* indicates how these critiques and analyses were beginning to push into mainstream liberal debate. As a result, we can see the provision of increasing space for intersectional and anti-racist analysis within the paper, and an effort to increase the representation of feminists of colour.[89] As part of this increasing visibility of Black feminism, the concept of intersectionality became introduced into the paper's feminist language. Having been briefly mentioned twice in comment pieces in 2010, the term was introduced more fully in a column by Bim Adewunmi in 2012, in the aftermath of the online arguments which followed Moran's infamous tweet.[90]

As discussed above, when feminist debates about intersectionality and privilege were picked up within the mainstream press, they became subject to intense backlash, defensiveness and ridicule. Although the most flagrant attacks on intersectionality have come from the right-wing press and the liberal *New Statesman*, the *Guardian* has also played its part in facilitating the containment of threats to the liberal status quo. Such responses have often focused particularly on race and trans issues (it is beyond the scope of my analysis to address the latter, but it should be noted that the *Guardian* has received significant critique for promoting transphobic perspectives).[91]

While comment articles about intersectionality and privilege in the *Guardian* usually acknowledge and principally support the argument that gender, race and class intersect to shape people's lives (with a few notable exceptions), such acknowledgements are often framed via a concurrent theme of trivialising grassroots intersectional feminist arguments.[92] This is exemplified in an article by regular columnist Zoe Williams, published in April 2013, titled 'Are you too white, rich, able-bodied and straight to be a feminist?'. Beginning by describing the article as 'a story about intersectionality', Williams summarises a recent online conflict in which the *New Statesman* deputy editor Helen Lewis played a key role as the subject of online criticism. 'A small but persistent Twitter intersectionality-core rounded on Lewis', Williams writes, going on to describe the critique of Lewis as an 'attack', quoting sexist terms of abuse allegedly used against Lewis. The piece highlights similar patterns of prominent white feminists being 'attacked' on Twitter by proponents of intersectionality. Williams bases her argument about the unfairness of these 'attacks' on the premise that a 'racist feminist just wouldn't make sense'. Considering Moran's case, she writes:

> Moran got on the wrong side of intersectionality when she said she 'didn't do race'. This made her a racist; also the mindless beneficiary of middle-class privilege, said critics. I weighed in, and said that not all feminists had to represent every perspective of feminism all the time. And middle class? She was raised on benefits. She's rich now, came the reply, plus she has a platform; ergo, she's part of the white, middle-class, straight, able-bodied, cis(gender) hegemony. To remain a true and respectful feminist with those privileges (never mind check them, it will take you long enough just to count them), your work must essentially be an act of atonement to all the people who are more marginalised than you are. As a feminist, you are occupying the space of the marginalised; to do so thoughtlessly is an act of trespass.

Ultimately, however, Williams concedes that inequalities between women do exist, highlighting some of the injustices experienced by trans women and women of colour in contemporary Britain, concluding:

> And that's the better reason to 'check your privilege' – not from some restrictive idea about how authentic you are, or whether you've endured the hardship to qualify as a progressive voice, but because not all prejudice is extinguished – some of it is just displaced. If someone else is taking the flak you would have got, in eras past, that flak is still your problem.[93]

On a surface level then, this article is supportive of the premise of intersectional analysis, and the need for those who benefit from whiteness, the class system and other structures of oppression to consider how this impacts their view of the world. However, it is worth considering other messages which the article transmits, and to judge which ones come across most strongly. Proponents of intersectionality, for instance, are characterised solely as members of a nameless and hysterical 'intersectionality-core' who 'round' on, 'attack' and abuse well-meaning white feminists. In her analysis of the online intersectionality debates around this time, Okolosie draws attention to the fact that 'Black feminism' and 'intersectionality' often became synonymous, and Black feminists were thereby implicitly constructed as those that abused high-profile white feminists online.[94] Both Eddo-Lodge and Okolosie write about an incident on a Radio 4 Woman's Hour feature at the end of 2013, in which Eddo-Lodge, Criado-Perez and Bates were interviewed about the year in feminism. As Eddo-Lodge raised the issue of racism within feminism, Criado-Perez responded by arguing that a 'big part of the problem is the way certain women use intersectionality as a cloak to abuse' high-profile white feminists.[95] Although Criado-Perez later apologised for the implication that it was Black feminists who had abused her online when this was not the case, the link being drawn between feminists of colour (and their implied mindless white followers), intersectionality and online abuse is clear, not just in this example, but also in many others. In several *Guardian* columns – specifically those by regular white feminist columnists – the words intersectionality and privilege appear in the vicinity of words like 'bullying', 'abuse' and 'attack'.[96] In a clear illustration of Ahmed's concept of 'sticky signs' (see Chapter 4), the proximity of these words affectively associates Black feminist critique of white feminism with bullying without the writer ever having to explicitly say this.[97] And as Eddo-Lodge points out, even if the connection is later refuted, the damage is already done.[98]

Another common line of argument is that talk of intersectionality and privilege 'silences' those who do not agree and shuts down debate, a point regular columnist Hadley Freeman has made repeatedly. In one column, for instance, she writes that '[c]ries of privilege-checking and intersectionality – both, objectively, good things – too often become tic-like terms of abuse and a means of shutting down conversation as opposed to opening it up'.[99] Suzanne Moore, another regular and high-profile columnist, makes a similar argument:

> Intersectionality is good in theory, though in practice, it means that no one can speak for anyone else. It is the dead-end where much queer politics, feminist politics and identity politics ends up. In its

own rectum. It refuses to engage with many other political discourses and becomes the old hierarchy of oppression.[100]

These dismissive claims of how intersectional politics function within feminism chime with that of Williams, quoted above, which suggests that what proponents of intersectionality are calling for is that anyone who is privileged in relation to race, class, disability and/or gender identity must simply spend all their time 'atoning' for these privileges, or otherwise remain silent. This rhetorical move, which equates critique with silencing, is neither novel nor innocent. Ironically, it is an effective strategy for shutting down critique. Exposing the connection between Helen Lewis' attacks on feminists of colour and the *New Statesman*'s (and its white, male millionaire owner's) increased profit margin, Flavia Dzodan writes how Lewis used her position to frame debates about intersectionality as one of women of colour bullying and harassing white feminist journalists. Dzodan importantly draws attention to the power structures within these debates, and who benefits at whose expense via their commodification. 'Any protestations are met with further discipline and silencing', she notes, exposing the expectation that feminists of colour 'are just to nod silently while white millionaires and the white feminists who assist them make money from our oppression'.[101]

Alongside blatant institutional inequalities, it is also worth returning to the racial underpinnings of liberalism here. On the liberal logic that conditions of debate are neutral, it can be said that the *Guardian*'s response to critiques of its whiteness, which has been to ensure the publication of more commentary by feminists of colour, has adequately addressed earlier exclusions, and thereby ensured that more 'voices' are heard. However, the premise that all voices can be heard equally lacks sustained attention to how power structures operate, both in terms of who has access to channels of public debate, but also how different voices are heard and different perspectives perceived. Within liberal feminist discussions in the *Guardian*, while the racial identity of the speaker may be brought into view through what they say or through the picture that accompanies the column, it is simultaneously presumed irrelevant to their ability to be heard and listened to. But of course whiteness frames the space within which these discussions have taken place. Even though there is a more diverse range of 'voices' participating in the *Guardian* discourse, the largely white and middle-class readership, and the dominant whiteness (in terms of ideology *and* editorial power) of the paper mean that there is not likely to be an equal hearing of different perspectives and arguments. The framing of the intersectionality debates as being among 'equals' within a power-evasive liberal framework, and the simultaneous depiction of those who are in fact more marginalised within them as abusive attackers does the work of ensuring that existing power relations prevail.

When anti-racist or other critiques gain visibility within the public sphere, the role of high-profile white feminist columnists becomes to ensure that they are seen to understand the issues at stake, while also reframing the debates to ensure that their relevance and central positions within them are not threatened. Their role is to articulate the 'reasonable', liberal position which claims to hear 'other' marginalised voices, encourages them to speak, but chides them when they become too angry or demanding. The dominance of these white feminist voices within the *Guardian* discourse – although 'other' voices are increasingly included – ensures that the white liberal norm is defended. The repeated claims that intersectionality might be good 'in theory' but not 'in practice' function to both trivialise and delegitimise anti-racist and intersectional feminisms. It reduces a wide range of critical interventions, analyses and perspectives on a diverse range of issues into a homogeneous group of Twitter bullies.

While the *Guardian*'s response to anti-racist challenge can be characterised as a form of liberal co-option and diffusion, it is at the same time clear that a more intersectional analysis *has* started to permeate the paper's feminist coverage and commentary. While this is a positive development, it is important to pay attention to the racialised dynamics through which this transformation has played out. The increasing adoption of intersectionality – both as a term and, to some extent, as a perspective – has been done alongside the dismissal of feminists of colour's work to get it on the agenda in the first place. Instead, a narrative of 'expanding diversity', as Mary-Jo Nadeau identifies in a different context (see Chapter 3), suggests that 'moments of inclusivity appear as autonomous developments disconnected from the context of broader struggles'.[102] White feminists are portrayed as having developed an intersectional analysis of their own accord, thereby maintaining their credibility. As Yasmin Gunaratnam observes about white feminist co-option of the concept: 'intersectionality has become a form of anti-racist capital for some white feminists, a currency that nods in the direction of Black feminist concerns but that does very little to dismantle racial thinking and privilege'.[103] Power relationships between feminists of colour and white feminists remain largely the same. The intersectionality and privilege debates thus illustrate how difference can be incorporated into a white liberal feminist framework, and even welcomed, as long as the white people involved do not have to give up any power.

CONCLUSION: LIBERAL APPROPRIATIONS

This chapter has highlighted how whiteness operates at both very explicit and more subtle levels within contemporary popular feminism, from some of the blatantly exclusive and imperial dimensions of the books to the more sophisticated presentation of a diversity of 'voices' and perspectives within recent *Guardian* coverage. The former is of course much easier to critique than the latter, and it may seem unwarranted to continue to criticise the *Guardian*'s representation of feminism given the changes its editors have implemented in more recent years. However, I would argue that a continuum between the two exists – one which ensures continued white control over the narrative of feminism, whether that is through the erasure of feminists of colour (as enacted by the books) or whether it is through the incorporation but subsequent reframing of intersectionality as a concept which enables abuse of white feminists.

While critiquing the books may seem to some to be taking them too seriously, it is unfortunately not simply the case that they are irrelevant and out-of-touch. Although activists and feminist bloggers have often been critical of the feminist politics espoused in these books – particularly as they are in many ways very gender- and hetero-normative – they have at the same time often been impelled to engage with them and their authors, simply because that is how popular culture works: it can be difficult to ignore. The books also garnered significant attention within the press at the time of their publication. Yet, notably, there was little attention to their racism within either the feminist blogosphere or the mainstream press (although Moran, as discussed, has been widely criticised for her comments on Twitter).[104] The fact that the imperial resonances and whiteness of these texts have been absent from public discourse about them is indicative of how ingrained normative white-ness is within mainstream British feminism. The authors, who are all journalists, have also had significant influence within public debates about feminism on the back of their books. Walter and Moran in par-ticular have become high-profile 'celebrity feminists' (Walter published a second book, *Living Dolls: The Return of Sexism*, in 2010, while Moran has published a number of popular non-fiction and fiction books in the wake of *How to Be a Woman*'s success).

The trajectory of debates about race within the *Guardian* highlights some of the dangers and costs of liberal politics. This is not a critique of the activists and writers who choose to write for or make use of the *Guardian* to promote anti-racist feminist work. Liberal media spaces can be effectively used to get certain messages into public debate, to bring attention to campaigns, and to chip away at hegemonic white-ness. Okolosie's regular columns, for instance, have put forward Black feminist analyses on a range of topics related to education, politics, popular culture and more.[105] Having anti-racist feminist perspectives within the public sphere matters. Yet, the 'cost of representation', as Eddo-Lodge so effectively describes in her book, is high. Following her appearance on Woman's Hour, Eddo-Lodge wrote of such media work as 'a double-edged sword': 'Though it sometimes feels like I am entering into a trap, I'm hyper-aware that if I don't accept these opportunities, black feminism will be mischaracterised and misrepresented by the pri-oritises of the white feminists taking part in the conversation.'[106]

In tracing the transformation of whiteness within popular liberal feminism, the analysis highlights how critique can effect change. However, as has been shown, different perspectives have been accommo-dated only up to the point where they do not threaten white hegemony and entitlement. The liberal framework thus very effectively depoliti-cises anti-racist critiques by reframing them and appropriating them, all the while continuing to evade an explicit discussion of the racialised power inequalities which ensure the continued unevenly stacked terms of the debate.

6

Feminist Complicities

The last three chapters have developed an analysis of what I am describing as white-centred feminism. This white-centred feminism is not, in the main, the same as the white feminism of the 1970s and 1980s – i.e. one that was more or less wholly oblivious to racism and differences between women. Instead, in general terms, what I am identifying as contemporary white-centred feminism positions itself as knowledgeable about race and difference, and as having taken anti-racist critiques of feminist whiteness on board. In different ways and to varying extents, it incorporates awareness of racial difference and acknowledgement of women of colour's work and experiences into its analysis, but it still centres white women as the normative, central subjects of feminism.

In Chapter 3, I examined narratives within contemporary academic texts which describe feminism as having developed from a white, ignorant (yet innocent) past to a race-aware and race-critical present. Such narratives imply or explicitly locate a moment of transformation after which white feminists became vigilant against ethnocentrism and whiteness in their theorising and praxis. As such, they leave the problems associated with white feminism in the past, and as requiring no further attention in the present. While some of these texts engage with racism as an axis of oppression which intersects with sexism, in others, race analysis is more or less entirely displaced, while simultaneously being *claimed* to have been incorporated.

Chapter 4 focused on texts which do recognise racism and whiteness as ongoing problems for feminist communities and which more substantially attempt to address such problems. However, these texts continue to centre white feminists in their analysis, by prioritising their experiences and engagements with anti-racist critiques and concepts such as intersectionality. In this way, they both highlight how feminists of colour have been marginalised within feminism and contribute towards their continued marginalisation. Women of colour become positioned as a minority group within feminism and white dominance within feminist communities is implied to be inevitable. While racism is acknowledged as a continuing problem for both Britain and feminism, it is constructed as something which is largely outside of white feminists' power to challenge.

Chapter 5 examined a more forceful new white feminism, as exhibited in three popular books aimed at a mainstream audience claiming to articulate a modern feminism for the twenty-first century. These books erase the context of racism entirely, and reproduce long-critiqued colonial representations of 'other' women, specifically women from the global South and Muslim women. The narratives which these books produce largely erase feminists of colour. The chapter also analysed representations of feminist activism in the liberal-left newspapers, the *Guardian* and the *Observer*, tracing how, as a result of anti-racist critiques, these have changed over the last decade from more or less entirely white towards an emphasis on diversity and intersectionality. Even so, as I argued, debates about intersectionality and privilege have been framed in ways which 'contain' the challenge of anti-racist critiques, and the liberal framework ensures the continued privileging of white feminist voices as those which are positioned to be most 'reasonable' within the debates. This has occurred alongside the representation of prominent white feminist activists as moral and selfless campaigners in terms which reproduce colonial norms of respectable white, middle-class femininity.

Although my analysis is focused on a relatively small number of books and newspaper articles, I suggest it has a broader relevance beyond the texts themselves. Although each of the books discussed has been authored by one or two individuals, they have not been written and published in isolation. Clare Hemmings' emphasis on 'knowledge practices as shared rather than individual' usefully highlights the collective process involved in knowledge production and publication.[1] Scholarship is a collaborative endeavour; published books are the end point of various collective processes, including engagement with circulating ideas, debates and prior scholarship, peer review, editing and conversations with colleagues. This goes equally for articles published in newspapers; as I stressed in Chapter 5, media content must be understood as the end product of collective, institutionalised processes. It is not a coincidence, then, that the books and articles which I have focused on all centre and reproduce whiteness in various ways. While I am not arguing that they are representative of British feminist scholarship and public discourse as a whole – clearly my focus on *white-centred* discourse indicates that they are not – I suggest that they provide evidence of a broader, dominant trend of theoretical and political frameworks which marginalise the work and analyses of feminists of colour, as well as the significance of racism, whiteness and coloniality.

As I hope is clear, but might be worth reiterating (see Chapter 1), the concepts of 'white-centred' and white feminisms are not used in any essentialist way to demarcate racial identity (i.e. white feminists) but to critically interrogate the focus and orientation of forms of feminist knowledge which reproduce racial hierarchies and ignorance about how whiteness functions. At the same time, in this chapter I also more explicitly address white feminists (a constituency of which I am a part) in order to call attention to ways in which white-centred feminist narratives and forms of knowledge can be interrupted, particularly through challenging their/our investments in white innocence.

Across the chapters, I have emphasised how white feminist innocence is maintained in order to legitimise white women's position at the centre of feminist politics. In narratives which frame feminist racism as existing only in the past (where it is acknowledged at all), the representation of contemporary white feminists as race aware implies that they are once again innocent, which provides an alibi for white women's continued dominance in the present. In the narratives which acknowledge feminist racism as an ongoing issue, white feminists are represented as concerned about such issues, yet they are ultimately positioned as having little power to change the dynamics of white dominance. This exonerates them from blame for racism, and prioritises their innocence above challenging racism. Imperial narratives which erase racism from feminism completely, such as those presented by the popular books, maintain a continuity of undisturbed white innocence. And the liberal media's elevation of white, middle-class feminists as intellectual leaders of the contemporary movement emphasises their moral innocence.

This repeated reassertion of white innocence plays a significant role in maintaining white racial dominance within feminist theorising and politics. To restate a point made in the introductory chapter, the assertion of innocence is *not* innocent, but rather a strategy for maintaining racial power. Following arguments such as Gloria Wekker's, Mary-Louise

Fellows and Sherene Razack's, Sarita Srivastava's and María Lugones' (see Chapter 1), I suggest that the contemporary white-centred feminist project's investment in maintaining white innocence signals a continuity with colonial ideals of a pure, moral and 'good' white femininity.[2] This investment disavows white women's involvement and complicity in the (continuous) project of colonial modernity, and white feminism's entanglement within this project. It indicates a refusal to fully engage with and take on board anti-racist critiques made by feminists of colour which stress the importance of attending to these complicities.

It is high time, then, for white feminists to divest from racial innocence. In order to consider what this entails, this chapter shifts attention from innocence towards complicity. In writing about the ways in which investments in critical discourses (including feminism and anti-racism) can become 'a way of not admitting one's complicity', Sara Ahmed suggests that 'complicity is a *starting point*: We are implicated in the worlds that we critique; being critical does not suspend any such implication.'[3] This chapter explores what such a starting point opens up in relation to white feminists' complicity in racism. The next section elaborates on theories of complicity and considers what a commitment to examining white feminist complicity involves. Following this, I return to the book's theme of narratives, focusing in particular on the need for white British feminists to interrogate their role in the erasure of Black British feminists' work from histories of feminism. I then turn to the importance of 'staying with' anti-racist critique, something which requires deep listening and a commitment to anti-racist self-education and resistance as ongoing work.

FROM INNOCENCE TO COMPLICITY

As long as we see ourselves as not implicated in relations of power, as innocent, we cannot begin to walk the path of social justice and to thread our way through the complexities of power relations.[4]

In *Looking White People in the Eye*, Razack interrogates the ways in which women are invested in not seeing themselves as complicit in other women's oppression. Emphasising systems of oppression as *interlocking* (rather than intersecting), Razack argues that such an analytical framework enables us to perceive the ways in which the different positions which women occupy are dependent upon each other (a point I mentioned briefly in Chapter 2). As Razack argues: 'Interlocking systems need one another, we learn how women are produced into positions that exist symbiotically but hierarchically. We begin to understand, for example, how domestic workers and professional women are produced so that neither exists without the other.'[5]

In Chapter 1, I introduced Razack's article written together with Mary Louise Fellows, which highlights how feminist debates about differences and inequalities between women easily descend into contentious and emotional position-staking, whereby individuals are much more likely to emphasise the ways in which they are oppressed and marginalised (i.e. innocent) rather than be willing to consider the ways in which they are oppressors. Fellows and Razack stress the emotional dimension of innocence, pointing out that while many feminists may have 'gained an intellectual understanding of complicity – how we, as women, participate in the oppression of one another ... we seldom *feel* this to be true'. They argue that this strong emotional investment in innocence stems from the fact that dominant groups define themselves against what they are not, and therefore members of dominant groups may 'experience an engulfment, a literal loss of self that can be extremely destabilizing' when their taken-for-granted sense of who they are is questioned.[6] Yet, without confronting such attachments to innocence, feminist movements are doomed to reproduce structures of oppression whereby more privileged groups of women may gain what Fellows and Razack describe as a 'toehold on respectability', but only within existing structures of dominance which will continue to subordinate other groups of women.

Razack develops this argument further in her book, in which she explores how systems of oppression interlock within specific contexts (in Razack's case, Canadian courtrooms and classrooms) to (re)produce hierarchical relations between different groups of women. By framing women's complicity in other women's oppression as a central concern, Razack shifts the ground of normative feminist enquiry, which tends to focus primarily on women's marginality and oppression. Instead, Razack suggests, feminists need to investigate 'how, at specific sites, patriarchy, white supremacy, and capitalism interlock to structure women differently and unequally'. In this way, she argues, '[o]ur strategies for change have less to do with being inclusive than they have to do with being accountable'. Such a 'politics of accountability' requires, for instance, recognition that advancements of predominantly white middle- and upper-class women within various institutions of power has been achieved largely at the expense of other groups of women, through the exploitation of their reproductive labour, the marginalisation of their political priorities and needs, and so on. When the interlocking nature of systems of oppression is centred within analysis, this shifts attention from illusory solidarities of women as a group towards the 'hierarchical relations among women', which Razack argues feminists must do if they truly wish to 'change the world'.[7]

Razack's book was published in 1998, yet her argument is still very timely, and her framework for a 'politics of accountability' is valuable for thinking through what is required to dismantle white-centred theorising and politics. The need for feminists to focus much more concerted attention on the ways in which more privileged groups of women are complicit in other women's oppression is clear when we examine contemporary dominant strands of British feminist theorising and public debate. This is of course not only relevant in relation to race, but also to class, disability and gender identity, among other structural axes of oppression, particularly at their intersections. Staying with the focus on race, though, while there is clearly more attention to race and/or ethnic differences between women, there is still widespread reluctance in considering how white women (actively or passively) participate in the oppression of women of colour.

Calls for attention to white feminist complicity in racism are often problematically interpreted as calling for a white feminist sense of guilt (as evident, for instance, in the debate about privilege in the *Guardian*, discussed in Chapter 5). But a focus on guilt stays unhelpfully within the moral framework of innocence, by implying that one must be either innocent or guilty. Barbara Applebaum's work developing a 'white complicity pedagogy' for engaging white students in discussions of racism usefully reconceptualises moral responsibility by shifting away from this dichotomy. She argues that it is necessary to move away from understandings of moral responsibility which presume that 'moral innocence is attainable'. In her words, '[b]ecause such notions of responsibility center the question "what can *I* do?" rather than the question "what needs to be done?" they can encourage moral solipsism, heroism and white narcissism'. Engaging with theories of white ignorance and innocence, as well as with feminist philosophers of justice, Applebaum argues for an understanding of moral responsibility which instead emphasises 'uncertainty, vulnerability and vigilance'. White ignorance, as Charles Mills argues (see Chapter 1), functions as a form of knowledge: a refusal to know about racism which, in Applebaum's words, *arrogantly parades as knowledge*. A white complicity pedagogy, therefore, aims to 'disrupt white certainty', enabling white people to acknowledge that they do *not* know better than people of colour about racism and to understand how white ignorance functions to maintain white privilege and power.[8] It also requires humility and vigilance in awareness that white people can reproduce racism even when there is no intention to do so. Applebaum locates white complicity as something which extends well beyond individual responsibility for intentionally racist actions. As she argues, all white people have a responsibility to examine the ways in which they are complicit in the maintenance of white supremacy, and then to act from the basis of that knowledge.

Attending to white (feminist) complicity in racism is necessary, not just as a form of ethical responsibility, but also because, as Razack emphasises, (women's) liberation is not otherwise possible. Analysing complicity, in other words, forms a crucial part of the puzzle in understanding how all subordinated groups of people are oppressed and dehumanised. This, it should be noted, also includes privileged white women. As Barbara Smith wrote in 1982:

White women don't work on racism to do a favour for someone else, solely to benefit Third World women. You have to comprehend how racism distorts and lessens your own lives as white women – that racism affects your chances for survival, too, and that it is very definitely your issue.[9]

This point is effectively captured by Gail Lewis in a recent interview by Hemmings for the journal *Feminist Theory*, in which they discuss whiteness and feminism. In noting how white women can make use of gendered forms of vulnerability in their interactions with Black women, Lewis gives the following example:

I mean the sort of classic thing that often black women/feminists will say when we get together: how unbearable it is that when you're with some white women and the question of race comes up and the white women will collapse into tears, like a classic performance of the fey little woman, who's not strong enough, like a little bird, that she might faint, and it feels like that has happened sooo often and it's just unbearable. That performance of the very gendered category that *you say* is a problem ... here you're enacting it against us, which then of course repositions *us* as not really women ...[10]

Lewis' description of the ways in which white women mobilise the heteropatriarchal construct of the weak childlike woman to assert their power over Black women – who do not have access to this patriarchal ideal of white (and to an extent also classed) femininity – speaks powerfully of the ways in which racism also 'distorts and lessens' white women's lives. By investing in discourses of white innocence, white women align themselves with a white supremacist patriarchy in ways which not only enforce the oppression of people of colour, but also their own patriarchal subjugation.

A 'politics of accountability', then, requires concerted white feminist attention to the ways in which white-centred and white-dominated feminist politics are entangled with white supremacy and coloniality. When such work starts with an acknowledgement that complicity is inescapable and innocence is impossible, defences can be lowered, opening up possibilities for different kinds of responses, questions and action to take shape.

DISRUPTING WHITE NARRATIVES

Here I want to revisit the book's focus on narratives through a lens of complicity, in order to highlight more concretely how white-centred narratives, such as the ones that I have discussed in the preceding chapters, are complicit in marginalising the intellectual projects of Black and postcolonial feminisms. I want to emphasise, in other words, how white-centred stories of feminism have material effects in terms of reproducing white dominance within feminist communities. As outlined in preceding chapters, the texts I have analysed give very variable attention to intersectional oppression, racism and whiteness, within both feminism and wider society. Across all of them, however, there is a unifying privileging of white feminist actors and perspectives – a continuous centring of white women as the main protagonists of the (British) feminist story. Stories of women of colour's organising and theorising are, in the majority of cases, not highly visible, or enter the narratives at the moment of critique. Crucially, the stories of Black *British* feminism are largely absent. The texts on the whole (with two exceptions) demonstrate minimal engagement with the work of British (and British-based) feminists of colour, while more frequently citing those from the US. Narratives rarely locate specific debates about race and feminism which have taken place in the British context, or consider the implications of these. The one text which does attend to such debates, i.e. Finn Mackay's *Radical Feminism* (see Chapter 4), does so mainly in order to argue that Black feminists were factually incorrect in their critiques of early Reclaim the Night marches.

More generally, the visibility of the work and perspectives of feminists of colour (whether from Britain or elsewhere) is also variable. In terms of theoretical engagement, a couple of the texts – specifically Angela McRobbie's *The Aftermath of Feminism* (see Chapter 3) and Prudence Chamberlain's *Feminist Fourth Wave* (see Chapter 4) – engage in depth with the work of individual feminists of colour, yet a number engage predominantly with the work of white feminists. In terms of positioning women of colour as part of feminist movements, at best they are described or implied as being part of diverse and inclusive contemporary movements or included as significant 'minority' constituents. At worst they are erased entirely. Despite these differences, when maintaining what Razack calls a 'wary eye for complicity' it becomes apparent that across all of the texts, there is insufficient attention given to the relationship *between* white feminists and feminists of colour as one structured by domination.[11] Even in analyses where white dominance is recognised as an ongoing problem for feminist politics, there is little attention to precisely *how* white feminists reproduce whiteness through the domination of feminists of colour (and women/people of colour more generally).

By focusing on complicity in relation to how stories are told, my aim here is to dislodge some of the 'common sense' truths inherent in stories which construct white feminists as the primary intellectual leaders and as 'naturally' at the centre of British feminism, by pointing to how such stories *require* the marginalisation (and in some instances, the complete erasure) of the work and perspectives of feminists of colour. To apply Applebaum's point about the need for uncertainty, recognising this complicity requires dislodging the certainty and authority with which white women are placed at the centre of the story, recognising that this certainty and authority is rooted in a 'white ignorance' which does not fully 'see' women of colour's contributions to the intellectual project of feminism. Drawing on (Fellows and) Razack's framework, a focus on complicity also requires questioning who is served by the current framing of these stories, and how they function to maintain relations of dominance between different groups of women. Foregrounding these frameworks opens up space for more questions and for different stories. It requires the placing of white-centred stories within a broader context of interlocking systems of oppression within the specificities of the British postcolonial context. Such a lens makes clear that it is precisely the marginalisation of Black and postcolonial feminisms which enables the story of white women as 'naturally' at the centre of British feminist theorising and politics to hold legitimacy.

Razack stresses that analyses of complicity cannot be performed in the abstract, but rather that the relations between differently positioned groups of people must be examined 'in a historical and site-specific way'.[12] The lack of engagement with local Black feminist histories is highly significant for understanding the ways in which white-centred feminism fails to interrogate its complicities in a meaningful way. Specifically, it enables white feminists to distance themselves from complicity in their own 'site-specific' contexts. When they engage with American Black feminist literature, this addresses a different historical and geographical context in which British feminists are less implicated. As Cecily Jones suggests about white British scholars' tendency to mainly cite African-American women: '[p]erhaps the voices of BME women closer to home make for less comfortable listening'.[13] Comfort is key here: maintaining white comfort requires not fully engaging with what women of colour 'closer to home' are saying. White comfort requires such 'voices' to be kept at bay, or to be addressing a different context. This point is also made by Lewis in an oral history interview in which she discusses the legacy of the Black feminist anthology *Charting the Journey* (see Chapter 2). Lewis reflects on the fact that while the book has been taken up within US Women's Studies courses, it is not well known in Britain, and she suggests that this is 'absolute testimony' to the ways in which white feminists were unable to see Black women's work 'as central to feminist politics in this country'. Instead, she points out, when white feminists set up Women's Studies programmes in Britain, 'they looked to the US for their women of colour scholarship'.[14] This highlights white women's complicity in the marginalisation of Black British feminist thought as feminism became institutionalised in the academy. This has material effects: white feminists' lack of engagement with Black feminists' work clearly contributes towards the structural marginalisation of women of colour within higher education institutions (see Chapter 2).

Narratives which presume that white women have always been the central actors in struggles for gender justice, whether in the British context or elsewhere, can be and have been contested through the centring of other histories of activism and theorising by women of colour. The assumption that women of colour's thought and organising can be 'tacked on' as additions to or critiques of a white feminist centre is steeped in white ignorance about the many different trajectories of such work. In *The Heart of the Race*, Beverley Bryan, Stella Dadzie and Suzanne Scafe document Black women's central roles in organising Black communities to survive and thrive in the hostile environment of 1950s, 1960s and 1970s Britain. They highlight the visionary leadership of Claudia Jones, originally from Trinidad, who arrived in England in 1956 after being deported from the US due to her activism as a member of the Communist Party, and went on to set up the *West Indian Gazette*, the first Black campaigning newspaper in Britain.[15] Jones is perhaps today most well known as the founder of the Notting Hill Carnival (in 1959), but her agitation for women's rights and theorising of Black women's 'triple oppression', however, is less well known.[16] Bryan, Dadzie and Scafe also write about Olive Morris who, among many other community organising activities, was one of the founders of the Brixton Black Women's Group and a member of the Black Panthers before she tragically died of cancer in 1979 at the age of 26. One of the women quoted in Bryan, Dadzie and Scafe's account about the development of the Brixton Black Women's Group suggests that Black women's organising in Britain in the 1970s was 'influenced far more, at the time, by what was happening in the liberation movements on the African continent' than they were by white women's activism.[17] In *Cartographies of Diaspora*, Avtar Brah also draws attention to South Asian women's 'long history of resistance and struggle, both in the sub-continent and in Britain'. The most well known of these are perhaps South Asian women workers' industrial disputes, such as that at the Grunwick photo processing plant in 1976–78, led by Jayaben Desai (documented in Amrit Wilson's *Finding a Voice*), but Brah stresses a wide variety of community organising which has been led by Asian women, noting that such work 'may not always take a form which is familiar to a Western observer or be crystallised around issues defined as relevant from a Western frame of reference'.[18] These are just some examples of the individual and collective leadership of women of colour which often is entirely erased from white-centred accounts of women's liberation organising in Britain.

To return to an example from the 1980s, discussed in Chapter 2, *Outwrite Women's Newspaper* constitutes another significant site of activism and theorising which holds important lessons and legacies for contemporary feminists. The *Outwrite* archive showcases a concrete effort to forge feminist coalitions across national, race and class divisions, constructing what may today be defined as transnational feminist theorising and politics. As I highlighted, it is recognised as an important piece of Black British feminist history, but it is largely neglected within white-dominated feminist accounts. This speaks to the ways in which Black-led feminist work is constructed as marginal to the overall British feminist story. If the history of *Outwrite* was recognised and foregrounded in accounts of British feminism's recent past (not just *Black* British feminism's), then a very different story can be told about feminist politics, practices and analyses of this era and its legacies for contemporary feminists. For one, it highlights that women of colour have been at the forefront of British feminist struggle and analysis. That they are rarely acknowledged as such within white-centred accounts is thereby exposed as a practice of erasure rather than a reflection of an empirical fact.

It is only because white women are so often assumed to be the central subjects of feminism that their stories and voices are repeatedly centred. By acknowledging a lack of knowledge about women of colour's activist and intellectual histories, and committing to educating themselves about these, white feminists can begin to address the ways in which their stories are complicit in the reproduction of white dominance. Crucially, in interrogating the ways in which white feminist stories have come to dominate, white feminists must resist repeating the familiar colonial gestures of inclusion – by, for example, adding women of colour's radical histories into an existing broader white-defined narrative. Such a process will simply add another chapter to the long history of white feminist co-option of women of colour's work. Instead, as per Applebaum's 'white complicity pedagogy', an approach guided by uncertainty, humility and vigilance requires interrogating and interrupting the imperial gesture inherent in attempts to tell the authoritative story of feminism. One way to disrupt such attempts is to turn attention towards moments of critique, resisting the urge to move on and assimilate or erase them from the narrative. In the following section, I address what staying with anti-racist critique entails and opens up.

STAYING WITH ANTI-RACIST CRITIQUE

Ahmed observes that when she talks about whiteness, white people often respond by asking her how they can resist it. Problematising such responses, she writes that

> [t]o respond to accounts of institutional whiteness with the question 'what can white people do?' is not only to return to the place of the white subject, but it is also to locate agency in this place. It is also to re-position the white subject as somewhere other than implicated in the critique.

She suggests that the desire to turn so quickly towards the need for a resolution is evidence of a resistance to hearing about racism. Such a response by white people indicates a desire to move on from the moment of anti-racist critique, and to move away from confronting their investment in white supremacy. While a response indicating a wish to 'do something' might in most cases be well intended, there is a continuity between such responses with other more expressly defensive ones which white people commonly exhibit when faced with anti-racist critique. Responding to a discussion of whiteness by immediately wishing to do something to resolve it becomes another way for white people to 'resist hearing about racism' by deflecting attention away from really listening to the critique being made. As Ahmed writes, '[i]f we want to know how things can be different *too quickly*, then we might not hear anything at all'.[19]

Ahmed highlights the importance of staying with critique and recognising one's complicities in oppressive systems, and considers what doing anti-oppressive, political work while doing so might entail. Here I draw on her insights to argue that white feminists must resist the imperative to repeatedly move on from critiques of racism and whiteness within feminism, and instead consider what staying with such critiques opens up. This requires better practices of listening to such critiques and an openness to hearing what they are communicating. Being able to hear critiques of white feminist racism without resorting to defensiveness requires a commitment to staying with complicity and accountability.

In the preceding chapters, I have identified two modes through which white-centred feminist analyses move on from anti-racist critique and the topic of white feminist racism (I have left the three popular books analysed in Chapter 5 out of the discussion here because they do not recognise that racism has ever been a problem for feminism). In the books discussed in Chapter 3, as summarised above, feminist whiteness is left in the past while contemporary white feminists are represented as race aware and attentive to difference. A similar process is evident within the debates about intersectionality and privilege in the *Guardian*, whereby white columnists quickly established themselves as knowledgeable about the meaning of these concepts, and as arbiters of just how far they should be applied. In both the books and the newspaper articles, then, the discussions move on from anti-racist critiques by positioning white feminists as now being knowledgeable about racism. They are implied to have successfully transcended, to return to Ahmed's words, being 'implicated in the critique'. The second mode of moving on, evident in the books discussed in Chapter 4, is generated by the sense of inevitability about the continuity of feminist whiteness these books exhibit. Constructing white dominance within contemporary feminist communities as more or less inevitable, whiteness becomes a backdrop against which feminists continue with 'business as usual'. In this way, the books move on from anti-racist critiques of feminist whiteness; attention shifts elsewhere, because to stay with the difficulty appears fruitless.

As I discussed in the conclusion of Chapter 3, claims of race criticality can function as a 'politics of declaration', as per Ahmed's theorisation.[20] Through their descriptions of feminism as having gone through a process of transformation in terms of recognising the significance of race and differences between women, the texts position (white) feminists as now knowledgeable about these topics. The white columnists position themselves similarly in the discussions of intersectionality and privilege in the *Guardian*. Yet, rather than challenging racism and whiteness, *the claim to knowledge* about the significance of race and whiteness often substitutes for sustained attention to how race and whiteness continuously shapes feminist theorising, spaces and politics. Without such sustained attention, such claims primarily serve a legitimising function for white feminists, which enables them to move on from continuing to attend to feminist whiteness. This claim to white feminist knowledge about race and racism is certainly not unique to the texts that I have discussed in this book, but is commonplace within contemporary feminist discussions.

My thoughts around the importance of staying with difficulty, and the implications of not doing so, were sharpened at an academic feminist conference I attended while working on this book. This was a conference heavily dominated by white feminists and their concerns. At different plenaries throughout the conference, a small number of delegates, including myself, raised questions about whiteness, in relation to the topics being discussed as well as in relation to the space of the conference. Answers were often vague and evasive. In the discussion following the final plenary, one of the only feminists of colour in the room spoke of what a difficult space the conference had been for her, and called for everyone to consider what it meant that hardly any women of colour had attended the conference (and some of those that had attended had only stayed for a short while). A silence ensued, followed by a few hesitant comments, and then, following another brief silence, one of the organisers noted the time and closed the discussion with some remarks about the difficulty of doing intersectional work, and the importance of continuing to address these issues beyond the conference. While silence can mean many things, and can certainly be problematic, in that moment it seemed to me an important acknowledgement. The silence was long, tense and uncomfortable and seemed at one level a collective recognition of the failure of anti-racism at the conference. All the white feminists who had attended the conference had to sit through that moment of failure and recognise our complicity in it. And as a conversation slowly started to take form, it appeared that a meaningful discussion could have taken place. But the conversation was wrapped up before it could develop (which would have likely required us to stay with some more silence).

Leaving the conference, I checked the Twitter hashtag. There were a number of tweets documenting the preceding discussion. Yet, moments later, tweets celebrating the conference started to appear, scattered with words such as 'success', 'wonderful', 'rewarding', 'inspiring', 'great' and 'amazing'. These tweets joined dozens of others which had similarly been celebrating the importance and success of the conference across the days it had run. Having just experienced the silence in the room, these tweets felt jarring to me. They seemed like an immediate push back; a defiant affirmation and implicit defence of the conference, despite its overwhelming whiteness. What did it mean that moments after hearing how the conference had failed feminists of colour, white feminists continued to celebrate its supposed success? While there were certainly useful and important aspects to the conference, it was strikingly clear to me in that moment that these were seen to override the fact of anti-racist failure, and that this was saying something powerful about the continued naturalisation of whiteness in academic feminism. It highlighted to me the ease with which white feminists can move on from anti-racist critique; the way in which the ongoing problems of whiteness can be momentarily acknowledged and then again put aside, to be dealt with in some other time and place (the perennial 'next time').

What would it have meant to stay in that moment of difficulty for longer? What different kinds of conversations and opportunities for collaborative work might have opened up as a result? Of course, it may have led to nothing, or the conversation might have got derailed, or turned towards white women's feelings, as these conversations often do.[21] The risks of further failure would have been high. However, the risk might still have been worth it. As Ien Ang argues, rather than attempting to minimise the difficulties in building equal relationships between differently racialised women, feminists would do well to see 'those painful moments at which communication seems unavoidably to *fail*' as useful starting points for addressing difference in ways which resist the politics of inclusion and presumed unity.[22] What would it have meant to allow the anti-racist critique to penetrate the celebration of the success of the conference? To take on board the recognition that, in fact, the conference was not successful? To allow ourselves to just stop and ask: what is so wrong with feminist academia that this is normal and acceptable? To refuse to move on with business as usual, and to refuse to give in to an assumption of inevitable whiteness, or chalk it on to the broader context of institutional racism and larger societal structures? While these are clearly relevant for understanding the whiteness of feminist academia, they are not an excuse for complacency. Feminists do have significant power over the spaces (conferences, networks, groups) that they create within academic institutions, as well as in other settings.

Staying with critique does not require immobilising guilt, but rather better and deeper forms of listening and attentiveness. It is worth remembering that the first part of the title of Hazel Carby's ground-breaking essay was 'White woman listen!' (see Chapter 2). White women's lack of willingness to really listen to what women of colour are telling them often lies at the core of Black feminist critiques of white feminisms. This lack of listening is a primary cause of the repetitive-ness frequently identified as a key feature of debates about racism within feminism. Elaine Swan emphasises listening as one way in which white feminists can begin to contribute to anti-racist praxis. This seems like an obvious point, but in practice it happens all too little. Swan urges white feminists, like herself, to 'undertake sustained reading of critical race and postcolonial theories and non-fiction in order to learn about our histories, whiteness and racism, to ground ourselves in practical, critical "self-work" guided by non-white discourses'. Learning about racism from the perspectives of people of colour, as Swan suggests, is necessary in order to understand and deconstruct the ways in which white ignorance functions as a knowledge system which conceals the truth about how white supremacy functions. She suggests that politi-cal listening for white feminists is about 'decentring' their attachments to white ways of seeing the world. This, she describes, 'require that we white people stop in our tracks, and repel our urge to turn away from racism and move into doing things that we think are right and good'.[23] This stopping in your tracks can be understood as a practice of *staying with* the realities of racism; about committing to understand these without seeking the comfort of innocence provided by white-centred ways of seeing the world.

This book in itself is an attempt to stay with critique. Yet, of course, while it critiques whiteness, this does not mean that it is not simul-taneously entangled in it. In particular, I am fully aware of how the mechanism of distancing looms large in this book – unavoidably my critiques of the works of other white feminists function to position me as potentially more 'critical' or more 'knowledgeable' about racism, which could again be understood as an attempt to position myself as a 'good' white feminist. Even though I claim to see myself as part of the argument and critiques that I am making, such a statement can itself function as a 'declaration of whiteness' whereby by declaring to see my complicity in whiteness, I simultaneously wish to transcend it. While writing this book, I have become acutely aware of and had to reckon with my own attachment to white innocence. I have deliberated considerably about the usefulness or not of the project and the extent to which it plays into versus challenges patterns of white-centredness and appropriation. Yet, these deliberations, in my experience, can lead down endless rabbit holes. And while reflecting on one's own practice and motivations is crucial, when white people make such processes extensively visible, this is ultimately not that helpful for anti-racist work. The display of white anxieties around whether you are 'doing it right' are of course still wrapped up in a moral framework of guilt versus innocence, and shifts the focus back towards white people and their intentions. I see this kind of critical reflective work as best done in private and/or together with other white people who are concerned with racism. There is also a limit to which such self-reflective work is actually useful, as highlighted by Sara de Jong in *Complicit Sisters*, a recently published study critically interrogating the self-understandings and self-reflections of women from the global North doing aid and development work with women from the global South. de Jong concludes her book by explaining her resistance to providing recommendations for how aid work can be done better. As she points out, women like those in her study are heavily invested in the idea of 'getting it right', and would welcome such recommendations, yet the problem with the unequal power relations between differently positioned women in the aid industry cannot ever be solved through 'more awareness and reflexivity'.[24] Given that these power inequalities are rooted in interlocking systems of oppression, they can ultimately only be effectively addressed through collective, ongoing struggle.

Foregrounding the need to stay with complicity, then, is not the same as presuming the inevitability of racism, but rather calls attention to the need to commit to ongoing anti-oppressive work. It is important to distinguish these because the latter, as highlighted above, can also encourage moving on, because it is perceived that there is nothing that can be done. Instead, 'staying with' requires an attentiveness to critique and continuous commitment to challenging racism, while recognising that one is never outside of the structural relations of race. In Applebaum's words, 'the white complicity claim does not reject the possibility of whites working to challenge racism. Instead, the white complicity claim calls for a specific type of vigilance that recognizes the dangers of presuming that one can transcend racist systems when one attempts to work to challenge racist systems.'[25]

It should also be stressed that staying with and listening to critique and people of colour's knowledge about racism is a beginning rather than an end point. It is what leads towards a deeper understanding of what other action is required. Such action cannot be predetermined prior to the work of listening and educating oneself about racism. Questions asking what white people should do are often problematic precisely because they skip over the step of really listening and learning. Doing the work of deep listening requires allowing what you hear to change your sense of yourself, your place in the world and what you do. As long as white feminists engage with discussions about race from a position of needing to be seen as innocent, then the impulse to move on from addressing feminist racism will always be strong. Yet, this impulse is contrary to what anti-racist work really requires, which is ongoing commitment and attention.

BREAKING THE CYCLE OF FEMINIST WHITENESS

In 2018, a book titled *Can We All Be Feminists?* edited by June Eric-Udorie, was published by Virago Press. Subtitled *Seventeen Writers on Intersectionality, Identity and Finding the Right Way Forward for Feminism*, the book highlights how contemporary mainstream feminism – a term Eric-Udorie uses interchangeably with white feminism – excludes and harms differently marginalised groups, including sex workers, women of colour, disabled women and trans women. Virago, which sprang up in the heat of the women's liberation movement in the 1970s, aims to promote women's and feminist writing to mainstream audiences. Notably, it is the same publisher which 20 years ago published Natasha Walter's *The New Feminism*. In some ways the two books are similar: they both take feminism itself as a subject and are concerned with finding 'the right way forward' for the movement. Of course, in other ways they are markedly different. While *The New Feminism* represents one specific white, middle-class and otherwise privileged perspective and claims it to be universal, *Can We All Be Feminists?* represents a multitude of marginalised perspectives and deconstructs such claims to universality. That such a book is considered marketable to a mainstream audience today says something about the moment we are in, in terms of feminism's current popularity, and the rise in visibility of intersectional discourses. Virago likely knows that if it published a book like Walter's today, it would come under significant critique.

We might see Virago's transformation from publishing a book promoting white feminism to publishing a book on intersectional feminism as evidence of increased race awareness within a white-dominated sector. However, this is not the first time this particular publisher has made such a journey. White-led feminist publishers like Virago came under critique for their lack of support for women of colour's work in the 1970s and early 1980s.[26] Subsequently, in 1978, Virago published Amrit Wilson's *Finding a Voice: Asian Women in Britain*. As Ranu Samantrai notes, the success of Wilson's book led to a 'scramble for manuscripts' on behalf of publishers which suddenly 'awoke to the marketing possibilities for texts by and about racialized women'. Virago, in its sudden rush to publish more women of colour, was even duped into publishing a book written by a white man, Toby Forward, pretending to be a South Asian woman, presuming the book's 'stereotype of the pathologically modest Muslim woman' to be an authentic representation.[27]

My point here is not to focus on the actions of this specific feminist publisher, but to draw attention to the circularity of debates about racism, power and privilege within feminist communities. As Jan McKenley highlighted in the letter quoted at the start of this book, debates about racism can be the centre of attention within white-dominated feminist communities at one point, giving the impression that things are changing, only to be 'forgotten' again a few years later. McKenley pinpoints one such moment in 1978. As discussed in Chapter 2, the early to mid 1980s constitute another significant time period in which such discussions took centre-stage. And as highlighted in Chapter 5, the early 2010s were also a significant moment for such conversations. I am not suggesting that this is a definitive account of debates about race in British feminism – there have of course been many such moments taking place within different spheres at different times, and with differing intensities – but these moments are, in my view, clearly significant in terms of their impact on mainstream, white-dominated feminist politics, theorising and spaces.

Over the decade that I have been working on different variations of this project (since starting my PhD in 2008), feminist discourse has changed significantly. In particular, online debates about white feminists' racism have reverberated far and wide. One oft-cited key moment was the widespread trending of the Twitter hashtag #solidarityisforwhitewomen, initiated by US Black feminist Mikki Kendall in August 2013 and taken up widely by feminists of colour in different geographic locations to name instances of white feminist racism and ignorance. The hashtag's popularity led to widespread media coverage and debate as well as academic study and reflection.[28] As a result of such interventions (online and off), as I have discussed, race has become a more prominently discussed topic among feminists, representations of feminists within the liberal media have become more diverse, and a language of intersectionality has become commonplace within activist and academic communities. Although intersectionality had already been described as a 'buzzword' in academia in 2008, it is notable that, with the exception of Walby's book, it is not an extensively discussed concept in the books analysed in Chapter 3, which were all published between 2009 and 2011, whereas it is in the books discussed in Chapter 4, which were published between 2015 and 2017.[29] With race and intersectionality relatively high on the agenda, this could then be seen as a potentially important moment of transformation. But the extent to which this moment is indicative of any deep-rooted change is questionable. As should be clear by now, anti-racist theories and critiques quickly become appropriated and commodified, depoliticised and assimilated into – or erased from – white-controlled narratives.

As I stressed in Chapter 1, in these times of resurgent heteropatriarchal (ironically, transnational) nationalisms – in Britain, as well as in many countries in Europe, in India, the US, Brazil and elsewhere – anti-racist, coalitional and transnational feminist politics are urgently needed. This is not to suggest that such work is not happening, but to call attention to the ongoing need to address whiteness and racism within feminism so that such movements can grow stronger and a politics of solidarity between differently racialised feminists can flourish. To some, the issues which I have raised in this book might appear trivial and the critiques misdirected – it is after all not generally liberal/left feminist academics, journalists or activists who are calling for closed borders or attacking Muslim women in the streets. But the extent to which whiteness destroys the possibilities of solidarity between differently racialised feminists should not be underestimated. bell hooks writes of her experience attending a conference of liberal academics, describing her increasing sense of fear as she noted how 'the usual arrangements of white supremacist hierarchy were mirrored in terms of who was speaking, of how bodies were arranged on the stage, of who was in the audience, of what voices were deemed worthy to speak and be heard'. She explains how this fear was 'a response to the legacy of white domination' which, to her dismay, was invisible to the white progressive people who surrounded her. As she stresses, if such people could so easily 'reproduce a version of the status quo and not "see" it, the thought of how racial politics would be played out "outside" this arena was horrifying'.[30] This draws attention to the continuity of white domination extending between the (in)actions of 'well-meaning' white liberals and those of more explicitly racist constituencies. When white feminists uncritically buy into the dominant racial 'common sense' they reproduce white ignorance: a refusal to fully know and see coloniality and racism, and to fully know and see people of colour.[31] Whiteness is a power structure which is held in place through maintaining its 'invisibility'. When it is repeatedly rendered invisible within white-dominated feminist communities this undermines any proclaimed commitments to inclusion and race criticality, and thus must continue to be repeatedly challenged.

Challenging feminist whiteness is increasingly urgent within the contemporary context because of the ways in which the current configuration of coloniality has involved a rising tide of what Sara Farris calls 'femonationalism' (after Jasbir Puar's 'homonationalism'), whereby a discourse of women's rights has been mobilised in the service of both state and popular anti-migrant and anti-Muslim racism.[32] The colonial construction of Black and Brown men as sexual threats has been reinvigorated for the twenty-first century within the context of the 'War on Terror', now with a veneer of 'gender equality' rhetoric. Yet, as Gargi Bhattacharyya points out, although feminists (at least those on the left) are more likely to oppose than support military interventions and racist legislation, the feminist arguments made by state actors and others 'who historically have had little interest in [women's] advancement' are often not 'easily distinguishable from those articulated by "real" feminists'. As Bhattacharyya continues, 'this imperial deployment is not pretend feminism, because the influence of feminist scholarship, lobbying and activism is readily apparent in its articulation'.[33] When feminist arguments are not explicitly anti-racist they become more easily amenable to such racist and imperial appropriations.

Rather than stressing feminism's innocence from racism, it is more useful to interrogate how feminist discourses collude with and are mobilised within the interlocking structures of white supremacy, heteropatriarchy and capitalism in order to challenge such complicities more incisively. Attachments to white feminist innocence obstruct such interrogations and lock feminist communities into cycle after cycle of repetitive debate. In this chapter I have argued that using complicity as a starting point for analysing white feminists' positions in relation to racism provides a better chance for interrupting such repetitions. I have highlighted white feminists' complicity in the marginalisation of histories of women of colour's thought and organising within the dominant stories of British feminism. Throughout the book I have interrogated the disconnection between Black and postcolonial versus white-centred feminist analysis, and I have argued that attention to the former exposes the latter's complicity in reproducing dominant racial discourses, including the presumption that white women are 'naturally' at the centre of feminist theorising and communities. Significantly, while Black and postcolonial feminisms situate gender analysis within the context of coloniality, white-centred feminisms often theorise gender without attention to this context. Yet, as I have highlighted, an analysis of coloniality is as crucial for understanding how gender operates today as it was in formal colonial times. White feminists must urgently attend to the colonial context in which contemporary feminisms are articulated, including the ways in which white womanhood and white feminist discourse are being mobilised for racist ends. To turn Razia Aziz's definition of white feminism on its head (see Chapter 1), counteracting the cycle of feminist whiteness requires a consideration of 'both the wider social and political context of power in which feminist utterances and actions take place, and the ability of feminism to influence that context'.[34] Such considerations must attend to how racism and whiteness function both in the world 'out there' and within feminist communities 'in here'. Rather than constantly attempting to move on from anti-racist critiques, it is crucial for white feminists to stay with and attend to them closely, in order to loosen the grip of white innocence and the way it functions to obstruct genuine engagement and commitment to anti-racist work. Critiques of whiteness (and other forms of domination) which have drawn attention to feminist complicities within interlocking structures of oppression have been and continue to be fundamental to the development of feminist analyses and politics, and need to be recognised and engaged with as such. Only then can the repetitive cycles of feminist whiteness be broken.

Notes

CHAPTER 1 'THAT OLD CHESTNUT': FEMINISM AND RACISM

1. Jan McKenley, 'On the Shelf' (letter), *Spare Rib*, 101 (December 1980) (p. 24).
2. Reni Eddo-Lodge, *Why I'm No Longer Talking to White People About Race* (London: Bloomsbury Circus, 2017) (pp. 167–8).
3. Nadine El-Enany, 'The Iraq War, Brexit and Imperial Blowback', *Truth Out* (6 July 2016), www.truth-out.org/opinion/item/36703-the-iraq-war-brexit-and-imperial-blowback (last accessed 17 October 2019).
4. Missing Migrants: Tracking Deaths Along Migratory Routes, https://missingmigrants.iom.int/region/mediterranean (last accessed 17 October 2019).
5. Nadine El-Enany, 'The Colonial Logic of Grenfell', *Verso* (3 July 2017), www.versobooks.com/blogs/3306-the-colonial-logic-of-grenfell (last accessed 4 October 2019).
6. Boris Johnson, 'Denmark Has Got It Wrong. Yes, the Burka Is Oppressive and Ridiculous – But That's Still No Reason to Ban It', *Telegraph* (5 August 2018), www.telegraph.co.uk/news/2018/08/05/denmark-has-got-wrong-yes-burka-oppressive-ridiculous-still/ (last accessed 24 January 2020).
7. Terese Jonsson et al., 'Anti-Racist Feminist Statement on Islamophobia' (21 August 2018), *Sideways Times*, https://sidewaystimesblog.wordpress.com/2018/08/21/anti-racist-feminist-statement-on-islamophobia/ (last accessed 24 January 2020).
8. Emine Saner, '"It Has Made Us Unsafe": Muslim Women on Fear and Abuse After Boris Johnson's Burqa Remarks', *Guardian* (14 August 2018), www.theguardian.com/world/2018/aug/14/unsafe-muslim-women-fear-abuse-boris-johnson-burqa (last accessed 24 January 2020).
9. Jack Peat, 'Far Right Figures Flooding to the Conservative Party', *London Economic* (19 December 2019), www.thelondoneconomic.com/politics/far-right-figures-flooding-to-the-conservative-party/19/12/ (last accessed 24 January 2020).
10. Naaz Rashid, 'Giving the Silent Majority a Stronger Voice? Initiatives to Empower Muslim Women as part of the UK's "War on Terror"', *Ethnic and Racial Studies*, 37:4 (2014), pp. 589–604 (p. 601).
11. Michaela Rogers, 'Funding Cuts Could Leave Victims of Domestic Violence with Nowhere to Go', *The Conversation* (22 June 2016), https://

theconversation.com/funding-cuts-could-leave-victims-of-domestic-violence-with-nowhere-to-go-61177 (last accessed 17 October 2019).

12. Sisters Uncut, www.sistersuncut.org/ (last accessed 17 October 2019).
13. Akwugo Emejulu and Leah Bassel, 'Minority Women, Austerity and Activism', *Race and Class*, 57:2 (2015), pp. 86–95 (p. 88).
14. *Channel 4 News*, 'Yarl's Wood: Undercover in the Secretive Immigration Centre' (2 March 2015), www.channel4.com/news/yarls-wood-immigration-removal-detention-centre-investigation (last accessed 17 October 2019). Diane Taylor, 'Dossier Calling for Yarl's Wood Closure Chronicles Decade of Abuse Complaints', *Guardian* (15 June 2015), www.theguardian.com/uk-news/2015/jun/15/yarls-wood-report-calling-for-closure-decade-abuse-complaints (last accessed 17 October 2019). Amelia Hill, 'Vulnerable Women "Still Locked Up in Yarl's Wood Immigration Centre"', *Guardian* (1 November 2017), www.theguardian.com/uk-news/2017/nov/01/vulnerable-women-still-locked-up-in-yarls-wood-immigration-centre (last accessed 17 October 2019).
15. Ruth Cain, 'Post-Truth and the "Metropolitan Elite" Feminist: Lessons from Brexit', *Feminists@Law*, 6:1 (2016), http://journals.kent.ac.uk/index.php/feministsatlaw/article/view/259/837 (last accessed 1 October 2019).
16. Nicola Rollock, *Staying Power: The Career Experiences and Strategies of UK Black Female Professors* (London: UCU, 2019), www.ucu.org.uk/media/10075/Staying-Power/pdf/UCU_Rollock_February_2019.pdf (last accessed 19 October 2019) (p. 4).
17. Julia Sudbury, *'Other Kinds of Dreams': Black Women's Organisations and the Politics of Transformation* (London: Routledge, 1998) (p. 199).
18. Hazel Carby, 'White Woman Listen! Black Feminism and the Boundaries of Sisterhood', in Centre for Cultural Studies (ed.), *The Empire Strikes Back: Race and Racism in 70s Britain* (London: Hutchinson, 1982), pp. 211–34 (p. 232).
19. Vron Ware, *Beyond the Pale: White Women, Racism and History*, 2nd edition (London: Verso, 2015). First published 1992. Ruth Frankenberg, *White Women, Race Matters: The Social Construction of Whiteness* (London: Routledge, 1993). Antoinette Burton, *Burdens of History: British Feminists, Indian Women, and Imperial Culture, 1865–1915* (London: University of North Carolina, 1994). Catherine Hall, *White, Male and Middle Class: Explorations in Feminism and History* (Cambridge: Polity Press, 1992).
20. Charles Mills, 'White Ignorance', in Shannon Sullivan and Nancy Tuana (eds), *Race and Epistemologies of Ignorance* (Ithaca, NY: State University of New York Press, 2007), pp. 13–38.
21. Avtar Brah, *Cartographies of Diaspora: Contesting Identities* (London: Routledge, 1996) (pp. 110–11).
22. Nydia A. Swaby, '"Disparate in Voice, Sympathetic in Direction": Gendered Political Blackness and the Politics of Solidarity', *Feminist Review*, 108 (2014), pp. 11–25 (p. 13).

23. Charmaine Jacobs, 'NUS Needs to Evaluate the Use of "Political Blackness" in the Student Movement' (May 2016), *Student Voices*, www.studentvoices. co.uk/2016/05/nus-needs-to-evaluate-use-of-political.html (last accessed 17 October 2019). Amarachi Ninette Iheke, 'NUS Black Students' Conference 2017: Politically Anti-Black' (29 May 2017), *Gal Dem*, gal-dem. com/nus-black-students-conference-2017-politically-anti-black/ (accessed 2 October 2019).

24. Razia Aziz, 'Feminism and the Challenge of Racism: Deviance or Difference?', in Helen Crowley and Susan Himmelweit (eds), *Knowing Women: Feminism and Knowledge* (Cambridge: Polity Press, 1992), pp. 291–305 (p. 296).

25. Suki Ali, 'Feminism and Postcolonial: Knowledge/Politics', *Ethnic and Racial Studies*, 30:2 (2007), pp. 191–212 (pp. 194–5).

26. Akwugo Emejulu and Francesca Sobande, 'Introduction: On the Problems and Possibilities of European Black Feminism and Afrofeminism', in Akwugo Emejulu and Francesca Sobande (eds), *To Exist Is to Resist: Black Feminism in Europe* (London: Pluto Press, 2019), pp. 3–9 (p. 4).

27. For example, Valerie Amos, Gail Lewis, Amina Mama and Pratibha Parmar (eds), *Many Voices, One Chant: Black Feminist Perspectives, Feminist Review*, Special issue, 17 (1984); Beverley Bryan, Stella Dadzie and Suzanne Scafe, *The Heart of the Race: Black Women's Lives in Britain* (London: Virago Press, 1985); Shabnam Grewal, Jackie Kay, Liliane Landor, Gail Lewis and Pratibha Parmar (eds), *Charting the Journey: Writings by Black and Third World Women* (London: Sheba Feminist Publishers, 1988); Brah, *Cartographies*; Heidi Safia Mirza (ed.), *Black British Feminism: A Reader* (London: Routledge, 1997); Sudbury, *'Other Kinds of Dreams'*; Ranu Samantrai, *AlterNatives: Black Feminism in the Postimperial Nation* (Stanford: Stanford University Press, 2002); Rahila Gupta (ed.), *From Homebreakers to Jailbreakers: Southall Black Sisters* (London: Zed Books, 2003); Amrit Wilson, *Dreams, Questions, Struggles: South Asian Women in Britain* (London: Pluto Press, 2006); Rashida L. Harrison, 'Towards a Transnational Black Feminist Discourse: Women Writing Against States of Imperialism, 1975–1989' (unpublished doctoral thesis, Michigan State University, 2012); Sukhwant Dhaliwal and Nira Yuval-Davis (eds), *Women Against Fundamentalism: Stories of Dissent and Solidarity* (London: Lawrence and Wishart, 2014); Joan Anim-Addo, Yasmin Gunaratnam and Suzanne Scafe (eds), *Black British Feminisms, Feminist Review*, Special issue (2014) (p. 108).

28. Emejulu and Sobande, *To Exist Is to Resist*.

29. Ali, 'Feminism and Postcolonial' (p. 195).

30. Lola Okolosie, 'Beyond "Talking" and "Owning" Intersectionality', *Feminist Review*, 108 (2014), pp. 90–6 (p. 91).

31. Kathleen Wilson, 'Empire, Gender and Modernity in the Eighteenth Century', in Philippa Levine (ed.), *Gender and Empire* (Oxford: Oxford University Press, 2004), pp. 14–45 (pp. 15–16, 21 and 44).

32. Oyèrónké Oyéwùmí, *The Invention of Women: Making an African Sense of Western Gender Discourses* (Minneapolis: University of Minnesota Press, 1997) (pp. 130, 142–6 and 124).

33. Ware, *Beyond the Pale* (p. 108).

34. Clare Midgley, 'Anti-Slavery and the Roots of "Imperial Feminism"', in Clare Midgley (ed.), *Gender and Imperialism* (Manchester: Manchester University Press, 1998), pp. 161–70 (pp. 163–5).

35. Burton, *Burdens of History*. Inderpal Grewal, *Home and Harem: Nation, Gender, Empire, and the Cultures of Travel* (London: Leicester University Press, 1996).

36. Ware, *Beyond the Pale* (p. 126).

37. Grewal, *Home and Harem* (pp. 76–8).

38. Mona L. Siegel, 'Western Feminism and Anti-Imperialism: The Women's International League for Peace and Freedom's Anti-Opium Campaign', *Peace and Change*, 36:1 (2011), pp. 34–61 (pp. 34 and 48).

39. Grewal, *Home and Harem* (pp. 77–8).

40. Denise Noble, 'Decolonizing Britain and Domesticating Women: Race, Gender, and Women's Work in Post-1945 British Decolonial and Metropolitan Liberal Reform Discourses', *Meridians: Feminism, Race, Transnationalism*, 13:1 (2015), pp. 53–77 (pp. 57–9 and 73).

41. Carby, 'White Woman Listen!' (p. 219).

42. Samantrai, *AlterNatives* (p. 23).

43. Burton, *Burdens of History* (p. 24).

44. For example, Sylvia Wynter, 'Unsettling the Coloniality of Being/Power/Truth/Freedom: Towards the Human, After Man, Its Overrepresentation – an Argument', *The New Centennial Review*, 3:3 (2003), pp. 257–337; Aníbal Quijano, 'Coloniality and Modernity/Rationality', *Cultural Studies*, 21:2–3 (2007), pp. 168–78; María Lugones, 'Heterosexualism and the Colonial/Modern Gender System', *Hypatia*, 22:1 (2007), pp. 186–209; Ramón Grosfoguel, 'The Structure of Knowledge in Westernized Universities: Epistemic Racism/Sexism and the Four Genocides/Epistemicides of the Long 16th Century', *Human Architecture: Journal of the Sociology of Self-Knowledge*, 11:1 (2013), pp. 73–90.

45. Quijano, 'Coloniality' (pp. 168–9).

46. Heidi Safia Mirza, 'Introduction', in Heidi Safia Mirza (ed.), *Black British Feminism: A Reader* (London: Routledge, 1997), pp. 1–28 (p. 3).

47. Sara Ahmed, 'Declarations of Whiteness: The Non-Performativity of Anti-Racism', *borderlands*, 3:2 (2004), www.borderlands.net.au/vol3no2_2004/ahmed_declarations.htm (last accessed 19 October 2019) (paragraphs 1–2).

48. Mills, 'White Ignorance' (pp. 16–8, 11 and 34).

49. María Lugones, *Pilgrimages Peregrinajes: Theorizing Coalition Against Multiple Oppressions* (Lanham, MD: Rowman & Littlefield, 2003) (p. 48–9).

50. Mariana Ortega, 'Being Lovingly, Knowingly Ignorant: White Feminism and Women of Color', *Hypatia*, 21:3 (2006), pp. 56–74 (pp. 58–60); Marilyn

Frye, *The Politics of Reality: Essays in Feminist Theory* (New York: Crossing Press, 1983).

51. Aileen Moreton-Robinson, *Talkin' Up to the White Woman: Indigenous Women and Feminism* (Queensland: University of Queensland Press, 2000) (pp. xxii and 144).

52. Gloria Wekker, *White Innocence: Paradoxes of Colonialism and Race* (London: Duke University Press, 2017) (p. 18).

53. bell hooks, 'Representing Whiteness in the Black Imagination', in Ruth Frankenberg (ed.), *Displacing Whiteness: Essays in Social and Cultural Criticism* (London: Duke University Press, 1997), pp. 165–79 (p. 169).

54. Barbara Applebaum, *Being White, Being Good: White Complicity, White Moral Responsibility, and Social Justice Pedagogy* (Plymouth: Lexington Books, 2010) (pp. 20 and 45). Italics in original.

55. Wekker, *White Innocence* (p. 79).

56. Mary Louise Fellows and Sherene Razack, 'The Race to Innocence: Confronting Hierarchical Relations Among Women', *Journal of Gender, Race and Justice*, 1 (1998), pp. 335–52 (p. 349).

57. Sarita Srivastava, '"You're Calling Me a Racist?" The Moral and Emotional Regulation of Antiracism and Feminism', *Signs: Journal of Women in Culture and Society*, 31:1 (2005), pp. 29–62 (pp. 30–5).

58. Eddo-Lodge, *Why I'm No Longer* (p. 165).

59. Frankenberg, *White Women* (pp. 142–3, 147, 167 and 188).

60. Ware, *Beyond the Pale*.

61. Ann Phoenix, 'Re-narrating Feminist Stories: Black British Women and Transatlantic Feminisms', in Kathy Davis and Mary Evans (eds), *Transatlantic Conversations: Feminism as Travelling Theory* (Farnham, Surrey: Ashgate, 2011), pp. 55–67 (p. 63).

62. Elizabeth Evans, *The Politics of Third Wave Feminism: Neoliberalism, Intersectionality, and the State in Britain and the US* (Basingstoke: Palgrave Macmillan, 2015) (p. 199).

63. Chandra Talpade Mohanty, *Feminism Without Borders: Decolonizing Theory, Practicing Solidarity* (London: Duke University Press, 2003) (pp. 106 and 116). The term 'politics of location' originates from Adrienne Rich, *Blood, Bread and Poetry: Selected Prose, 1975–1985* (New York: Norton & Company, 1986).

64. Lord Ashcroft, 'How the United Kingdom Voted on Thursday ... and Why', *Lord Ashcroft Polls* (24 June 2016), http://lordashcroftpolls.com/2016/06/how-the-united-kingdom-voted-and-why/ (last accessed 19 October 2019).

65. Richard Hayton, 'The UK Independence Party and the Politics of Englishness', *Political Studies Review*, 14:3 (2016), pp. 400–10.

66. David Owen, 'Variations in National Identity, Diversity and Integration within the UK', presented at UK Data Service Conference, University of Manchester (17 July 2015), https://warwick.ac.uk/fac/soc/ier/people/

dowen/conferences/20150715_d_owen.pptx (last accessed 19 October 2019).

67. Ahmed, 'Declarations of Whiteness'.

68. Fiona Probyn, 'Playing Chicken at the Intersection: The White Critic of Whiteness', *borderlands*, 3:2 (2004), www.borderlands.net.au/vol3no2_2004/probyn_playing.htm (last accessed 11 April 2019) (paragraph 17).

69. Sara Ahmed, *Living a Feminist Life* (London: Duke University Press, 2017) (p. 148).

70. Humaira Saeed (ed.), *Race Revolt*, 1–5 (2007–10).

71. bell hooks, *Outlaw Culture: Resisting Representations* (London: Routledge, 1994) (p. 67).

72. Sara Ahmed, *On Being Included: Racism and Diversity in Institutional Life* (London: Duke University Press, 2012); Sara Ahmed, *Willful Subjects* (London: Duke University Press, 2014).

73. Clare Hemmings, 'Telling Feminist Stories', *Feminist Theory*, 6:2 (2005), pp. 115–39 (p. 118).

74. Clare Hemmings, *Why Stories Matter: The Political Grammar of Feminist Theory* (London: Duke University Press, 2011) (p. 229, n. 16).

75. Stuart Hall, 'The Work of Representation', in Stuart Hall (ed.), *Representation: Cultural Representations and Signifying Practices* (London: Sage, 1997), pp. 13–74 (p. 61).

CHAPTER 2   BRITISH FEMINISMS
IN THE AFTERMATH OF EMPIRE

1. Heidi Safia Mirza, 'Introduction', in Heidi Safia Mirza (ed.), *Black British Feminism: A Reader* (London: Routledge, 1997), pp. 1–28 (pp. 4–5). Italics in original.

2. Barnor Hesse and S. Sayyid, 'Narrating the Postcolonial Political and the Immigrant Imaginary', in N. Ali, V.S. Kalra and S. Sayyid (eds), *A Postcolonial People: South Asians in Britain* (London: Hurst & Company, 2006), pp. 13–31 (p. 21).

3. Errol Lawrence, 'Just Plain Common Sense: The "Roots" of Racism', in Centre for Contemporary Cultural Studies (ed.), *The Empire Strikes Back: Race and Racism in 70s Britain* (London: Routledge, 1982), pp. 47–94 (p. 75).

4. Stuart Hall, 'Old and New Identities, Old and New Ethnicities', in Les Back and John Solomos (eds), *Theories of Race and Racism: A Reader* (Abingdon, Oxon: Routledge, 2000), pp. 144–53 (p. 147).

5. John Solomos, Bob Findlay, Simon Jones and Paul Gilroy, 'The Organic Crisis of British Capitalism and Race: The Experience of the Seventies', in Centre for Contemporary Cultural Studies (ed.), *The Empire Strikes Back: Race and Racism in 70s Britain* (London: Routledge, 1982), pp. 9–46 (pp.

11, 9 and 15); see also A. Sivanandan, *A Different Hunger: Writings on Black Resistance* (London: Pluto Press, 1982).

6. Solomos et al., 'Organic Crisis' (p. 27).

7. Vron Ware, *Beyond the Pale: White Women, Racism and History*, 2nd edition (London: Verso, 2015 (p. 228). First published 1992.

8. Hazel Carby, 'White Woman Listen! Black Feminism and the Boundaries of Sisterhood', in Centre for Cultural Studies (ed.), *The Empire Strikes Back: Race and Racism in 70s Britain* (London: Hutchinson, 1982), pp. 211–234 (pp. 212 and 221).

9. Amrit Wilson, 'Creating Revolutionary Change', *Outwrite Women's Newspaper*, 71 (December 1988) (p. 11).

10. Valerie Mason-John and Ann Khambatta, *Lesbians Talk: Making Black Waves* (London: Scarlett Press, 1993) (p. 12).

11. OWAAD, 'Editorial', *FOWAAD! Newsletter of the Organisation of Women of Asian and African Descent*, 1 (1979) (p. 2).

12. Ann Phoenix, 'Re-narrating Feminist Stories: Black British Women and Transatlantic Feminisms', in Kathy Davis and Mary Evans (eds), *Transatlantic Conversations: Feminism as Travelling Theory* (Farnham, Surrey: Ashgate, 2011), pp. 55–67 (p. 60).

13. Angela Y. Davis, *Women, Race and Class* (London: The Women's Press, 1982) (p. 182).

14. OWAAD, 'Campaign Against the Corrie Bill', *FOWAAD! Newsletter of the Organisation of Women of Asian and African Descent*, 2 (1979) (pp. 4–5).

15. On the history of eugenics and its relationships to feminism, see also Valerie Amos and Pratibha Parmar, 'Challenging Imperial Feminism', *Feminist Review*, 17 (1984), pp. 3–19 (pp. 12–13).

16. Natalie Thomlinson, 'The Colour of Feminism: White Feminists and Race in the Women's Liberation Movement', *History*, 97:327 (2012), pp. 453–75 (pp. 455–7 and 469).

17. Ware, *Beyond the Pale* (pp. 25 and 19).

18. Roisin Boyd, 'Women Speak Out Against Zionism', *Spare Rib*, 121 (1982), pp. 22–3.

19. *Spare Rib* Collective, 'Sisterhood ... Is Plain Sailing', *Spare Rib*, 132 (1983), p. 24.

20. Linda Bellos, untitled letter, *London Women's Liberation Newsletter*, 319 (1983).

21. Pratibha Parmar, 'Other Kinds of Dreams', *Feminist Review*, 31 (1989), pp. 55–65 (p. 56).

22. Bellos, untitled letter.

23. Faversham Women's Group, untitled letter, *Spare Rib*, 134 (September 1983) (p. 44).

24. The seven demands of the women's liberation movement were agreed at the annual women's liberation conferences held between 1970 and 1978. These were: (1) Equal pay; (2) Equal educational and job opportunities; (3) Free

contraception and abortion on demand; (4) Free 24-hour nurseries; (5) Legal and financial independence for all women; (6) The right to a self-defined sexuality. An end to discrimination against lesbians; and (7) Freedom for all women from intimidation by the threat or use of violence or sexual coercion regardless of marital status; and an end to the laws, assumptions and institutions which perpetuate male dominance and aggression to women. Sisterhood and After, 'Women's Liberation: A National Movement', www.bl.uk/sisterhood/articles/womens-liberation-a-national-movement (last accessed 16 January 2020).

25. Jan Parker, untitled contribution, *Spare Rib*, 132 (July 1983), p. 26.

26. *Spare Rib* Collective, 'Editorial', *Spare Rib*, 134 (September 1983) (p. 4).

27. See e.g. letters from Hilary Britten, Penny Pattenden and Lesley Saunders, *Spare Rib*, 134 (September 1983), pp. 44–5.

28. *Spare Rib* Collective, 'Editorial', *Spare Rib*, 115 (February 1982) (p. 3).

29. Thomlinson, 'The Colour of Feminism' (p. 473).

30. Amos and Parmar, 'Challenging Imperial Feminism' (p. 4).

31. Valerie Amos, Gail Lewis, Amina Mama and Pratibha Parmar, 'Editorial', *Feminist Review*, 17, pp. 1–2 (p. 1).

32. Feminist Review Editorial Collective, 'Editorial', *Feminist Review*, 40 (1992).

33. Amina Mama, 'Black Women, the Economic Crisis and the British State', *Feminist Review*, 17 (1984), pp. 21–35; Parita Trivedi, 'To Deny Our Fullness: Asian Women in the Making of History', *Feminist Review*, 17 (1984), pp. 37–50; Gail Carmen and Shaila Pratibha, 'Becoming Visible: Black Lesbian Discussions', *Feminist Review*, 17 (1984), pp. 53–72.

34. Amos et al., 'Editorial' (p. 1).

35. Michèle Barrett and Mary McIntosh, 'Ethnocentrism and Socialist-Feminist Theory', *Feminist Review*, 20 (1985), pp. 23–47.

36. Kum-Kum Bhavnani and Margaret Coulson, 'Transforming Socialist-Feminism: The Challenge of Racism', *Feminist Review*, 23 (1986), pp. 81–92 (p. 83).

37. Heidi S. Mirza, 'The Dilemma of Socialist Feminism: A Case for Black Feminism', *Feminist Review*, 22 (1986), pp. 103–5 (p. 103).

38. Chandra Talpade Mohanty, 'Under Western Eyes: Feminist Scholarship and Colonial Discourses', *Feminist Review*, 30 (1988), pp. 61–88 (p. 62).

39. Parmar, 'Other Kinds of Dreams' (p. 57).

40. Phoenix, 'Re-narrating Feminist Stories' (p. 62).

41. Feminist Review Editorial Collective, 'A *Feminist Review* Roundtable on the Un/Certainties of the Routes of the Collective and the Journal', *Feminist Review*, 80 (2005), pp. 198–219 (p. 202).

42. Gail Lewis and Clare Hemmings, '"Where Might We Go If We Dare": Moving Beyond the "Thick, Suffocating Fog of Whiteness" in Feminism', *Feminist Theory* (2019), https://doi.org/10.1177%2F1464700119871220 (p. 7).

43. Feminist Review Editorial Collective, 'A *Feminist Review* Roundtable' (p. 201).

44. Feminist Review Editorial Collective, 'Editorial' (pp. 2–3).

45. Feminist Review Editorial Collective, 'A *Feminist Review* Roundtable' (pp. 201–3).

46. Outwrite Collective, 'Editorial Policy', *Outwrite Women's Newspaper*, 1 (1982), p. 2.

47. Ranu Samantrai, *AlterNatives: Black Feminism in the Postimperial Nation* (Stanford: Stanford University Press, 1982) (p. 7).

48. Outwrite Collective, 'Editorial Policy' (p. 2).

49. Margot Farnham, 'Interview with Shaila Shah, Teresa Hope, Frances Ellery and Nanda Sirker', *Trouble and Strife*, 15 (Spring 1989), pp. 46–52 (p. 46).

50. For an overview of all of the main stories the paper published, see Outwrite Collective, 'Outwrite: The Issues Covered', *Outwrite Women's Newspaper*, 71 (December 1988), pp. 20–1.

51. For example, Outwrite Collective, untitled, *Outwrite Women's Newspaper*, 13 (April 1983), p. 6; Outwrite Collective, 'Stop This Racism', *Outwrite Women's Newspaper*, 10 (January 1983), pp. 1 and 10.

52. For example, Sue F., 'Sisters Speak Out', *Outwrite Women's Newspaper*, 2 (April 1982), p. 1; Sisters Against Disablement, 'Sisters Against Disablement', *Outwrite Women's Newspaper*, 16 (July 1983), p. 2.

53. For example, Outwrite Collective, 'Women's Hospital – Fight for Life', *Outwrite Women's Newspaper*, 11 (February 1983), pp. 1 and 8–9 (p. 1); Outwrite Collective, 'Occupying for Change: South London Women's Hospital', *Outwrite Women's Newspaper*, 31 (December 1984), pp. 10–11; Shaila Shah, '"Not the Gentle Touch": Violent Eviction Does Not Deter Campaigners', *Outwrite Women's Newspaper*, 36 (May 1985), p. 5.

54. Rashida L. Harrison, 'Towards a Transnational Black Feminist Discourse: Women Writing Against States of Imperialism, 1975–1989' (unpublished doctoral thesis, Michigan State University, 2012) (pp. 159 and 182).

55. Samantrai, *AlterNatives* (p. 11).

56. See e.g. discussions in *London Women's Liberation Newsletter*, 278 (27 July 1982) and 279 (3 August 1982); Dena Attar, 'An Open Letter on Anti-Semitism and Racism', *Trouble and Strife*, 1 (Winter 1983), pp. 13–16.

57. See e.g. Gabrielle Griffin (ed.), *Feminist Activism in the 1990s* (London: Taylor & Francis, 1995); Sukhwant Dhaliwal and Nira Yuval-Davis (eds), *Women Against Fundamentalism: Stories of Dissent and Solidarity* (London: Lawrence and Wishart, 2014); Rahila Gupta (ed.), *From Homebreakers to Jailbreakers: Southall Black Sisters* (London: Zed Books, 2003).

58. Shabnam Grewal, Jackie Kay, Liliane Landor, Gail Lewis and Pratibha Parmar (eds), *Charting the Journey: Writings by Black and Third World Women* (London: Sheba Feminist Publishers, 1988) (pp. 2–3).

59. On the politics of naming fields, see e.g. Suki Ali, 'Feminism and Postcolonial: Knowledge/Politics', *Ethnic and Racial Studies*, 30:2 (2007),

pp. 191–212 (pp. 194–5); Lola Young, 'What Is Black British Feminism?', *Women: A Cultural Review*, 11:1/2 (2000), pp. 45–60.

60. Mirza, 'Introduction' (p. 5).
61. Razia Aziz, 'Feminism and the Challenge of Racism: Deviance or Difference?', in Helen Crowley and Susan Himmelweit (eds), *Knowing Women: Feminism and Knowledge* (Cambridge: Polity Press, 1992), pp. 291–305 (p. 292).
62. Avtar Brah, *Cartographies of Diaspora: Contesting Identities* (London: Routledge, 1996) (p. 108).
63. Suki Ali, 'Black Feminist Praxis: Some Reflections on Pedagogies and Politics in Higher Education', *Race Ethnicity and Education*, 12:1 (2009), pp. 79–86 (p. 82).
64. Gail Lewis, *'Race', Gender, Social Welfare: Encounters in a Postcolonial Society* (Cambridge: Polity Press, 2000) (pp. 34, 37 and 203).
65. Brah, *Cartographies* (pp. 186–7).
66. Kalwant Bhopal, *White Privilege: The Myth of the Post-Racial Society* (Bristol: Policy Press, 2018).
67. Yasmin Gunaratnam, *Researching 'Race' and Ethnicity: Methods, Knowledge and Power* (London: Sage, 2003) (p. 17).
68. Gail Lewis, talk at The Birkbeck Institute for Social Research, 'Citizenship, Gender and Diversity' (28 September 2012). Online recording: https://backdoorbroadcasting.net/2012/09/citizenship-gender-and-diversity/ (last accessed 21 October 2019).
69. Gail Lewis, 'Only Connect? The Difficult Imperatives of Being Minor', *European Journal of Women's Studies*, 20:1 (2013), pp. 3–7 (p. 5).
70. Brah, *Cartographies* (p. 109).
71. Kimberlé Crenshaw, 'Demarginalizing the Intersection of Race and Sex: A Black Feminist Critique of Antidiscrimination Doctrine, Feminist Theory and Antiracist Politics', *University of Chicago Legal Forum* (1989), pp. 139–67.
72. Kimberlé W. Crenshaw, 'Mapping the Margins: Intersectionality, Identity Politics and Violence Against Women of Color', *Stanford Law Review*, 43:6 (1991), pp. 1241–99.
73. Sumi Cho, Kimberlé Crenshaw and Leslie McCall, 'Toward a Field of Intersectionality Studies: Theory, Applications, and Praxis', *Signs: Journal of Women in Culture and Society*, 38:4 (2013), pp. 785–810.
74. Jennifer C. Nash, 'Re-thinking Intersectionality', *Feminist Review*, 89 (2008), pp. 1–15 (p. 2).
75. Avtar Brah and Ann Phoenix, 'Ain't I a Woman? Revisiting Intersectionality', *Journal of International Women's Studies*, 5:3 (2004), pp. 75–86 (p. 76).
76. The Combahee River Collective, 'A Black Feminist Statement', in Gloria T. Hull, Patricia Bell Scott and Barbara Smith (eds), *All the Women Are White, All the Blacks Are Men, But Some of Us Are Brave: Black Women's Studies* (New York: The Feminist Press, 1982), pp. 13–22 (p. 13).

77. Patricia Hill Collins, *Black Feminist Thought* (Abingdon, Oxon: Routledge, 2000) (pp. 21 and 246).

78. Sherene Razack, *Looking White People in the Eye: Gender, Race and Culture in Courtrooms and Classrooms* (Toronto: University of Toronto Press, 1998) (p. 13).

79. Sara Salem, 'Intersectionality and Its Discontents: Intersectionality as Traveling Theory', *European Journal of Women's Studies*, 25:4 (2018), pp. 403–18 (pp. 408 and 406). Italics in original.

80. In addition to Salem and sources cited below, see also Vivien M. May, '"Speaking into the Void"? Intersectionality Critiques and Epistemic Backlash', *Hypatia*, 29:1 (2014), pp. 94–112; Barbara Tomlinson, 'Colonizing Intersectionality: Replicating Racial Hierarchy in Feminist Academic Arguments', *Social Identities: Journal for the Study of Race, Nation and Culture*, 19:2 (2013), pp. 254–72.

81. Gail Lewis, 'Experiencing Intersectionality and Feminist Displacements', *Signs: Journal of Women in Culture and Society*, 38:4 (2013), pp. 869–92 (pp. 872 and 884).

82. Sirma Bilge, 'Intersectionality Undone: Saving Intersectionality from Feminist Intersectionality Studies', *Du Bois Review*, 10:2 (2013), pp. 405–24 (p. 418).

83. Sara Ahmed, *On Being Included: Racism and Diversity in Institutional Life* (London: Duke University Press, 2012) (p. 195, n. 18); see also Gloria Wekker, *White Innocence: Paradoxes of Colonialism and Race* (London: Duke University Press, 2017) (pp. 70–3).

84. Clare Hemmings, *Why Stories Matter: The Political Grammar of Feminist Theory* (London: Duke University Press, 2011).

85. Lynne Segal, *Why Feminism? Gender, Psychology, Politics* (Cambridge: Polity Press, 1999) (p. 4).

86. Young, 'What Is Black British Feminism?' (pp. 50, 46, 49 and 53–4). Italics in original.

87. Nirmal Puwar, 'Making Space for South Asian Women: What Has Changed since Feminist Review Issue 17?', *Feminist Review*, 66 (2000), pp. 131–46 (pp. 134–6).

88. Nirmal Puwar, *Space Invaders: Race, Gender and Bodies Out of Place* (Oxford: Berg, 2004).

89. Sara Ahmed, 'Embodying Diversity: Problems and Paradoxes for Black Feminists', *Race, Ethnicity and Education*, 12:1 (2009), pp. 41–52 (p. 44).

90. Ahmed, *On Being Included* (p. 151).

91. Ahmed, 'Embodying Diversity' (p. 42).

92. See e.g. Deborah Gabriel and Shirley Anne Tate (eds), *Inside the Ivory Tower: Narratives of Women of Colour Surviving and Thriving in British Academia* (London: UCL Institute of Education Press, 2017); Azeezat Johnson, Remi Joseph-Salisbury and Beth Kamunge (eds), *The Fire Now: Anti-Racist Scholarship in Times of Explicit Racial Violence* (London: Zed

Books, 2018); Gurminder K. Bhambra, Dalia Gebrial and Kerem Nişancioğlu, *Decolonising the University* (London: Pluto Press, 2018).

93. Heidi Safia Mirza and Yasmin Gunaratnam, "'The Branch on Which I Sit": Reflections on Black British Feminism', *Feminist Review*, 108 (2014), pp. 125–33 (pp. 131 and 126).

94. Joan Anim-Addo, 'Activist-Mothers Maybe, Sisters Surely? Black British Feminism, Absence and Transformation', *Feminist Review*, 108 (2014), pp. 44–60 (p. 54).

95. Bhopal, *White Privilege* (p. 52).

96. Samantrai, *AlterNatives* (pp. 2–3).

CHAPTER 3   LEAVING FEMINIST WHITENESS BEHIND: NARRATIVES OF TRANSCENDENCE IN THE ERA OF DIFFERENCE

1. Angela McRobbie, *The Aftermath of Feminism: Gender, Culture and Social Change* (London: Sage, 2009); Kath Woodward and Sophie Woodward, *Why Feminism Matters: Feminism Lost and Found* (Basingstoke: Palgrave Macmillan, 2009); Catherine Redfern and Kristin Aune, *Reclaiming the F Word: The New Feminist Movement* (London: Zed Books, 2010); Shelley Budgeon, *Third Wave Feminism and the Politics of Gender in Late Modernity* (Basingstoke: Palgrave Macmillan, 2011); Sylvia Walby, *The Future of Feminism* (Cambridge: Polity Press, 2011).

2. Sara Ahmed, *Living a Feminist Life* (London: Duke University Press, 2017).

3. Angela McRobbie, 'Post-Feminism and Popular Culture', *Feminist Media Studies*, 4:3 (2004), pp. 255–64. As of October 2019, Google Scholar listed over 3100 citations for *The Aftermath of Feminism* and over 1400 citations for the 2004 article.

4. Woodward and Woodward, *Why Feminism Matters* (p. 18); Walby, *Future* (pp. 1–2).

5. McRobbie, *Aftermath* (pp. 1, 26–30 and 164).

6. Kimberly Springer, 'Third Wave Black Feminism?', *Signs: Journal of Women in Culture and Society*, 27:4 (2002), pp. 1059–82 (p. 1061).

7. Woodward and Woodward, *Why Feminism Matters* (p. 168).

8. Redfern and Aune, *Reclaiming the F Word* (chapters 1, 3 and 6).

9. For example, Kira Cochrane, 'Feminism Is Not Finished', *Guardian* (24 July 2010), www.theguardian.com/lifeandstyle/2010/jul/24/feminism-not-finished-not-uncool (last accessed 21 October 2019); Cassandra Jardine, 'Feminism Is Showing Signs of Life', *Telegraph* (9 March 2010), www.telegraph.co.uk/lifestyle/7400365/Feminism-is-showing-signs-of-life.html (last accessed 21 October 2019); Susie Mesure, 'The March of the New Feminists', *Independent* (29 November 2009), www.independent.co.uk/news/uk/home-news/the-march-of-the-new-feminists-1830514.html (last accessed 21 October 2019); No author, 'New Feminism Has Started the

Fight-Back at Last', *Evening Standard* (7 June 2010), www.standard.co.uk/news/new-feminism-has-started-the-fight-back-at-last-6477572.html (last accessed 21 October 2019); Susan Hogan, 'Reclaiming the F Word: The New Feminist Movement', *Times Higher Education* (1 July 2010), www.timeshighereducation.co.uk/story.asp?sectioncode=26&storycode=412277 (last accessed 21 October 2019).

10. Redfern and Aune, *Reclaiming the F Word*. With the exception of a new preface, the two editions are substantially the same.
11. Walby, *Future* (pp. 9 and 1–2).
12. McRobbie, *Aftermath* (pp. 152–6).
13. Walby, *Future* (p. 162).
14. Clare Hemmings, 'Telling Feminist Stories', *Feminist Theory*, 6:2 (2005), pp. 115–139 (pp. 122–3).
15. Redfern and Aune, *Reclaiming the F Word* (p. x).
16. Carli-Ria Rowell, 'Reclaiming the F Word' (review), *Sociological Research Online* (2014), www.socresonline.org.uk/19/1/reviews/3.html (last accessed 21 October 2019).
17. Redfern and Aune, *Reclaiming the F Word* (pp. 19 and 115; see also pp. 126, 30 and 107).
18. Ibid. (p. 154).
19. Ibid. (pp. xi and 207).
20. Ibid. (pp. 236, 6 and 205).
21. Walby, *Future* (pp. 64 and 61).
22. Ibid. (pp. 5, 26–51 and 53–5).
23. Mary-Jo Nadeau, 'Troubling Herstory: Unsettling White Multiculturalism in Canadian Feminism', *Canadian Woman Studies/Les Cahiers de la Femme*, 27:2/3 (2009), pp. 6–13 (pp. 11 and 9).
24. Walby, *Future* (p. 61).
25. McRobbie, *Aftermath* (pp. 25, 30 and 9).
26. Ibid. (p. 13).
27. See e.g. Kum-Kum Bhavnani and Margaret Coulson, 'Transforming Socialist-Feminism: The Challenge of Racism', *Feminist Review*, 23 (1986), pp. 81–92.
28. No author, 'Composite Report from the Sunday Workshops on Socialist Feminism', *Scarlet Women: Journal of the Socialist Feminist Current of the WLM* (July 1979) (p. 8).
29. Trinh T. Minh-ha, *Woman, Native, Other: Writing Postcoloniality and Feminism* (Bloomington, IN: Indiana University Press, 1989); Chandra Talpade Mohanty, 'Under Western Eyes: Feminist Scholarship and Colonial Discourses', *Feminist Review*, 30 (1988), pp. 61–88; Gayatri Chakravorty Spivak, *Can the Subaltern Speak? Marxism and the Interpretation of Culture* (Urbana: University of Illinois Press, 1988), pp. 271–313.
30. Hazel Carby, 'White Woman Listen! Black Feminism and the Boundaries of Sisterhood', in Centre for Cultural Studies (ed.), *The Empire Strikes Back:*

Race and Racism in 70s Britain (London: Hutchinson, 1982), pp. 211–234 (p. 230).

31. Woodward and Woodward, Why Feminism Matters (pp. 4 and 50).

32. Ibid. (pp. 15–16).

33. Hemmings, 'Telling Feminist Stories' (p. 123).

34. Budgeon, Third Wave Feminism (pp. 5, 8, 25–6).

35. Ibid. (pp. 8 and 25–6).

36. Woodward and Woodward, Why Feminism Matters (p. 16).

37. Ibid. (pp. 85–9).

38. Ibid. (pp. 87, 109, 89 and 166).

39. Ibid. (pp. 16, 23 and 15; for references to Walker, see pp. 14, 21, 43 and 50–1).

40. Ibid. (pp. 2–4).

41. Aileen Moreton-Robinson, Talkin' Up to the White Woman: Indigenous Women and Feminism (Queensland: University of Queensland Press, 2000) (p. 144).

42. Woodward and Woodward, Why Feminism Matters (p. 166).

43. Budgeon, Third Wave Feminism (p. 128).

44. Rebecca L. Clark Mane, 'Transmuting Grammars of Whiteness in Third-Wave Feminism: Interrogating Postrace Histories, Postmodern Abstraction, and the Proliferation of Difference in Third-Wave Texts', Signs: Journal of Women in Culture and Society, 38:1 (2012), pp. 71–97 (p. 77).

45. Budgeon, Third Wave Feminism (p. 8).

46. Clark Mane, 'Transmuting' (pp. 79 and 89).

47. Budgeon, Third Wave Feminism (pp. 8 and 168).

48. Avtar Brah, Cartographies of Diaspora: Contesting Identities (London: Routledge, 1996) (pp. 117 and 95–127).

49. Walby, Future (pp. 61–2, 64 and 125–46).

50. Ibid. (pp. 126, 128–38, 161–2).

51. Ibid. (pp. 7–8).

52. Ibid. (pp. 17 and 126).

53. Sara Salem and Vanessa Thompson, 'Old Racisms, New Masks: On the Continuing Discontinuities of Racism and the Erasure of Race in European Contexts', Nineteen Sixty Nine: An Ethnic Studies Journal, 3:1 (2016), https://escholarship.org/uc/item/98p8q169 (last accessed 21 October 2019) (p. 3).

54. Weiner in ibid. (p. 3).

55. Salem and Thompson, 'Old Racisms' (p. 3).

56. Walby, Futures (p. 160).

57. Ibid. (p. 145).

58. Gurminder K. Bhambra, 'Whither Europe?', Interventions, 18:2 (2016), pp. 187–202 (pp. 198–9).

59. Peo Hansen and Stefan Jonsson, 'Another Colonialism: Africa in the History of European Integration', Journal of Historical Sociology, 27:3 (2014), pp. 442–61 (p. 454).

60. Missing Migrants: Tracking Deaths Along Migratory Routes, https://missingmigrants.iom.int/region/mediterranean (last accessed 17 October 2019).

61. Walby, *Future* (p. 6).

62. McRobbie, *Aftermath* (pp. 69 and 146–7).

63. Redfern and Aune, *Reclaiming the F Word* (pp. 204–5).

64. Valerie Wagner, 'In the Name of Feminism', in Diane Elam and Robyn Wiegman (eds), *Feminism Beside Itself* (New York: Routledge, 1995), pp. 119–30 (p. 128).

65. Ien Ang, 'I'm a Feminist But ... "Other" Women and Postnational Feminism', in Reina Lewis and Sara Mills (eds), *Feminist Postcolonial Theory: A Reader* (Edinburgh: Edinburgh University Press, 2003), pp. 190–206 (pp. 190 and 203). Italics in original.

66. Redfern and Aune, *Reclaiming the F Word* (p. 17).

67. Ang, 'I'm a Feminist But ...' (p. 203).

68. McRobbie, *Aftermath* (pp. 164–70 and 151).

69. Nicola Rollock, 'Unspoken Rules of Engagement: Navigating Racial Microaggressions in the Academic Terrain', *International Journal of Qualitative Studies in Education*, 25:5 (2012), pp. 517–32; Shirley Anne Tate, 'Racial Affective Economies, Disalienation and "Race Made Ordinary"', *Ethnic and Racial Studies*, 37:13 (2013), pp. 2475–90; Kalwant Bhopal, *The Experiences of Black and Minority Ethnic Academics: A Comparative Study of the Unequal Academy* (Abingdon: Routledge, 2015); Heidi Safia Mirza, 'Decolonizing Higher Education: Black Feminism and the Intersectionality of Race and Gender', *Journal of Feminist Scholarship*, 7/8 (2015), pp. 1–12; Claire Alexander and Jason Arday, *Aiming Higher: Race, Inequality and Diversity in the Academy* (London: Runnymede Trust, 2015), www.runnymedetrust.org/uploads/Aiming%20Higher.pdf (last accessed 21 October 2019).

70. Heidi Safia Mirza, '"One in a Million": A Journey of a Post-Colonial Woman of Colour in the White Academy', in Deborah Gabriel and Shirley Anne Tate (eds), *Inside the Ivory Tower: Narratives of Women of Colour Surviving and Thriving in British Academia* (London: Institute of Education Press, 2017), pp. 39–53 (p. 39).

71. Joan Anim-Addo, 'Activist-Mothers Maybe, Sisters Surely? Black British Feminism, Absence and Transformation', *Feminist Review*, 108 (2014), pp. 44–60 (p. 56).

72. Suki Ali, 'Feminism and Postcolonial: Knowledge/Politics', *Ethnic and Racial Studies*, 30:2 (2007), pp. 191–212 (p. 203).

73. Aída Hurtado and Abigail J. Stewart, 'Through the Looking Glass: Implications of Studying Whiteness for Feminist Methods', in Michelle Fine, Lois Weis, Linda C. Powell and L. Mun Wong (eds), *Off White: Readings on Race, Power, and Society* (London: Routledge, 1997), pp. 297–311 (pp. 300–3).

74. Gail Lewis and Clare Hemmings, "'Where Might We Go If We Dare": Moving Beyond the "Thick, Suffocating Fog of Whiteness" in Feminism', *Feminist Theory* (2019), https://doi.org/10.1177%2F1464700119871220 (p. 9).

75. Sara Ahmed, 'Declarations of Whiteness: The Non-Performativity of Anti-Racism', *borderlands*, 3:2 (2004), www.borderlands.net.au/vol3no2_2004/ ahmed_declarations.htm (last accessed 19 October 2019) (paragraph 11).

CHAPTER 4   INEVITABLE WHITENESS?
ABSOLVING WHITE FEMINIST DOMINANCE

1. Elizabeth Evans, *The Politics of Third Wave Feminisms: Neoliberalism, Intersectionality, and the State in Britain and the US* (Basingstoke: Palgrave Macmillan, 2015); Finn Mackay, *Radical Feminism: Feminist Activism in Movement* (Basingstoke: Palgrave Macmillan, 2015); Prudence Chamberlain, *The Feminist Fourth Wave: Affective Temporality* (Cham, Switzerland: Springer Nature, 2017).

2. Evans, *Politics* (pp. 10 and 39–59).

3. Mackay, *Radical Feminism* (p. 15).

4. Ibid. (pp. 15 and 227–38). On transphobia in radical feminism, see e.g. Ray Filar, 'You Can't Smash the Patriarchy with Transphobia', *The F-Word* (3 September 2011), https://thefword.org.uk/2011/09/radical_feminism_ transphobia/ (last accessed 21 October 2019); Laura, 'There's Nothing Radical About Transphobia', *The F-Word* (17 May 2012), https://thefword. org.uk/2012/05/theres_nothing/ (last accessed 21 October 2019); Sophie Lewis, 'How British Feminism Became Anti-Trans', *New York Times* (7 February 2019), www.nytimes.com/2019/02/07/opinion/terf-trans-women-britain.html (last accessed 21 October 2019); Sam Hope, *A Feminist Challenging Transphobia* (blog), https://feministchallengingtransphobia. wordpress.com/ (last accessed 21 October 2019).

5. Chamberlain, *Feminist Fourth Wave* (pp. 10 and 186).

6. Evans, *Politics* (pp. 3 and 87–110).

7. Mackay, *Radical Feminism* (pp. 19, 135 and 101).

8. Chamberlain, *Feminist Fourth Wave* (pp. 52 and 74).

9. See e.g. Astrid Henry, *Not My Mother's Sister: Generational Conflict and Third Wave Feminism* (Bloomington, IN: Indiana University Press, 2004); Stacey Gillis, Gillian Howie and Rebecca Munford (eds), *Third Wave Feminism: A Critical Exploration*, 2nd edition (Basingstoke: Palgrave Macmillan, 2007); Jonathan Dean, 'Who's Afraid of Third Wave Feminism?', *International Feminist Journal of Politics*, 11:3 (2009), pp. 334–52; Jonathan Dean and Kristin Aune, 'Feminism Resurgent? Mapping Contemporary Feminist Activisms in Europe', *Social Movement Studies*, 14:4 (2015), pp. 375–95.

10. Kimberly Springer, 'Third Wave Black Feminism?', *Signs: Journal of Women in Culture and Society*, 27:4 (2002), pp. 1059–82 (p. 1061).
11. Chamberlain, *Feminist Fourth Wave* (p. 51).
12. Evans, *Politics* (pp. 5 and 38).
13. Chamberlain, *Feminist Fourth Wave* (pp. 36–9).
14. Ibid. (pp. 29 and 4).
15. Evans, *Politics* (pp. 49–50).
16. Mackay, *Radical Feminism* (pp. 6–7).
17. Ibid. (p. 136).
18. Ibid. (pp. 51–2).
19. Ibid. (pp. 17–18).
20. Sara Ahmed, 'Embodying Diversity: Problems and Paradoxes for Black Feminists', *Race, Ethnicity and Education*, 12:1 (2009), pp. 41–52 (p. 42).
21. Avtar Brah, *Cartographies of Diaspora: Contesting Identities* (London: Routledge, 1996); Gail Lewis, *'Race', Gender, Social Welfare: Encounters in a Postcolonial Society* (Cambridge: Polity Press, 2000); Gail Lewis, 'Only Connect? The Difficult Imperatives of Being Minor', *European Journal of Women's Studies*, 20:1 (2013), pp. 3–7; Yasmin Gunaratnam, *Researching 'Race' and Ethnicity: Methods, Knowledge and Power* (London: Sage, 2003).
22. Evans, *Politics* (pp. 8 and 204).
23. Ibid. (pp. 91–2).
24. Ibid. (p. 89).
25. Ibid. (p. 90).
26. Ibid. (pp. 50 and 52–3).
27. Sirma Bilge, 'Intersectionality Undone: Saving Intersectionality from Feminist Intersectionality Studies', *Du Bois Review*, 10:2 (2013), pp. 405–24.
28. Sumi Cho, Kimberlé Crenshaw and Leslie McCall, 'Toward a Field of Intersectionality Studies: Theory, Applications, and Praxis', *Signs: Journal of Women in Culture and Society*, 38:4 (2013), pp. 785–810 (p. 788).
29. Evans, *Politics* (pp. 57 and 59).
30. Ibid. (pp. 59 and 39).
31. Ibid. (pp. 59, 39 and 57).
32. Bilge, 'Intersectionality Undone' (pp. 405 and 407–8).
33. Evans, *Politics* (p. 57).
34. Cho et al., 'Toward a Field' (pp. 789 and 791).
35. Evans, *Politics* (pp. 49–51).
36. Ibid. (pp. 88–90).
37. Chamberlain, *Feminist Fourth Wave* (p. 167).
38. Ibid. (p. 117); Black Women's Blueprint et al., 'An Open Letter from Black Women to Slutwalk Organizers', *Huffington Post* (27 September 2011), www.huffpost.com/entry/slutwalk-black-women_b_980215 (last accessed 21 October 2019).
39. Mikki Kendall, '#SolidarityIsForWhiteWomen: Women of Color's Issue with Digital Feminism', *Guardian* (14 August 2013), www.theguardian.

com/commentisfree/2013/aug/14/solidarityisforwhitewomen-hashtag-feminism (last accessed 21 October 2019); @tgirlinterruptd et al., 'This Tweet Called My Back', *Model View Culture* (13 December 2014), https://modelviewculture.com/pieces/thistweetcalledmyback (last accessed 21 October 2019).

40. Lola Okolosie, 'Beyond "Talking" and "Owning" Intersectionality', *Feminist Review*, 108 (2014), pp. 90–6 (p. 92).

41. Chamberlain, *Feminist Fourth Wave* (p. 139).

42. Jessica Elgot, '#killallwhitemen Row: Charges Dropped Against Student Diversity Officer', *Guardian* (3 November 2015), www.theguardian.com/world/2015/nov/03/bahar-mustafa-charges-dropped-killallwhitemen-row (last accessed 21 October 2019).

43. Chamberlain, *Feminist Fourth Wave* (pp. 142–6 and 150).

44. Ibid. (pp. 168–71).

45. Ibid. (p. 171).

46. Uma Narayan, *Dislocating Cultures: Identities, Traditions and Third-World Feminism* (New York: Routledge, 1997); Chandra Talpade Mohanty, 'Under Western Eyes: Feminist Scholarship and Colonial Discourses', *Feminist Review*, 30 (1988), pp. 61–88.

47. Chamberlain, *Feminist Fourth Wave* (pp. 169 and 174).

48. Ibid. (p. 178).

49. Sara Ahmed, 'Affective Economies', *Social Text*, 22:2 (2004), pp. 117–39. For Chamberlain's use of Ahmed, see Chamberlain, *Feminist Fourth Wave* (chapter 4).

50. Naaz Rashid, *Veiled Threats: Representing 'the Muslim Woman' in UK Public Policy Discourses* (Bristol: Policy Press, 2016) (p. 32).

51. Liz Fekete, *A Suitable Enemy: Racism, Migration and Islamophobia in Europe* (London: Pluto Press, 2009); Arun Kundnani, *The Muslims Are Coming! Islamophobia, Extremism and the Domestic War on Terror* (London: Verso, 2014).

52. Kundnani, *The Muslims* (section 2, paragraph 22 of 'Introduction' in ebook).

53. HM Government, *Revised Prevent Duty Guidance: For England and Wales* (2015), https://assets.publishing.service.gov.uk/government/uploads/system/uploads/attachment_data/file/445977/3799_Revised_Prevent_Duty_Guidance__England_Wales_V2-Interactive.pdf (last accessed 21 October 2019).

54. See e.g. Open Society Justice Initiative, *Eroding Trust: The UK's Prevent Counter-Extremism Strategy in Health and Education* (New York: Open Society Foundations, 2016), www.justiceinitiative.org/uploads/f87bd3ad-50fb-42d0-95a8-54ba85dce818/eroding-trust-20161017_0.pdf (last accessed 21 October 2019); Barbara Cohen and Waqas Tufail, 'Prevent and the Normalization of Islamophobia', in Farah Elahi and Omar Khan (eds),

Islamophobia: Still a Challenge for Us All. A 20th-Anniversary Report (London: The Runnymede Trust, 2017).

55. Rashid, *Veiled Threats* (p. 178).

56. Gurminder Bhambra, 'Europe Won't Resolve the "Migrant Crisis" Until It Faces Its Own Past', *The Conversation* (1 September 2015), https://theconversation.com/europe-wont-resolve-the-migrant-crisis-until-it-faces-its-own-past-46555 (last accessed 21 October 2019).

57. bell hooks, *Feminist Theory: From Margin to Center* (Boston, MA: South End Press, 1984).

58. Mackay, *Radical Feminism* (pp. 91–2).

59. Ibid. (p. 93).

60. Bhavnani and Coulson, cited in Mackay, *Radical Feminism* (p. 94).

61. Mackay, *Radical Feminism* (p. 95).

62. RTN Hackney organisers, untitled letter, *London Women's Liberation Newsletter*, 261 (30 March 1982); Liz Dew, 'Some Confused Thoughts on Reclaim the Night Marches', *London Women's Liberation Newsletter*, 261 (30 March 1982).

63. Mackay, *Radical Feminism* (pp. 96, 100–1).

64. Ibid. (pp. 96 and 99).

65. Angela Davis, *Women, Race and Class* (London: The Women's Press, 1982) (p. 185).

66. Vron Ware, *Beyond the Pale: White Women, Racism and History*, 2nd edition (London: Verso, 2015) (p. 181). First published 1992.

67. Hazel Carby, '"On the Threshold of Woman's Era": Lynching, Empire and Sexuality in Black Feminist Theory', *Critical Inquiry*, 12:2 (1985), pp. 262–77 (p. 270).

68. Ware, *Beyond the Pale* (p. 38).

69. Davis, *Women, Race and Class* (pp. 181–2 and 178).

70. Mackay, *Radical Feminism* (pp. 42, 45, 76, 278).

71. Valerie Amos and Pratibha Parmar, 'Challenging Imperial Feminism', *Feminist Review*, 17 (1984), pp. 3–19 (p. 14). The quote in the last sentence comes from Vron Ware, 'Imperialism, Racism and Violence Against Women', *Emergency*, 1 (Winter 1983/84), pp. 25–30.

72. Kum-Kum Bhavnani, 'Contribution to "A Decade in Feminism"', *Spare Rib*, 150 (January 1985) (p. 23).

73. Sara Ahmed, *On Being Included: Racism and Diversity in Institutional Life* (London: Duke University Press, 2012) (p. 210, n. 8).

74. Thank you to Sarah Keenan for drawing my attention to the legal connotations of this framing.

75. Philomena Essed, 'Everyday Racism', in David Theo Goldberg and John Solomos (eds), *A Companion to Racial and Ethnic Studies* (Oxford: Blackwell Publishers, 2002), pp. 202–16 (p. 210).

76. Mary Louise Fellows and Sherene Razack, 'The Race to Innocence: Confronting Hierarchical Relations Among Women', *Journal of Gender, Race and Justice*, 1 (1998), pp. 335–52.

77. Kay Stephens, '"Asian Grooming Gangs": Media, State and the Far Right', *Institute of Race Relations* (8 March 2019), www.irr.org.uk/news/asian-grooming-gangs-media-state-and-the-far-right/ (last accessed 21 October 2019); Stefanie C. Boulila and Christiane Carri, 'On Cologne: Gender, Migration and Unacknowledged Racisms in Germany', *European Journal of Women's Studies*, 24:3 (2017), pp. 286–93.

78. Pragna Patel, 'Third Wave Feminism and Black Women's Activism', in Heidi Safia Mirza (ed.), *Black British Feminism* (London: Routledge, 1997), pp. 255–68.

79. Heidi Safia Mirza and Yasmin Gunaratnam, '"The Branch on Which I Sit": Reflections on Black British Feminism', *Feminist Review*, 108 (2014), pp. 125–33 (p. 127); Sara Ahmed, 'Black Feminism as Life-Line', *feministkilljoys* (27 August 2013), https://feministkilljoys.com/2013/08/27/black-feminism-as-life-line/ (last accessed 21 October 2019).

CHAPTER 5   LIBERAL WHITENESS
AND THE 'NEW' FEMINISM

1. Angela McRobbie, *The Aftermath of Feminism: Gender, Culture and Social Change* (London: Sage, 2009); Gabrielle Griffin (ed.), *Feminist Activism in the 1990s* (London: Taylor & Francis, 1995).

2. Catherine Redfern and Kristin Aune, *Reclaiming the F Word: The New Feminist Movement* (London: Zed Books, 2010).

3. Natasha Walter, *The New Feminism* (London: Virago Press, 1999); Ellie Levenson, *The Noughtie Girl's Guide to Feminism* (Oxford: Oneworld Publications, 2009); Caitlin Moran, *How to Be a Woman* (UK: Ebury Press, 2011).

4. For example, Kat Banyard, *The Equality Illusion: The Truth About Women and Men Today* (London: Faber & Faber, 2010); Hadley Freeman, *Be Awesome: Modern Life for Modern Ladies* (London: Fourth Estate, 2013); Laura Bates, *Everyday Sexism* (London: Simon & Schuster, 2014); Caroline Criado-Perez, *Do It Like a Woman: ... and Change the World* (London: Portobello Books, 2015); Deborah Frances-White, *The Guilty Feminist: From Our Noble Goals to Our Worst Hypocrisies* (London: Virago Press, 2018). The latter fits my selection criteria, but was published after the research for this chapter had been completed.

5. Kira Cochrane (ed.), *Women of the Revolution: Forty Years of Feminism* (London: Guardian Books, 2010).

6. Kaitlynn Mendes, *Feminism in the News: Representations of the Women's Movement since the 1960s* (Basingstoke: Palgrave Macmillan, 2011) (p. 147).

7. Charles W. Mills, 'Racial Liberalism', *PMLA*, 123:5 (2008), pp. 1380–97 (p. 1380).

8. Loretta Kensinger, '(In)Quest of Liberal Feminism', *Hypatia*, 12:4 (1997), pp. 178–97 (p. 184).

9. Mills, 'Racial Liberalism' (p. 1386).

10. Carole Pateman, *The Sexual Contract* (Cambridge: Polity Press, 1988).

11. bell hooks, *Feminist Theory: From Margin to Center* (Boston, MA: South End Press, 1984) (pp. 20–1).

12. See e.g. Open Society Justice Initiative, *Eroding Trust: The UK's Prevent Counter-Extremism Strategy in Health and Education* (New York: Open Society Foundations, 2016), www.justiceinitiative.org/uploads/f87bd3ad-50fb-42d0-95a8-54ba85dce818/eroding-trust-20161017_0.pdf (last accessed 21 October 2019).

13. Reni Eddo-Lodge, *Why I'm No Longer Talking to White People About Race* (London: Bloomsbury Circus, 2017) (pp. ix–x).

14. Joanne Hollows and Rachel Moseley, 'Popularity Contests: The Meanings of Popular Feminism', in Joanne Hollows and Rachel Moseley (eds), *Feminism in Popular Culture* (Oxford: Berg, 2006), pp. 1–23.

15. Sarah Banet-Weiser, Rosalind Gill and Catherine Rottenberg, 'Postfeminism, Popular Feminism and Neoliberal Feminism?', *Feminist Theory* (2019), https://doi.org/10.1177/1464700119842555.

16. Rosalind Gill, 'Post-Postfeminism? New feminist Visibilities in Postfeminist Times', *Feminist Media Studies*, 16:4 (2016), pp. 610–30 (pp. 614–18).

17. For instance, 'feminism' was the most looked-up word of the year in 2017 in Merriam-Webster's online dictionary: No author, 'Merriam-Webster's 2017 Words of the Year', www.merriam-webster.com/words-at-play/word-of-the-year-2017-feminism/feminism (last accessed 18 October 2019).

18. Redfern and Aune, *Reclaiming the F Word*.

19. Many of the original blog posts no longer exist, but for some context read: brownfemipower, no title, *bfpfinal* (16 April 2008), https://bfpfinal.wordpress.com/2008/04/16/3/ (last accessed 21 October 2019); Ann, 'Brownfemipower, WOC, and the Appropriation of Lives Lived', *Beautiful, Also, Are the Souls of my Black Sisters* (11 April 2008), https://kathmanduk2.wordpress.com/2008/04/11/brownfemipower-woc-and-the-appropriation-of-lives-lived/ (last accessed 21 October 2019); Anonymous, 'An Open Letter to the White Feminist Community', *Dear White Feminists* (17 April 2008), https://dearwhitefeminists.wordpress.com/ (last accessed 21 October 2019).

20. As above, but see Factora-Borchers, 'A Book Is Never Just a Book: Thoughts on Full, Frontal Feminism', *myecdysis* (24 May 2007), www.myecdysis.com/2007/05/a-book-is-never-just-a-book-thoughts-on-full-frontal-feminism/ (last accessed 21 October 2019); Kate Tuttle, 'The Jungle Book', *The Root* (3 June 2008), www.theroot.com/the-jungle-book-1790899895 (last accessed 21 October 2019).

21. For example, zoora moosa, 'Race and Gender in Blogland', *The F-Word* (10 August 2007), www.thefword.org.uk/blog/2007/08/race_and_gender (last accessed 21 October 2019); zoora moosa, 'Three Suggestions re Feminism and White Privilege (1)', *The F-Word* (30 April 2008), www.thefword.org.

uk/blog/2008/04/three_suggestio (last accessed 21 October 2019); Annika Spalding, 'Whose Feminism Is It?', *The F-Word* (September 2008), www.thefword.org.uk/features/2008/09/feminism_of_tod (last accessed 21 October 2019); Terese Jonsson, 'Piercing the Whitening Silence', *The F-Word* (March 2009), www.thefword.org.uk/features/2009/03/piercing_the_wh (last accessed 21 October 2019); Holly Combe, 'Oppression Olympics: The Privilege Paradox?', *The F-Word* (23 August 2010, www.thefword.org.uk/blog/2010/08/oppression_olym (last accessed 21 October 2019).

22. Black Feminists UK, 'Learning from the Journey to Here for the Journey to Come', *Black Feminists* (13 October 2011), www.blackfeminists.org/2011/10/13/learning-from-the-journey-to-here-for-the-journeys-to-come/ (last accessed 5 September 2013).

23. MsAfropolitan, 'Riot, Rage and Rebellion', *Black Feminists* (10 August 2011), www.blackfeminists.org/2011/08/10/riot-rage-and-rebellion/ (last accessed 5 September 2013); Charmaine Elliott, 'I Loot, Therefore I Am', *Black Feminists* (10 August 2011), www.blackfeminists.org/2011/08/10/i-loot-therefore-i-am/ (last accessed 5 September 2013); Lola Okolosie, 'We Need to Listen', *Black Feminists* (12 August 2011), www.blackfeminists.org/2011/08/12/we-need-to-listen/ (last accessed 5 September 2013); Donolea, 'Justice for One But Not for All', *Black Feminists* (5 January 2012), www.blackfeminists.org/2012/01/05/justice-for-one-but-not-for-all/ (last accessed 5 September 2013); Lola Okolosie, 'Racism: A Clear and Present Danger', *Black Feminists* (5 January 2012), www.blackfeminists.org/2012/01/05/racism-a-clear-and-present-danger/ (last accessed 5 September 2013); Anonymous, 'Let Us Talk About Racism When Discussing Identity, Belonging and Multiculturalism', *Black Feminists* (7 February 2011), www.blackfeminists.org/2011/02/07/let-us-talk-about-racism-when-discussing-identity-belonging-and-multiculturalism/ (last accessed 5 September 2013).

24. Adunni Adams, 'Feminism Is Not All White', *Black Feminists* (10 April 2012), www.blackfeminists.org/2012/04/10/feminism-is-not-all-white/ (last accessed 5 September 2013); Aisha Zakira, 'Response to the Guardian's Article "Why Is India So Bad for Women?"', *Black Feminists* (31 July 2012), www.blackfeminists.org/2012/07/31/response-to-the-guardians-article-why-is-india-so-bad-for-women/ (last accessed 5 September 2013).

25. Bim Adewunmi, 'What the Girls Spat on Twitter Tells Us About Feminism', *Guardian* (8 October 2012), www.theguardian.com/commentisfree/2012/oct/08/girls-twitter-feminism-caitlin-moran (last accessed 21 October 2019).

26. Stephanie Phillips, 'How to Be A RESPONSIBLE Woman', *Black Feminists* (9 October 2012), www.blackfeminists.org/2012/10/09/how-to-be-a-responsible-woman-caitlin-moran-lena-dunham/ (last accessed 13 September 2013); Leslie O'Neil, 'Caitlin Moran and Lena Dunham – "Girls" I'm All Too familiar with', *Black Feminists* (12 October 2012), www.

blackfeminists.org/2012/10/12/caitlin-moran-lena-dunham-girls-im-all-too-familiar-with/ (last accessed 13 September 2013); Natalie Ntim, 'We Need to Talk About Privilege', Black Feminists (22 October 2012), www.blackfeminists.org/2012/10/22/we-need-to-talk-about-privilege/ (last accessed 13 September 2013); Lianne, 'Dear Vagenda Editors ...', Black Feminists (23 October 2012), www.blackfeminists.org/2012/10/23/dear-vagenda-editors/ (last accessed 5 September 2013).

27. Phillips, 'How to Be'.

28. Louise Mensch, 'How About Some Reality-Based Feminism?', Guardian (30 May 2013), www.theguardian.com/commentisfree/2013/may/30/reality-based-feminism-louise-mensch (last accessed 18 October 2019); Julie Burchill, 'Don't You Dare Tell Me to Check My Privilege', The Spectator (22 February 2014), www.spectator.co.uk/2014/02/dont-you-dare-tell-me-to-check-my-privilege/ (last accessed 18 October 2019); Nick Cohen, 'How to Defend the Arts Using Liberal Values', The Spectator (1 October 2015), https://blogs.spectator.co.uk/2015/10/how-to-defend-the-arts-using-liberal-values/ (last accessed 18 October 2019); Tom Midlane, 'The Problem with Privilege-Checking', New Statesman (17 December 2012), www.newstatesman.com/politics/2012/12/problem-privilege-checking (last accessed 18 October 2019); Sadie Smith, 'There's No Point in Online Feminism If It's an Exclusive Mean Girls Club', New Statesman (21 March 2013), www.newstatesman.com/voices/2013/03/theres-no-point-online-feminism-if-its-exclusive-mean-girls-club (last accessed 18 October 2019).

29. Lola Okolosie, 'Beyond "Talking" and "Owning" Intersectionality', Feminist Review, 108 (2014), pp. 90–6 (pp. 90–3).

30. Rhiannon Lucy Cosslett and Holly Baxter, 'In Defence of Caitlin Moran and Populist Feminism', New Statesman (22 October 2012), www.newstatesman.com/lifestyle/2012/10/defence-caitlin-moran-and-populist-feminism (last accessed 21 October 2019).

31. Lianne, 'Dear Vagenda Editors'.

32. Gurminder K. Bhambra, 'Brexit, Trump, and "Methodological Whiteness": On the Misrecognition of Race and Class', The British Journal of Sociology, 68:S1 (2017), pp. S214–S232.

33. Eddo-Lodge, Why I'm No Longer (p. 165).

34. No author, 'The Guardian – Readership Figures', Media.Info (2014), https://media.info/newspapers/titles/the-guardian/readership-figures (last accessed 21 October 2019).

35. Walter, New Feminism (pp. 5–6, 63–4, 148 and 22).

36. Ibid. (p. 148).

37. For example, Southall Black Sisters, Against the Grain: Southall Black Sisters 1979–1989. A Celebration of Struggle and Survival (London: Southall Black Sisters, 1990).

38. Heidi Mirza, 'All White Now: Take a Closer Look at the Picture Painted in the Press of Britain's New Feminism. See Any Black Women? Heidi Safia

Mirza Doesn't and Says It Is Time They Were There', *Guardian* (2 February 1998) (p. 5).

39. Levenson, *Noughtie* (pp. 215 and xvii).

40. Ibid. (pp. xiv–xv and 209).

41. For example, Miranda Sawyer, 'How to Be a Woman By Caitlin Moran – Review', *Observer* (26 June 2011), www.theguardian.com/books/2011/jun/26/caitlin-moran-how-be-woman (last accessed 18 October 2019); Katy Guest, 'How to Be a Woman, By Caitlin Moran', *Independent* (3 July 2011), www.independent.co.uk/arts-entertainment/books/reviews/how-to-be-a-woman-by-caitlin-moran-2305805.html (last accessed 18 October 2019); Laurie Penny, Selma James, Zohra Moosa and Bella Mackie, 'Caitlin Moran's Feminist Handbook: Panel Verdict', *Guardian* (20 June 2011), www.theguardian.com/commentisfree/2011/jun/20/caitlin-moran-how-to-be-a-woman (last accessed 18 October 2019).

42. Moran, *How to Be a Woman* (pp. 12 and 77).

43. Levenson, *Noughtie* (p. xvi).

44. Moran, *How to Be a Woman* (p. 81).

45. Katherine Viner, 'Learning to Love Our Cellulite', *Guardian* (24 February 1999), www.theguardian.com/theguardian/1999/feb/24/features11.g23 (last accessed 21 October 2019); Lisa Jardine, 'Growing Up with Greer', *Observer* (7 October 1999), www.theguardian.com/books/1999/mar/07/society (last accessed 21 October 2019); Barbara Ellen, 'Germaine to the Issue', *Observer* (16 July 2000), www.theguardian.com/theobserver/2000/jul/16/features.magazine7 (last accessed 21 October 2019); Melissa Benn, 'Trailblazer of Feminism', *Guardian* (22 July 2000), www.theguardian.com/books/2000/jul/22/society (last accessed 21 October 2019); Rebecca Allison, 'The Term Has Been Equated with Hatred of Men', *Guardian* (2 July 2003), www.theguardian.com/uk/2003/jul/02/gender.women1 (last accessed 22 October 2019).

46. Benn, 'Trailblazer'; Gaby Wood, 'Call Me a Feminist', *Observer* (16 September 2001), www.theguardian.com/theobserver/2001/sep/16/featuresreview.review (last accessed 22 October 2019); Polly Toynbee, 'Feminism Today: The Myth of Women's Lib', *Guardian* (6 June 2002), www.theguardian.com/world/2002/jun/06/gender.pollytoynbee (last accessed 22 October 2019); Guardian staff, 'Timeline: Equality for Women', *Guardian* (2 July 2003), www.theguardian.com/politics/2003/jul/02/women.gender1 (last accessed 22 October 2019); Julie Bindel, 'Marching to Freedom', *Guardian* (22 November 2006), www.theguardian.com/society/2006/nov/22/publicvoices.crime (last accessed 22 October 2019); Louise France and Eva Wiseman, 'The New Feminists', *Observer* (9 September 2007), www.theguardian.com/lifeandstyle/2007/sep/09/women (last accessed 22 October 2019); Melissa Benn, 'A Most Unshowy Feminist Icon', *Guardian* (22 October 2008), www.theguardian.com/lifeandstyle/2008/oct/22/women-highereducation-sheila-rowbotham-feminism (last accessed 22

October 2019); Carole Cadwalladr, 'It's Been a Long Journey – and We're Not There Yet', *Observer* (7 December 2008), www.theguardian.com/ lifeandstyle/2008/dec/07/women-equality-rights-feminism-sexism-women-s-liberation-conference (last accessed 22 October 2019); Rachel Cooke, 'How Far Have We Come in 80 Years?', *Observer* (7 December 2008), www.guardian.co.uk/lifeandstyle/2008/dec/07/women-equality-rights-feminism (last accessed 22 October 2019); Viv Groskop, 'The Feminist Year Ahead', *Guardian* (8 January 2010), www.theguardian.com/ lifeandstyle/2010/jan/08/the-feminist-year-ahead (last accessed 22 October 2019); Kira Cochrane, 'Forty Years of Women's Liberation', *Guardian* (26 February 2010), www.theguardian.com/lifeandstyle/2010/feb/26/forty-years-womens-liberation (last accessed 22 October 2019); Charlotte Raven, 'How the "New Feminism" Went Wrong', *Observer* (26 February 2010), www.theguardian.com/lifeandstyle/2010/feb/26/forty-years-womens-liberation (last accessed 22 October 2019); Rachel Cooke, 'The Funny Side of Feminism', *Observer* (7 March 2010), www.theguardian.com/ commentisfree/2010/mar/07/susan-brownmiller-greer-feminism (last accessed 22 October 2019); Mariella Frostrup, 'Feminism's Global Challenge: With One Voice', *Observer* (6 March 2011), www.theguardian. com/society/2011/mar/06/feminism-global-challenge-one-voice (last accessed 22 October 2019); Kat Banyard, 'How to Create a Feminist Future', *Guardian* (16 August 2011), www.theguardian.com/lifeandstyle/the-womens-blog-with-jane-martinson/2011/aug/16/feminist-suffragette-school-activists (last accessed 22 October 2019).

47. Diane Abbott, 'A Race Against Time', *Guardian* (10 July 2008), www. theguardian.com/commentisfree/2008/jul/10/gender.women (last accessed 22 October 2019); Robin Morgan, Charlotte Raven, Amrit Wilson, Selma James, Gail Lewis and Nawal El Saadawi, 'International Women's Day: In Defence of Feminist Dissent', *Guardian* (7 March 2014), www.theguardian. com/commentisfree/2014/mar/07/international-womens-day-defence-feminist-dissent-argued-priorities (last accessed 22 October 2019); Zoe Williams and Polly Russell, 'Spare Rib: The Top 10 Reads from the Archives', *Guardian* (28 May 2015), www.theguardian.com/lifeandstyle/womens-blog/2015/may/28/spare-rib-the-top-10-reads-from-the-archives (last accessed 22 October 2019). For commemoration of WLM conferences, see e.g. Cochrane, 'Forty years of Women's Liberation'.

48. Bindel, 'Marching'; Sian Norris, 'Let's Make Some Noise', *Guardian* (26 November 2008), www.guardian.co.uk/lifeandstyle/2008/nov/26/women-feminism-groups (last accessed 22 October 2019); Kira Cochrane, 'Feminism Is Not Finished', *Guardian* (24 July 2010), www.guardian.co.uk/ lifeandstyle/2010/jul/24/feminism-not-finished-not-uncool (last accessed 22 October 2019); Lizzy Davies, 'Feminism Is Back and We Want to Finish the Revolution, Say Activists', *Guardian* (5 August 2011), www.theguardian. com/world/2011/aug/05/feminism-resurgent-activists (last accessed 22

October 2019); Alexandra Topping, 'Feminists Hail Explosion in New Grassroots Groups', *Guardian* (9 April 2012), www.guardian.co.uk/ world/2012/apr/09/feminists-hail-explosion-grassroots-groups (last accessed 22 October 2019)); Kira Cochrane, 'The Fourth Wave of Feminism: Meet the Rebel Women', *Guardian* (10 December 2013), www.theguardian. com/world/2013/dec/10/fourth-wave-feminism-rebel-women (last accessed 22 October 2019); Joan Smith, 'The Great Feminist Revival', *Guardian* (14 May 2013), www.theguardian.com/lifeandstyle/2013/ may/14/feminism-slutwalks-spare-rib (last accessed 22 October 2019); Laura Bates, '2014: A Year of Brave, Inspiring, Young Feminists', *Guardian* (18 December 2014), www.theguardian.com/lifeandstyle/womens-blog/2014/dec/18/year-of-brave-youg-inspirational-feminist-role-models (last accessed 22 October 2019).

49. Jess McCabe, 'Leading from the Front Page', *Guardian* (13 July 2007), www. theguardian.com/media/2007/jul/13/pressandpublishing.genderissues (last accessed 22 October 2019); Norris, 'Let's Make Some Noise'; Cochrane, 'Feminism Is Not Finished'; Banyard, 'How to Create a Feminist Future'; Topping, 'Feminists Hail'; Natalie Bennett, 'A Post-Feminist Age? Think Again', *Guardian* (9 February 2007), www.theguardian.com/education/ 2007/feb/09/highereducation.uk (last accessed 22 October 2019).

50. Charles Mills, 'White Ignorance', in Shannon Sullivan and Nancy Tuana (eds), *Race and Epistemologies of Ignorance* (Ithaca, NY: State University of New York Press, 2007), pp. 13–38 (pp. 16, 11 and 35).

51. For example, Walter, *New Feminism* (pp. 41, 148 and 257); Levenson, *Noughtie* (pp. xviii–xix); Moran, *How to Be a Woman* (pp. 81 and 88).

52. Walter, *New Feminism* (pp. 45–6).

53. Levenson, *Noughtie* (p. 26).

54. Valerie Amos and Pratibha Parmar, 'Challenging Imperial Feminism', *Feminist Review*, 17 (1984), pp. 3–19 (p. 3).

55. Levenson, *Noughtie* (p. xviii).

56. Walter, *New Feminism* (pp. 88 and 98).

57. Ibid. (pp. 211 and 213).

58. Moran, *How to Be a Woman* (p. 81).

59. Walter, *New Feminism* (pp. 51–2).

60. Chandra Talpade Mohanty, 'Under Western Eyes: Feminist Scholarship and Colonial Discourses', *Feminist Review*, 30 (1988), pp. 61–88 (pp. 61 and 79).

61. Levenson, *Noughtie* (pp. 6–8).

62. Ibid. (pp. 157–9).

63. Moran, *How to Be a Woman* (p. 87). Italics in original.

64. Lila Abu-Lughod, *Do Muslim Women Need Saving?* (Cambridge, MA: Harvard University Press, 2013).

65. Moran, *How to Be a Woman* (pp. 134–5).

66. Ibid. (pp. 137–8).

67. Ibid. (p. 98).

68. Walter, *New Feminism* (p. 175); Levenson, *Noughtie* (p. 195).
69. Walter, *New Feminism* (p. 173).
70. Ranu Samantrai, *AlterNatives: Black Feminism in the Postimperial Nation* (Stanford: Stanford University Press, 1982).
71. Amos and Parmar, 'Challenging Imperial Feminism' (p. 4).
72. For example, Kira Cochrane, 'Natasha Walter: "I Believed Sexism in Our Culture Would Wither Away. I was Entirely Wrong"', *Guardian* (25 January 2010), www.theguardian.com/lifeandstyle/2010/jan/25/natasha-walter-feminism-sexism-return (last accessed 22 October 2019); Cochrane, 'Feminism Is Not Finished'; Jane Martinson, 'Why Mumsnet and Social Media Are Important New Forums for Feminism', *Guardian* (30 August 2013), www.theguardian.com/lifeandstyle/2013/aug/30/mumsnet-social-media-forums-feminism (last accessed 22 October 2019); Davies, 'Feminism Is Back'; Kira Cochrane, Suzanne Moore, Natasha Walter, Jessica Valenti, Nawal El Saadawi and Bidisha, 'Forty Years of Women's Lib', *Guardian* (11 March 2011), www.theguardian.com/lifeandstyle/2011/mar/11/forty-years-of-womens-lib (last accessed 22 October 2019); Kira Cochrane, 'Why Kat Banyard Is the UK's Most Influential Young Feminist', *Guardian* (10 September 2010), www.theguardian.com/lifeandstyle/2010/sep/10/kat-banyard-influential-young-feminist (last accessed 22 October 2019); Jane Martinson, '10 Lessons I've Learned from Being Guardian Women's Editor', *Guardian* (2 September 2014), www.theguardian.com/lifeandstyle/2014/sep/02/jane-martinson-10-things-learned-womens-editor-guardian (last accessed 22 October 2019); Emine Saner, 'Why Romola Garai Wants Tesco to Lose the Lads' Mags', *Guardian* (29 July 2013), www.theguardian.com/lifeandstyle/the-womens-blog-with-jane-martinson/2013/jul/29/romola-garai-tesco-lads-mags (last accessed 22 October 2019); Vanessa Thorpe, 'What Now for Britain's New-Wave Feminists – After Page 3 and £10 Notes?', *Observer* (27 July 2013), www.theguardian.com/world/2013/jul/27/new-generation-of-feminists-set-agenda (last accessed 22 October 2019); Tracey McVeigh, 'Meet the New Wave of Activists Making Feminism Thrive in a Digital Age', *Observer* (1 June 2013), www.theguardian.com/world/2013/jun/01/activists-feminism-digital (last accessed 22 October 2019); Topping, 'Feminists Hail'; Lizzy Davies, 'Feminist Summer School: Training the New Generation of "Suffragettes"', *Guardian* (14 August 2011), www.theguardian.com/world/2011/aug/14/feminism-summer-school-uk-feminista (last accessed 22 October 2019); Davies, 'Feminism Is Back'; Jane Martinson, 'What Does Feminism Mean to You?', *Guardian* (22 October 2012); Tess Reidy, 'Young Feminists Join Together to "Organise a World Without Sexism"', *Guardian* (17 August 2013), www.theguardian.com/world/2013/aug/17/new-feminism-feminista-summer-school (last accessed 22 October 2019); Kira Cochrane, 'The Women Fighting Sexism in the Media – from Page 3 to Politics', *Guardian* (27 November 2012), www.theguardian.com/

media/2012/nov/27/women-fighting-sexism-media-page-3 (last accessed 22 October 2019); Decca Aitkenhead, 'Laura Bates Interview: "Two Years Ago, I Didn't Know What Feminism Meant"', *Guardian* (24 October 2014), www.theguardian.com/world/2014/jan/24/laura-bates-interview-everyday-sexism (last accessed 22 October 2019).

73. Nicholas Lezard, 'How to Be a Woman By Caitlin Moran – Review', *Guardian* (6 March 2012), www.theguardian.com/books/2012/mar/06/how-woman-caitlin-moran-review (last accessed 22 October 2019); Annabel Pitcher, 'My Hero: Caitlin Moran', *Guardian* (11 January 2013), www.theguardian.com/books/2013/jan/11/caitlin-moran-annabel-pitcher (last accessed 22 October 2019); Alex Clark, 'Caitlin Moran: "Let's All Go and Be Feminists in the Pub"', *Observer* (19 June 2011), www.theguardian.com/theobserver/2011/jun/19/caitlin-moran-feminism-interview (last accessed 22 October 2019); Aida Edemariam, 'The Saturday Interview: Caitlin Moran', *Guardian* (18 June 2011), www.theguardian.com/theguardian/2011/jun/18/caitlin-moran-interview-book-extract (last accessed 22 October 2019).

74. Cochrane, 'Natasha Walter'.

75. Clare Midgley, 'Anti-Slavery and the Roots of "Imperial Feminism"', in Clare Midgley (ed.), *Gender and Imperialism* (Manchester: Manchester University Press, 1998), pp. 161–70.

76. Cochrane, 'Why Kat Banyard'.

77. Aitkenhead, 'Laura Bates Interview'.

78. For example, Natasha Walter, 'I Was Wrong About Porn', *Guardian* (21 May 2005), www.theguardian.com/media/2005/may/21/gender.world (last accessed 22 October 2019); Natalie Hanman, 'We Must Rebel Against Raunch', *Guardian* (21 June 2006), www.theguardian.com/commentisfree/2006/jun/21/actionspeakslouderthanword (last accessed 22 October 2019); Bindel, 'Marching'; Julie Bindel, 'Fighting Fear', *Guardian* (23 November 2007), www.theguardian.com/commentisfree/2007/nov/23/fightingfear (last accessed 22 October 2019); Rachel Bell, 'University Challenge', *Guardian* (9 February 2007), www.theguardian.com/education/2007/feb/09/highereducation.uk (last accessed 22 October 2019); Suswati Basu, 'Lads' Mags: The Great Cover-Up, *Guardian* (15 October 2010), www.theguardian.com/lifeandstyle/2010/oct/15/lads-magazines-feminist-protests (last accessed 22 October 2019); Topping, 'Feminists Hail'; Cochrane, 'The Women Fighting Sexism'; Kira Cochrane, 'Page 3's Days May Finally Be Numbered, as Online Activism Makes Its Mark', *Guardian* (23 August 2013), www.theguardian.com/lifeandstyle/the-womens-blog-with-jane-martinson/2013/aug/23/online-activism-page-3-campaign (last accessed 22 October 2019).

79. Simon Hattenstone, 'Caroline Criado-Perez: "Twitter Has Enabled People to Behave in a Way They Wouldn't Face to Face"', *Guardian* (4 August 2013), www.theguardian.com/lifeandstyle/2013/aug/04/caroline-criado-perez-

twitter-rape-threats (last accessed 22 October 2019); Jane Martinson, 'Caroline Criado-Perez: "I Speak as Someone Psychologically Scarred"', *Guardian* (19 December 2013), www.theguardian.com/world/2013/dec/19/stories-of-2013-caroline-criado-perez-twitter (last accessed 22 October 2019); Ursula Kenny, 'Q&A with Caroline Criado-Perez: "What Happened to Me Was a Wake-Up Call for Society"', *Guardian* (3 May 2015), www.theguardian.com/world/2015/may/03/caroline-criado-perez-interview-what-happened-to-me-was-a-wake-up-call (last accessed 22 October 2019).

80. @tgirlinterruptd et al., 'This Tweet Called My Back', *Model View Culture* (13 December 2014), https://modelviewculture.com/pieces/thistweetcalledmyback (last accessed 22 October 2019).

81. Izzi I., 'The State of Online Harassment: Decentering Whiteness and Colonization', *Model View Culture* (15 December 2015), https://modelviewculture.com/pieces/the-state-of-online-harassment-decentering-whiteness-and-colonization (last accessed 22 October 2019). See Rachelle Hampton, 'The Black Feminists Who Saw the Alt-Right Threat Coming', *Slate* (23 April 2019), https://slate.com/technology/2019/04/black-feminists-alt-right-twitter-gamergate.html (last accessed 22 October 2019).

82. Azmina Dhrodia, 'Unsocial Media: Tracking Twitter Abuse Against Women MPs', *Medium* (3 September 2017), https://medium.com/@Amnesty Insights/unsocial-media-tracking-twitter-abuse-against-women-mps-fc28aeca498a (last accessed 22 October 2019).

83. For example, Caroline Criado-Perez, 'Rape Threats on Twitter Won't Get Women to Shut Up. If We Shout Back We'll Win', *Independent* (27 July 2013), www.independent.co.uk/voices/comment/rape-threats-on-twitter-wont-get-women-to-shut-up-if-we-shout-back-well-win-8734859.html (last accessed 18 October 2019); Mark Blunden, 'Caroline Criado-Perez: How I Won My Banknote Battle ... and Defied Rape Threat Trolls', *Evening Standard* (26 November 2015), www.standard.co.uk/news/london/caroline-criadoperez-how-i-won-my-banknote-battle-and-defied-rape-threat-trolls-a3123956.html (last accessed 18 October 2019); No author, 'Arrest After Twitter Threats Against Women's Campaigner', *Channel 4 News* (28 July 2013), www.channel4.com/news/twitter-abuse-arrest-caroline-criado-perez (last accessed 18 October 2019).

84. Jonathan Dean, 'Feminism in the Papers', *Feminist Media Studies*, 10:4 (2010), pp. 391–407.

85. Cochrane, 'The Fourth Wave'.

86. Kira Cochrane, *All the Rebel Women* (London: Guardian Books, 2013) (location 923), Kindle ebook.

87. Abbott, 'A Race'.

88. Chitra Nagarajan and Lola Okolosie, 'You Don't Need an MA in Gender Studies to Know That Race Matters to Feminism', *Guardian* (23 October

2012), www.guardian.co.uk/commentisfree/2012/oct/23/race-matters-to-feminism (last accessed 22 October 2019).

89. Lola Okolosie, 'As a Black Feminist, I See How the Wider Movement Fails Women Like My Mother', *Guardian* (9 December 2013), www.theguardian.com/commentisfree/2013/dec/09/black-feminist-movement-fails-women-black-minority (last accessed 22 October 2019); Morgan et al., 'International Women's Day'; Laura Bates, 'Sexism, Double Discrimination and More Than One Kind of Prejudice', *Guardian* (31 March 2014), www.theguardian.com/lifeandstyle/womens-blog/2014/mar/31/laura-bates-everyday-sexism-double-discrimination-intersectionality (last accessed 22 October 2019); Eliza Anyangwe, 'Misogynoir: Where Racism and Sexism Meet', *Guardian* (5 October 2015), www.theguardian.com/lifeandstyle/2015/oct/05/what-is-misogynoir (last accessed 22 October 2019).

90. Adewunmi, 'What the Girls Spat'; Renee Martin, 'I'm Not a Feminist (and There Is No But)', *Guardian* (10 April 2010), www.guardian.co.uk/commentisfree/2010/apr/10/white-feminism-black-woman-womanism (last accessed 22 October 2019); Cath Elliott, 'Feminists Must Not Be Deterred By a Backlash', *Guardian* (2 July 2010), www.theguardian.com/commentisfree/2008/jul/02/gender.equality (last accessed 22 October 2019).

91. See e.g. Sam Levin, Mona Chalabi and Sabrina Siddiqui, 'Why We Take Issue with the Guardian's Stance on Trans Rights in the UK', *Guardian* (2 November 2018), www.theguardian.com/commentisfree/2018/nov/02/guardian-editorial-response-transgender-rights-uk (last accessed 22 October 2019); Patrick Strudwick, 'The Guardian Newspaper Has Lost Two Trans Employees Over Its Reporting on Trans Issues', *Buzzfeed* (15 August 2019), www.buzzfeed.com/patrickstrudwick/two-transgender-employees-quit-guardian-transphobia (last accessed 22 October 2019).

92. Mensch, 'How About Some Reality-Based Feminism?'

93. Zoe Williams, 'Are You Too White, Rich, Able-Bodied and Straight to Be a Feminist', *Guardian* (18 April 2013), www.theguardian.com/commentisfree/2013/apr/18/are-you-too-white-rich-straight-to-be-feminist (last accessed 22 October 2019).

94. Okolosie, 'Beyond "Talking"' (pp. 92–3).

95. Criado-Perez, quoted in ibid. (p. 93).

96. Suzanne Moore, 'I Don't Care If You Were Born a Woman or Became One', *Guardian* (9 March 2013), www.theguardian.com/commentisfree/2013/jan/09/dont-care-if-born-woman (last accessed 22 October 2019); Hadley Freeman, 'Sheryl Sandberg Never Claimed She Was Writing a Feminist Manifesto, So Why This Chorus of Jeers?', *Guardian* (12 March 2013), www.theguardian.com/commentisfree/2013/mar/12/sheryl-sandberg-feminist-manifesto-jeers (last accessed 22 October 2019); Hadley Freeman, 'Check Your Privilege! Whatever That Means', *Guardian* (5 June 2013), www.theguardian.com/society/2013/jun/05/check-your-privilege-means (last

accessed 22 October 2019); Hadley Freeman, 'Feminist Infighting Only Takes Our Eyes Off the Real Struggle', *Guardian* (25 February 2014), www.theguardian.com/commentisfree/2014/feb/25/feminist-infighting-eyes-off-real-struggle (last accessed 22 October 2019).

97. Sara Ahmed, 'Affective Economies', *Social Text*, 22:2 (2004), pp. 117–39.

98. Eddo-Lodge, *Why I'm No Longer* (p. 164).

99. Freeman, 'Feminist Infighting'. See also Freeman, 'Sheryl Sandberg'; Freeman, 'Check Your Privilege!'.

100. Moore, 'I Don't Care'.

101. Flavia Dzodan, '"Misogofeminists" and the White Men Who Profit from Silencing Critiques', *Red Light Politics* (21 January 2014), https://redlightpolitics.info/post/74943518671/misogofeminists-and-the-white-men-who-profit (last accessed 22 October 2019).

102. Mary-Jo Nadeau, 'Troubling Herstory: Unsettling White Multiculturalism in Canadian Feminism', *Canadian Woman Studies/Les Cahiers de la Femme*, 27:2/3 (2009), pp. 6–13 (p. 9).

103. Heidi Safia Mirza and Yasmin Gunaratnam, '"The Branch on Which I Sit": Reflections on Black British Feminism', *Feminist Review*, 108 (2014), pp. 125–33 (p. 128).

104. For example, Melissa Benn, 'Making It', *London Review of Books*, 20:3 (1998), pp. 20–1, www.lrb.co.uk/v20/no3/melissa-benn/making-it (last accessed 22 October 2019); Libby Brooks, 'Time for a Good Scrap About What Our Feminism Really Is', *Guardian* (23 July 2009), www.theguardian.com/commentisfree/2009/jul/23/feminism-debate-infighting-gender (last accessed 22 October 2019); Laurie Penny, 'Beyond Noughtie Girls', *The F-Word* (August 2009), www.thefword.org.uk/reviews/2009/08/beyond_noughtie (last accessed 22 October 2019); Penny et al., 'Caitlin Moran's Feminist Handbook: Panel Verdict'; Alison Flood, 'Caitlin Moran's How to Be a Woman Wins Public Vote for Book of the Year', *Guardian* (23 December 2011), www.theguardian.com/books/2011/dec/23/caitlin-moran-book-of-the-year (last accessed 22 October 2019).

105. For example, Lola Okolosie, 'Rotherham's Abuse was Bred in a Toxic Mix of Class, Sexual and Racial Bigotry', *Guardian* (28 August 2014), www.theguardian.com/commentisfree/2014/aug/28/rotherham-abuse-class-sex-racial-bigotry (last accessed 22 October 2019); Lola Okolosie, 'Our Nauru Vigil Highlighted the Abuse Asylum Seekers Also Face in the UK', *Guardian* (30 August 2016), www.theguardian.com/commentisfree/2016/aug/30/nauru-vigil-abuse-asylum-seekers-uk-nauru-files-australian (last accessed 22 October 2019); Lola Okolosie, 'Racism in Schools Isn't Just Part of the Grim Past – It's Hiding in Plain Sight', *Guardian* (7 July 2017), www.theguardian.com/commentisfree/2017/jul/07/racism-schools-bame-pupils-teachers (last accessed 22 October 2019).

106. Eddo-Lodge, *Why I'm No Longer* (pp. 148–9).

CHAPTER 6   FEMINIST COMPLICITIES

1. Clare Hemmings, *Why Stories Matter: The Political Grammar of Feminist Theory* (London: Duke University Press, 2011) (p. 21).

2. Gloria Wekker, *White Innocence: Paradoxes of Colonialism and Race* (London: Duke University Press, 2017); Mary Louise Fellows and Sherene Razack, 'The Race to Innocence: Confronting Hierarchical Relations Among Women', *Journal of Gender, Race and Justice*, 1 (1998), pp. 335–52; Sarita Srivastava, '"You're Calling Me a Racist?" The Moral and Emotional Regulation of Antiracism and Feminism', *Signs: Journal of Women in Culture and Society*, 31:1 (2005), pp. 29–62; María Lugones, *Pilgrimages Peregrinajes: Theorizing Coalition Against Multiple Oppressions* (Lanham, MD: Rowman & Littlefield, 2003).

3. Sara Ahmed, 'Critical Racism/Critical Sexism', *feministkilljoys* (19 December 2013), https://feministkilljoys.com/2013/12/19/critical-racismcritical-sexism/ (last accessed 22 October 2019). Italics in original.

4. Sherene Razack, *Looking White People in the Eye: Gender, Race and Culture in Courtrooms and Classrooms* (Toronto: University of Toronto Press, 1998) (p. 22).

5. Ibid. (p. 13).

6. Fellows and Razack, 'The Race to Innocence' (pp. 337 and 343). Italics in original.

7. Razack, *Looking* (p. 160).

8. Barbara Applebaum, *Being White, Being Good: White Complicity, White Moral Responsibility, and Social Justice Pedagogy* (Plymouth: Lexington Books, 2010) (pp. 5, 39 and 185). Italics in original.

9. Barbara Smith, 'Racism and Women's Studies', in Gloria T. Hull, Patricia Bell Scott and Barbara Smith (eds), *All the Women Are White, All the Blacks Are Men, But Some of Us Are Brave: Black Women's Studies* (New York: The Feminist Press, 1982), pp. 48–51 (p. 49).

10. Gail Lewis and Clare Hemmings, '"Where Might We Go If We Dare": Moving Beyond the "Thick, Suffocating Fog of Whiteness" in Feminism', *Feminist Theory* (2019), https://doi.org/10.1177%2F1464700119871220 (pp. 7–8). Italics in original.

11. Razack, *Looking* (p. 14).

12. Ibid. (p. 12).

13. Cecily Jones, 'Falling Between the Cracks: What Diversity Means for Black Women in Higher Education', *Policy Futures in Education*, 4:2 (2006), pp. 145–59 (pp. 153–4).

14. Sisterhood and After, 'Black feminist Texts', www.bl.uk/learning/histcitizen/sisterhood/view.html#id=143433&id2=143140 (last accessed 22 October 2019).

15. Beverley Bryan, Stella Dadzie and Suzanne Scafe, *The Heart of the Race: Black Women's Lives in Britain* (London: Virago Press, 1985), pp. 128–40.

16. For an in-depth exploration of Jones' politics, see Carole Boyce Davies, *Left of Karl Marx: The Political Life of Black Communist Claudia Jones* (Durham: Duke University Press, 2008).

17. Bryan et al., *Heart of the Race* (pp. 151–5 and 148).

18. Avtar Brah, *Cartographies of Diaspora: Contesting Identities* (Oxon: Routledge, 1996) (p. 81); Amrit Wilson, *Finding a Voice: Asian Women in Britain*, 2nd edition (Montreal: Daraja Press, 2018).

19. Sara Ahmed, 'A Phenomenology of Whiteness', *Feminist Theory*, 8:2 (2016), pp. 149–68 (pp. 164–5). Italics in original.

20. Sara Ahmed, 'Declarations of Whiteness: The Non-Performativity of Anti-Racism', *borderlands*, 3:2 (2004), www.borderlands.net.au/vol3no2_2004/ahmed_declarations.htm (last accessed 19 October 2019).

21. Srivastava, 'You're Calling Me a Racist'; Lewis and Hemmings, 'Where Might'.

22. Ien Ang, 'I'm a Feminist But ... "Other" Women and Postnational Feminism', in Reina Lewis and Sara Mills (eds), *Feminist Postcolonial Theory: A Reader* (Edinburgh: Edinburgh University Press, 2003), pp. 190–206 (p. 193). Italics in original.

23. Elaine Swan, 'What Are White People to Do? Listening, Challenging Ignorance, Generous Encounters and the "Not Yet" as Diversity Research Praxis', *Gender, Work and Organization*, 24:5 (2017), pp. 547–63 (pp. 549, 556, 554 and 560).

24. Sara de Jong, *Complicit Sisters: Gender and Women's Issues Across North-South Divides* (Oxford: Oxford University Press, 2017) (p. 198).

25. Applebaum, *Being White* (p. 20).

26. See e.g. Outwrite Collective, 'Black Woman Talk to Outwrite', *Outwrite Women's Newspaper*, 25 (May 1984), pp. 8–9.

27. Ranu Samantrai, *AlterNatives: Black Feminism in the Postimperial Nation* (Stanford: Stanford University Press, 2002) (pp. 17–18).

28. For example, Anushay Hossain, 'American Woman: How Feminism Is Changing the Identity Discourse', *Forbes* (9 September 2013), www.forbes.com/sites/worldviews/2013/09/09/american-woman-how-feminism-is-changing-the-identity-discourse/ (last accessed 22 October 2019); Arit John, 'The Year in #SolidarityIsForWhiteWomen and Twitter Feminism', *The Atlantic* (31 December 2013), www.theatlantic.com/entertainment/archive/2013/12/year-solidarityisforwhitewomen-and-twitter-feminism/356583/ (last accessed 22 October 2019); Rachel Kuo, 'Racial Justice Activist Hashtags: Counterpublics and Discourse Circulation', *New Media and Society*, 20:2 (2018), pp. 495–514; Tegan Zimmerman, '#Intersectionality: The Fourth Wave Feminist Twitter Community', *Atlantis*, 38:1 (2017), pp. 54–70.

29. Kathy Davis, 'Intersectionality as Buzzword: A Sociology of Science Perspective on What Makes a Feminist Theory Successful', *Feminist Theory*, 9:1 (2008), pp. 67–85.

30. bell hooks, 'Representing Whiteness in the Black Imagination', in Ruth Frankenberg (ed.), *Displacing Whiteness: Essays in Social and Cultural Criticism* (London: Duke University Press, 1997). pp. 165–79 (p. 177).

31. Charles Mills, 'White Ignorance', in Shannon Sullivan and Nancy Tuana (eds), *Race and Epistemologies of Ignorance* (Ithaca, NY: State University of New York Press, 2007), pp. 13–38.

32. Sara R. Farris, *In the Name of Women's Rights: The Rise of Femonationalism* (London: Duke University Press, 2017); Jasbir K. Puar, *Terrorist Assemblages: Homonationalism in Queer Times* (London: Duke University Press, 2007).

33. Gargi Bhattacharyya, *Dangerous Brown Men: Exploiting Sex, Violence and Feminism in the War on Terror* (London: Zed Books, 2008) (p. 8).

34. Razia Aziz, 'Feminism and the Challenge of Racism: Deviance or Difference?', in Helen Crowley and Susan Himmelweit (eds), *Knowing Women: Feminism and Knowledge* (Cambridge: Polity Press), pp. 291–305 (p. 296).

Index

Abbott, Diane, 137, 149, 151
academia
    and Black British feminism, 58–63;
        Athena Swan, 62–3; 'decolo-
        nise' campaigns, 62; feminist
        academia, 11, 19, 44–7, 57,
        58–63, 92–4, 95, 173–5; feminist
        whiteness and racism within,
        7, 11, 17–18, 19, 26, 28, 59–63,
        77–9, 92–5, 168–9, 173–5; insti-
        tutional whiteness and racism
        within, 6, 34, 58–63, 93–4, 180;
        marketisation of higher educa-
        tion, 63; narratives of academic
        feminism and women's studies,
        77–9; white feminist academ-
        ics, 17–18, 59–63, 83, 93–4, 95;
        women of colour's experiences
        in, 6, 62, 58–63, 173
accountability, 120, 172
    'politics of accountability'
        (Razack), 163–4, 166; white
        women's/feminist evasion or
        deferral of, 17, 94, 97, 98, 125
activist feminism (interaction with
        popular feminism), 129–33
Adewunmi, Bim, 152
*Aftermath of Feminism: Gender,
    Culture and Social Change, The*
    (McRobbie, 2009), 67, 68–9, 71,
    76–8, 80, 89, 92–5, 167, 179
*Against Our Will: Men, Women and
    Rape* (Brownmiller, 1975), 120
Ahmed, Sara, 16, 23, 25, 28, 58, 61, 68,
        96, 104, 114, 122, 124, 162, 171–2
aid industry, 176
Ali, Nimco, 111–12
Ali, Suki, 9–10, 52, 53–4, 94

Amos, Valerie, 44–5, 120, 122, 124,
        140, 144
Ang, Ien, 91–2, 174
Anglo-American (term), 21–2
Anim-Addo, Joan, 62, 94
anti-imperialist feminism, 13, 24, 39,
        47–9, 75
antisemitism, 40–3
Apna Haq, 11
Applebaum, Barbara, 19, 164–5, 167,
        171
Aune, Kristin, 67, 126, 130
    *see also Reclaiming the F Word: The
        New Feminist Movement*
austerity, 2, 5
Aziz, Razia, 9, 52, 181

Banyard, Kat, 145, 147–8
Barrett, Michèle, 45
Bassel, Leah, 5
Bates, Laura, 145, 148, 154
Baxter, Holly, 132
Bellos, Linda, 40–2
Bhambra, Gurminder, 87–8
Bhattacharyya, Gargi, 180–1
Bhavnani, Kum-Kum, 41, 43, 44, 45,
        46, 47, 117, 120–2, 124
Bhopal, Kalwant, 62–3
Bilge, Sirma, 57–8, 59, 106–8
Blackness, definitions of, 8–9
Black resistance to state racism, 35,
        36
Black British Academics network, 62
Black British feminism, 6, 8–11, 24,
        32–3, 36–8, 43–65, 103, 116–22,
        170
    and academia, 58–63; and wave
        narratives, 124; deconstructing

217

coloniality, 15, 19, 115, 128, 166, 180, 181
and knowledge production, 18
see also white femininity and coloniality
Combahee River Collective, 55
Complicit Sisters: Gender and Women's Issues Across North-South Divides (de Jong, 2017), 176
complicity, 19, 23, 162–6
'white complicity pedagogy' (Applebaum), 164, 171; white feminist complicity in racism, 18, 44, 48, 59–63, 64, 83, 93, 119–23, 162, 164–81
Conservative Party/government, 2, 4, 5, 35–6, 49, 50
Corrie Bill (1979), campaign against, 38–9
Cosslett, Rhiannon Lucy, 132
Coulson, Margaret, 45, 117
Crenshaw, Kimberlé, 54–5, 71, 86, 87, 88, 103, 106, 107, 108
Criado-Perez, Caroline, 145, 148, 154
critique (anti-racist), 27–8
Black feminist critique represented as 'bullying' and 'silencing', 154–5; depoliticising of, 129, 150–8, 179; framed as 'accusation', 122; staying with, 171–7, 181–2; white-centred representations of 77–80, 84–5; white feminist erasure of, 75–6; white feminist responses to, 20

Dadzie, Stella, 10, 169
Daly, Mary, 134
Daughters of Eve, 111–13
Davis, Angela, 119–20
de Jong, Sara, 176
Dean, Jonathan, 150
decolonial theory, 15
Depo Provera, 39

Desai, Jayaben, 170
Dhrodia, Azmina, 149
difference, 54–8, 74, 80, 81–6, 91, 174
discourse, definition, 29
diversity, language of, 61
Dunham, Lena, 131
Dworkin, Andrea, 134
Dzodan, Flavia, 155

Eddo-Lodge, Reni, 1, 20, 128, 130, 154, 158
El-Enany, Nadine, 3
Emejulu, Akwugo, 5, 10
Empire Strikes Back: Race and Racism in 70s Britain, The (CCCS, 1982), 34–5
English Defence League, 4
'Englishness', 22–3
Equality Illusion: The Truth about Men and Women Today, The (Banyard, 2010), 145
equality politics, 127–8, 134, 135, 139–40
Eric-Udorie, June, 177
Essed, Philomena, 122
'ethnic minorities', 52–3, 104
Europe/European Union, 2–3, 87–8, 113–14, 115
European colonialism, 11–12, 19; European feminist debates about intersectionality, 57–8; 'Fortress Europe', 3; race-evasiveness in European scholarship, 87
see also Brexit
Evans, Elizabeth, 21–2
see also The Politics of Third Wave Feminism: Neoliberalism, Intersectionality, and the State in Britain and the US
Everyday Sexism, 109, 112, 145
'extremism', 113–15

Factora-Borchers, Lisa (Sudy), 130
Farris, Sara, 180

Mills, Charles, 8, 16, 127, 139
minoritisation, 52–4, 104, 112, 116, 125, 159–60
Mirza, Heidi, 10, 15–16, 33, 45, 51, 62, 93, 124, 134–5, 152
Mohanty, Chandra, 22, 45, 77, 78, 112, 142, 144
Moore, Suzanne, 154–5
Moran, Caitlin, 126, 131–2, 151, 152, 157–8
    see also How to Be a Woman
Moreton-Robinson, Aileen, 17–18, 83
Morris, Olive, 103, 169
Moseley, Rachel, 129
multiculturalism, 112–16
Muslim Women's Network UK, 109
Mustafa, Bahar, 110, 111

Nadeau, Mary-Jo, 75, 156
Nagarajan, Chitra, 151–2
Narayan, Uma, 112
narratives, feminist
    construction of, 24, 28–30, 68; marginalisation/erasure of Black British feminism within white-centred feminist narratives, 72, 90, 102, 108–9, 129–30, 135, 139, 166–71; narratives of feminist past as white, 133–9, 159–60, 161; positioning of racism within white-centred feminist narratives, 68; white-centred narratives of 'before and after' race awareness, 66, 72–81, 94–5, 95–6, 159, 161
    see also wave analogy/narratives and women's liberation movement
Nash, Jennifer, 55
National Abortion Campaign, 38
National Front, 39
National Union of Students, 8
nationalism, 2–3, 23, 34, 179–80
    and national identity. 35–6

Nationality Act, 1948, 14
Nationality Act, 1981, 14, 43, 48
neoliberalism, 2, 63, 69, 70, 76, 83, 87, 98, 107–8, 135
New Feminism, The (Walter, 1998), 126–7, 133–5, 138, 139–40, 141–2, 144–5, 146, 157, 177–8
New Statesman, 132, 152–3, 155
No Fly on the Wall, 11
Noble, Denise, 13–14
Notting Hill Carnival, 169
Noughtie Girl's Guide to Feminism, The (Levenson, 2009), 126–7, 135, 138, 140–1, 142–3, 144–5, 157

Observer, 23, 30–1, 160
    see also Guardian
Okolosie, Lola, 11, 110–11, 131–2, 151–2, 154, 158
online discussions
online feminist discussion, 1, 10–11, 129–33
    discussions and conflicts about racism and intersectionality, 131–2, 152–4, 179; feminist blogosphere, 130; online abuse, 111, 148–9; women of colour's labour online, 110–11, 130, 149
Organisation of Women of Asian and African Descent (OWAAD), 37–9, 50, 103, 137, 151
Ortega, Mariana, 17–18
'Other Kinds of Dreams': Black Women's Organisations and the Politics of Transformation (Sudbury, 1998), 10
othering
    of Black women, 141; of Muslim women, 105, 143, 160, 178; of women from the global South, 141–3, 160; of working-class women, 141

Thanks to our Patreon Subscribers:

Abdul Alkalimat
Andrew Perry

Who have shown their generosity and comradeship in difficult times.

The Pluto Press Newsletter

Hello friend of Pluto!

Want to stay on top of the best radical books
we publish?

Then sign up to be the first to hear about our
new books, as well as special events,
podcasts and videos.

You'll also get 50% off your first order with us
when you sign up.

Come and join us!

Go to bit.ly/PlutoNewsletter